Huts

A place beyond

D1629773

LESLEY RIDDOCH

Luath Press Limited

EDINBURGH

www.luath.co.uk

*To Manhal Nassif, Morwenna Wood and Jacqui Calder
whose surgical, medical, herbal and caring skills
mean I'm happily trotting about today.*

First published 2020
Reprinted with minor revisions 2020

ISBN: 978-1-913025-63-2

Printed and bound by
Printed and bound by Clays Ltd., Bungay

Typeset in 10.5 point Sabon

LESLEY RIDDOCH is an award-winning broadcaster, writer, journalist, independence campaigner and land reform activist. She writes weekly columns for *The Scotsman* and *The National* and is a contributor to *The Guardian*, BBC *Question Time, Scotland Tonight* and *Any Questions*. She is founder and Director of Nordic Horizons, a policy group that brings Nordic experts to the Scottish Parliament and produces a popular weekly podcast. Lesley has presented *You and Yours* on BBC Radio 4, *The Midnight Hour* on BBC2 and *The People's Parliament* and *Powerhouse* on Channel 4. She founded the Scottish feminist magazine *Harpies and Quines*, won two Sony awards for her daily Radio Scotland show and edited *The Scotswoman* – a 1995 edition of *The Scotsman* written by its female staff. She was a trustee of the Isle of Eigg Trust that pioneered the successful community buyout in 1997. She has presented and co-produced films about the Faroes, Iceland and Norway and during lockdown, presented *Declaration*, a film celebrating the 700th anniversary of the Declaration of Arbroath. Lesley was awarded a PhD in July 2020 and lives near the sea in north Fife.

To Riddoch, the humble hut is a birthright to which Scots
have long since been denied. On the page and in person,
Riddoch is persuasive.
SUNDAY TIMES

Huts: A Place Beyond *puts access to the countryside for*
recreation by ordinary folk centrestage. And it's a great page
turner too. I haven't waited so eagerly for a book for ages
and it surpassed expectations. Lesley Riddoch has managed
to take a mad fringe idea, give it respectability and put it in
the context of the wider northern world, quite apart from
publicising the largely lost radical working-class movements
of the early twentieth century.
CHRIS BALLANCE, CARBETH HUTTERS

An entertaining as well as a cogent argument for the develop-
ment of a hutting culture which is common place in other
countries of the north and which would bring us into better
balance with our natural environment at a time when we
need that more than ever.
SUNDAY NATIONAL

A fascinating tale of why Scotland's history of recreational hut culture is so far from the European norm. Lesley brings a blend of academic rigour, journalistic flair and entertaining story-telling to this neglected topic and makes a compelling case for a renaissance of the Scottish hut.
ANDY WIGHTMAN

Food for thought and full of insights and great anecdotes.
SARA SHERIDAN

Contents

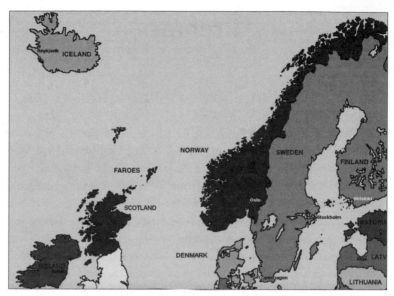

Scotland, Norway and our North Sea, Arctic and Baltic neighbours.

In this book the Norwegian word *hytte*, is used to mean hut, cabin or cottage. Observing Norwegian grammatical rules would lead to many variations. So, the singular form will be used throughout (ie *hytte* as opposed to *hytter*, *en hytte*, *hyttene*). Norwegian words (except proper names) will be shown in italics with their English meaning afterwards in brackets.

Preface

THIS STORY STARTS in the 1960s, with annual pilgrimages to my parents' family homes in Wick and Banffshire each summer holiday. Other folk round us in Belfast headed for the coast or destinations in the sun. But my dad drove our family (Mum, wee brother and myself) first to the Larne–Stranraer ferry and then overland on an epic annual car journey to some of the remotest parts of Scotland. Thus began my fascination with The North. That physical connection ended when my grandparents died and their council-owned homes passed on to new tenants. But the emotional link and the echo of their northern lives travelled with us. Everywhere. My dad recited the Doric poems of the North East every night into a reel-to-reel Grundig tape recorder – much to the mock annoyance of his truly fascinated offspring. Decades later, his regular use of the Doric 'quine' made *Harpies and Quines* an obvious title for a scurrilous feminist magazine I co-founded in the early '90s. My Caithness mother's quiet sense of outrage about land clearances and her fascination for almost all things Norwegian was infectious – even though she was never that keen on the Great Outdoors. I only ever coaxed her uphill to the bothy I rented for seven eventful and eccentric years on one solitary but memorable occasion.

So finally, in 2010, I put all these parts of my life together and embarked on a PhD comparing the hut and cabin traditions of Scotland and Norway. Ten long years, some great friends in Hammerfest and Lindøya and a basic proficiency in Norwegian later, this book is the result.

I'd like to thank Professor Donna Heddle, whose UHI Northern Studies course first prompted me to consider academic research and whose comments as an external examiner helped fine tune the PhD. Thanks also for the inspiration provided by Professor John Bryden, whose determination to connect Scotland to the wider Nordic region is nothing short of heroic. I'm grateful to my supervisors Profs Allan McInnes and Richard Finlay from Strathclyde University and Jon Vidar Sigurdsson from Oslo University for their belief and encouragement and to Dr Fiona Watson who spent her own valuable time helping me restructure the PhD when I was on the verge of quitting. Dr Ali Cathcart helped me shape mountains of material into coherent form with humour, genuine interest and gently applied academic rigour and Strathclyde University granted several extensions to the PhD submission because of my involvement in two referendums, four elections, three books and some serious health issues. Thanks to Caitlin DeSilvey and Janice Marshall for letting me read and quote from their own research '*When Plotters Meet*': *Edinburgh's Allotment Movement 1921–2001* and *Holidays in East Lothian with focus on Seton Sands*, respectively. Scott McGregor let me use Dundee University library to write up my PhD and Murray Ferris, the son of Carbeth pioneer William Ferris shared his personal archive of letters, newspaper cuttings and photographs. Chris Ballance, Gerry Loose and other Carbeth hutters gave access to their historical material and members of the Thousand Huts campaign including Karen Grant, Ninian Stuart and Donald McPhillimy diligently reminded me that the story of hutting and the determination of our thrawn forebears really does matter.

The generosity of Norwegians has also been amazing. I'd like to thank the Norwegian Consul in Scotland Mona Røhne and Honorary Consul David Windmill for arranging the study visit that brought me to Hammerfest. Thanks also to the Yggdrasil Mobility Programme funded by the Research Council of Norway for financing a three month stay at Oslo University in 2011. Dr Ellen Rees, Knut Kjeldstadli and Oivind Bratberg offered reassuring encouragement as I embarked on research in a new country and a faltering new language. Ingun Grimstad Klepp and Inger Johanne Lyngø gave access to their fascinating anthropological paper on the hytte islands (which then became case studies for my PhD) and answered innumerable questions ten long years after publication. Thanks also to Finn Arne Jørgensen and Dieter Müller from Umeå University who directed me towards relevant Nordic literature at the outset; Knut Are Tvedt, author of the comprehensive Oslo Byleksikon who helped me understand the wider context of Oslo life in the 1920s and my stalwart Scottish, Oslo-based friend Sarah Prosser and fellow Norwegian language learner, Professor of Outdoor Education and patriotic Kiwi, Pip Lynch for their constant humour and optimism. Tutta and Ola Normann and their friends on Lindøya managed endless queries and regular visits with ready smiles and strong coffee. Oddmund Østebø took time off work to explain the expansion of huts on neighbouring Nakholmen. My friend Inger Lise Svendsen took me round her extended family and the Arctic hutting community of Skaidi on her snowmobile, helping me piece together the story of its origins in glamorous style. I'm also hugely grateful to Creative Scotland for a small grant which let me take two months away from weekly newspaper column-writing to turn the completed PhD into this rather different fusion of story-telling and research.

Thanks finally to all my friends and particularly Chris Smith who rarely enjoyed a holiday for the best part of a decade without finding himself in the middle of yet another undiscovered hutting community.

Introduction

HUTS.

Wee wooden huts. Not sheds at the bottom of the garden, not yurts, pods or cabins hired by the week, not upmarket self-catering accommodation nor family houses in remote areas used as second homes.

I'm talking about modest, self-built, low-impact wooden huts – located in woodland, generally without electricity and in constant use every weekend and all summer long. Huts, like the Broons' mythical yet fondly remembered but 'n' ben.

Wee makeshift places, owned by individual families and handed down to each new generation as the ultimate family heirloom.

Huts – situated in the country but most dearly loved by folk who live in city flats without gardens or access to nature.

Wee, wooden huts.

Could half a million of them sprinkled throughout the woodlands of Scotland transform our health, happiness and democracy?

Well, apart from the amount of sheer uncomplicated fun such low-impact weekend retreats would bring to our (mostly) cooped up, indoor and urbanised leisure lives, Scotland would finally be a place where enjoying the countryside isn't the sole preserve of the very wealthy or the very hardy.

If every family could own a hut, many of Scotland's 'stuck' problems would be solved. Our bizarrely unequal system of land and forest ownership would be a distant memory; small plots would be available and affordable; forests would be filled with huts, not just timber operations; forest owners would be local communities, not just wealthy folk chasing tax breaks and large companies; planners would change rules to approve makeshift modest weekend homes and Scots would get out of cities to relax, not out of their heids.

Stuga, mokki, sommerhus, bach, cabaña, dacha, gite, *hytte* and cabins – modest weekend, wooden huts are common everywhere at wooded latitudes from Canada through the northern states of America and the Nordic/Baltic states to Russia.

Everywhere that is, except Scotland.

In Norway there are almost 500,000 wooden huts – one per ten Norwegians.

In Scotland there are fewer than 600 wooden huts – one per 8,035 Scots.

Does that matter? I think it does.

The average Scot finds it hard to physically escape the pressures of daily life – perhaps it's no coincidence we over-indulge in liquid and chemical escapes. What we need is to spend meaningful time in the restorative company of nature instead.

Research shows that time in nature produces measurable reductions in anxiety, blood pressure and stress whilst boosting feelings of self-esteem and wellbeing. Japanese doctors prescribe 'forest bathing' (*shinrin–yoku*) to strengthen the immune system, Scandinavian parents choose outdoor over indoor kindergarten, and for Richard Louv, who coined the phrase 'Nature Deficit Disorder' in *Last Child in the Woods*, academic studies are finally proving what he intuitively understood: 'Nature is not only nice to have, but it's a have-to-have for physical health and cognitive functioning.'[1]

And that means more than just looking from a car window. It means immersion.

Think about the last time you went for a spring walk in some natural woodland. Your absorption in small things quickly becomes vast – you try to identify trees by their leaves, or even their bark, notice that wild garlic and bluebells grow under some species not others, wonder why ash trees flower so late, or whether young nettles really do make delicious soup. Of course, the minute you get home (or even back in the car or on the bike), the immediacy of that natural environment fades to be replaced with the sights, smells, sounds and thus the stressful imperatives of everyday life. It's inevitable.

The good news is that the calming reverie returns as soon as immersion in nature resumes. The bad news is that such regular contact with the great outdoors is on the wane, especially amongst children. Ask the lexicographers. There was an outcry in 2015 when *The Oxford Junior Dictionary* was found to have removed the following redundant words: acorn, adder, ash, beech, bluebell, buttercup, catkin, conker, cowslip, cygnet, dandelion, fern, hazel, heather, heron, ivy, kingfisher, lark, mistletoe, nectar, newt, otter, paster and willow.

How scary. How depressing. When we now know that time spent rebalancing lives in nature does so much for the spirit. It reminds us that the world of work is not the only important dimension in our lives and the assigned role that comes with employment or unemployment, not our only identity. As the explorer and humanitarian Fridjhof Nansen put it his inaugural address as Rector of the University of St Andrews: 'We all have a Land of Beyond to seek in our life... Our part is to find the trail that leads to it.'[2]

But how do we do that? Without time spent in nature and regular access to that green gateway, how easy is it for the urban majority to spend unconstrained hours, pressure-free days, undemanding weeks even, immersed in nature?

The answer for Norwegians and just about every other nationality at our wooded latitude is simple – in huts.

The mystery of Scotland's missing huts has always bothered me – not least because I rented a stone-built bothy for seven glorious years after a series of professional accidents brought me to the lovely, forgotten slopes of Glen Buchat, 45 minutes' drive from Aberdeen. My 'hut' was actually a shepherd's house, abandoned in the 1960s. It had a great roof, two bedrooms and an amazing view thanks to its elevated location – 1,200 feet above fields of tatties, neeps and banks of heather. There was no electricity, road access or running water and over the empty decades, the hut had become the domain of animals. It took years of weekend and summer stays to fix things up and learn to calm down about sharing that space. A herd of elephants dancing in clogs at night signalled only the return of field-mice to the attic. A wedged-shut door didn't warn of a secret invader – just heavy rain the night before. Cows wandered outside – part of their water trough served as my floating, makeshift fridge.

I loved the freedom and the small, unpredictable adventures that bubbled up during every stay. Yet I knew only a handful of people who felt the same. When I was sufficiently persuaded of the merits of country life, I let go of the bothy and moved to a small house in rural Perthshire – filled immediately with my responsible, serious self and worldly possessions. That Norwegian balance of tame urban weeks and carefree country weekends and summers was over. I had become a normal Scot again with one fixed abode. But the experience never left me. Or the question that then arose.

Why do Scots have the smallest number of huts, cabins, bolt-holes and mountain retreats of any country in the world at a wooded latitude? After a decade of research, one thing's for sure. Today's sad reality is not the result of apathy or inaction by our grandparents' generation. During the 1920s and '30s, working people across Europe escaped the pressure, disease and squalor of TB-ridden cities by building weekend huts round big cities and Scots were just as active as Norwegians, Germans, Portuguese and Danes. Carbeth, Seton Sands, Barry Downs – all these large hutting communities began life during the interwar years. But elsewhere after World War Two, hutting developed. Cars were de-rationed, incomes rose, guaranteed leisure time increased and hutters (especially in Norway) went in search of individual *hytte* locations that were less coveted by land-hungry city councils and more adventurous than the old, densely packed and tightly regulated communal sites. Since land in Norway is owned by tens of thousands of citizens, that was fairly easy to do. So 'ordinary' Norwegians bought individual hut sites at low prices in the most stunning fjord-side locations, and the 1960s saw a huge expansion in *hytte* numbers.

In Scotland though, hutting was about to grind to a halt. The original wartime sites – with huts crammed in cheek by jowl – were still popular, but needed renewal. They didn't get it. Instead, from the 1970s onwards, hutters faced eviction and most hut sites were gentrified out of existence by councils and planners with a fierce dislike for the non-symmetrical, unplanned, makeshift and self-built. New individual plots couldn't be found in Scotland thanks to high land prices, closed forests, and distant, unapproachable landowners. So, a Norwegian-style 'cabin' culture failed to take root in Scotland, mostly because it wasn't possible to get a foot on the land and partly because long centuries of feudalism have left Scotland with an aesthetic of emptiness, which lies embedded and unquestioned at the heart of our planning system today.

Some folk speculate that Scots perhaps lack a real appetite for rural life after being urbanised and industrialised earlier than every other European nation. That would make sense – but it just isn't true.

The evidence shows that Scots shared the common desire of all Nordic and North European people for a permanent and modest wee retreat amongst the spectacular forests, lochs and mountains of their own country. But beyond setting up a few celebrated, communal sites, one enduring aspect of Scottish life made the realisation of that dream impossible – Scots, alone in Europe, could never, ever, ever own a piece of land to call their own.

So hut numbers soared in Norway after WW2, but halved here. At the same time, the number of detached family houses used as holiday homes more than doubled, helping create the impression (unique to Britain) that second homes are inherently elitist. This book aims to challenge that perception. Of course, second homes are currently the preserve of a privileged few. Of course, it's unhelpful to have precious first homes taken from the rural housing stock to sit half-empty and under-occupied. But designating family homes as 'first homes' in perpetuity – as they do in Norway – could help stop that practice. In Norway *boplikt* (the duty of place) has been in operation for 70 years, placing burdens in title deeds that mean first homes can only be sold to other permanent residents and second homes must be bought by other second homers. This has effectively created two separate housing markets and stopped locals from being trumped by wealthier incoming holiday homers.

So, hutting has generally thrived in Norway alongside, not instead of, vibrant rural communities. Scotland could do the same thing – but that would mean action in the sacred market place and intervention on land reform. And for what – so that folk can sit in auld wooden sheds?

This perhaps is the nub of the problem.

The pitifully low value we have learned to place on our own leisure lives and our relationships with nature. Most urban Scots aspire to lead modern, busy, cosmopolitan lives a world distant from the grinding poverty experienced by their parents. It's not a bad aspiration, but it's turned us away from their makeshift world – away from self-built, low-key and small, regular adventures towards large, expensive, commercial and organised 'fun'. So wooden huts, that are regarded as priceless family heirlooms in Norway, just look like shabby, slightly embarrassing shanties here – especially to decision-makers. That's the legacy of feudalism and whilst it's not the fault of Scotland's professionals, taking steps to end this long exile from nature certainly is their call.

Currently, Scots live to work, because no other place calls us away. Norwegians by contrast, work to live, because the *hytte* is always beckoning. It's not too late to change that situation around. If Scotland's second homes were less like someone else's first home and more like the modest, purpose-built wooden huts that fill forests across the world at our northern latitude, their reputation might improve and so might our leisure lives. It just needs people to rediscover their appetite for low-impact weekends on the land – and politicians to act.

Displacing locals is not what hutting does.

It's what the growth of upmarket holiday homes in the absence of hutting has done.

So, why shouldn't the ordinary Scots family have their ain wee but 'n' ben? One fifth of Scotland's landmass is currently a giant, empty, barren grouse moor, beyond local use, taxation or criticism. I'm not suggesting it all gets divvied up, planted out with trees, with clumps of huts in between. But in areas nearest to towns and cities – why not? Is the biggest threat facing rural Scotland really the near universal desire to have a wee holiday home – if that could be satisfied by modest wooden huts – or the pervasive, unacknowledged and chronic land scarcity we seem unable to name let alone tackle?

Let's rethink.

The process of removing Scots from our own countryside (except as grateful, obedient day trippers) is almost complete. Foreign visitors with stronger currencies outplan and outbid locals for scarce and increasingly expensive self-catering cottages, Bed and Breakfasts and even campsite pitches, while long-term lets for local workers have long since become Airbnbs. Caravans are a good alternative for many, but it's almost impossible to get planning permission for a lone, picturesquely sited van and organised sites simply replicate the conditions of city life, without any of the usual security against sudden rule changes and evictions.

Everywhere else, the citizens of a country are taken out of the cut-throat commercial holiday market and insulated from competition with wealthier foreign tourists by having their own humble huts. So why not here too?

Are Scots content, or just resigned to exclusion from one of the world's most sought-after natural habitats? Have we become such delicate, risk-averse, indoor wee flooers that spending summers and weekends in wooden huts just seems unhygienic and scary? Have we lost the belief we can build them? Does the prospect of unpackaged leisure time fill us with dread?

My bet is that most folk would be out there in a flash – learning to use native trees, build wooden huts and undo centuries of damaging distance from nature – given half the chance. The chance their families were never given.

So, here's the thing. In some respects, Scotland and Norway are very alike. But nothing sets the two northern neighbours further apart than the way they use leisure time.

Every weekend most Norwegians go to their hut or cabin. Every weekend most Scots do not. This book tries to describe what Scots are missing.

CHAPTER ONE

Arctic awakening

IT'S 6AM ON 14 MARCH 2009.

A tiny single-engine plane sits on the runway at Tromsø airport like a giant frozen insect half-heartedly rousing itself for flight. The carriage shudders as the propeller gathers speed. But after a few minutes of noise and vibration the blades slow again to a disappointing standstill. Moments later the same build-up sets the seat belt buckles rattling and the little Cessna almost lurches forward. Once again, the engine whine peaks and fades and the blades falter to a full stop.

Inside, I find myself thinking of balsa wood, sweet-smelling, near-drinkable white glue and model aircraft.

What has this got to do with hutting in Scotland?

Bear with me.

I'm on a week's trip round Norway arranged by the ever-helpful Norwegian Consul in Scotland, Mona Røhne. It's meant to end in the 'Arctic Capital' Tromsø, but the relative proximity of the world's northernmost town is hard to resist. Especially since plucky, utterly remote Hammerfest has strong connections with my mum's home town of Wick. Both like-sized small towns sit in the north of their respective countries. Both were once major fishing ports. But Arctic Hammerfest is now a thriving hub of world-beating, renewable technology that may yet extract energy from Scotland's fastest-flowing waters, 15 miles from struggling Wick. In 2009, Hammerfest Strøm announced plans to build turbines ultimately destined for the Pentland Firth. Hammerfest's population then was just 9,000 – slightly larger than Wick. And while the impact of ice ages means settlement in Caithness clearly preceded Hammerfest, it's pretty clear which North Sea sibling is the Big Sister now.

So this small Arctic hop is irresistible.

But the plane still isn't moving.

Scanning my three sleeping fellow passengers, I peer from

the window to see if the scheduled flight to Hammerfest looks entirely normal. A quick scan establishes the plane looks real enough, though the door isn't completely closed.

Outside only the lights of the tiny airport building are lit. It is 6.15am. We have no competition for our slot on the single runway, set within the deep snow like a dark exclamation mark. So why aren't we moving?

The cockpit door slides back and the pilot extracts himself with difficulty, opens the side door, bending to avoid hitting his head and steps carefully onto one of the wings. He bounces on the pliant fuselage a couple of times before swinging back through the door and into his faded blue leather seat. Smiling cheerfully at the stewardess he strains to read a thermometer gauge. A few more words are exchanged and the cycle of powering up and decelerating resumes. I look round. Everyone else is still asleep.

Suddenly, I realise the plane is de-icing. Snow on the wings is a small matter on the ground, but at 20,000 feet and temperatures of minus 30, light fluffy stuff becomes heavy and solid very fast. I smile at having unravelled this little mystery and feel somehow initiated.

Fully 15 minutes after the first engine surge, the plane finally taxies into position and without further fuss lifts cleanly into the clear March sky.

An Arctic Dawn.

I turn the words over slowly in my mind and conjure up images of high-flying sea eagles, low-flying Amelia Earharts and icebound Arctic explorers. All somehow at home in this epic, glowing terrain where jagged mountains turn into hard, squat lumps beneath us as the plane soars into the low, horizontal rays of the rising sun. I look down to see myth meet landscape. Here is the very route taken by the loving, resilient and faithful Gerda in the tale of the Snow Queen – travelling sometimes on the back of a reindeer, pounding hooves over narrow fringes of beaten, barren land; skating sometimes fast and light across thin ice, flying finally across the thick, slow, freezing, deadly Arctic. All to reach her brother and loosen winter's grip on his heart. At each new lofty latitude, with each new loss of reassuring habitat and animal companion, she comes to know what all on Odin's escalator understand, that the journey to the heart of another is endless. That the journey itself is all.

'Coffee?'

The stewardess looks inquiringly at her moist eyed passenger.

'Thanks – with milk,' I glance back quickly to the end of Europe taking place below. Molten gold is being laid down in long, sun strips and it seems important to keep at least one watery eye on the whole process.

'It's an amazing sight,' I venture, restraining the urge to share anything like my full emotional truth.

'Yes, the morning flight is the best time to fly north. The view on the other side is also good. You can move if you like.'

I try to convey a smile of helpless gratitude to Gerda's long-lost spiritual cousin and jump across a chasm of tectonic proportions to face East – towards Russia and the Urals, endless harsh terrain with meaningless borders, the remnants of salt mines and… it takes a few seconds to get a sense of proportion. We are nowhere near the Russian border.

I remember a conversation with some young Russian women from Murmansk and Arkhangelsk, who'd been given a year at Tromsø University as a reward for studying Norwegian language and culture. They found it hard to cope with the isolation of their new 'western-style' student accommodation. Living in single rooms and silent dormitories without the noise of mothers, fathers, brothers, sisters and cousins, they felt lonely and disconnected. But this was the price of progress in the new Russia. The most talented had to venture far beyond the comforting apron strings of home. Still, Tromsø clearly hadn't turned out to be the reward break they expected. I wondered where they would really like to go for a big event, like a special birthday. Three of the four were instantly agreed – St Petersburg. The fourth, after some encouragement to consider the whole of Europe, chose Rome, but after a few raised eyebrows and sideways looks from her colleagues added that her entire family would have to come too.

'Might you not head to Oslo or Stockholm or Helsinki?'

Sensing my surprise at their lack of curiosity about Scandinavia, the would-be Italian traveller – the youngest of the student group – started positioning our coffee cups around the table to make her point.

'Here we are in Arkhangelsk,' delivering the city's name in its full, scything Slavic splendour.

'To get to Murmansk,' her 'r' curled like a little chocolate shaving, 'is almost two hours away by plane. And yet we are neighbours in Russia. This is our next city. To come here to Tromsø we must fly first two hours to Murmansk and then two hours more. We are not close to Norway. Nothing is close.'

I try to imagine this. Neighbours two hours distant by plane and 21 hours distant by road. Neighbours that defy every aspect of the word save the most basic. The next people. Another 13 hours' drive to the next big clump of people in Tromsø – all partners in total isolation. Fellow travellers in a wilderness that should defy human existence as surely as the parched deserts of Nevada or the lion-infested plains of the Masai Mara.

They say Murmansk comes from the local Sami word *murman*, meaning 'the edge of the earth.'

I gaze down again on the primeval landscape with a keener sense of proportion. Of course, these aren't the Urals or any bit of Russia – that vast country lies in another cloudy time zone altogether. These ancient hills are more likely to be the interior of Norwegian Finnmark, the land of the nomadic reindeer Sami, whose every turf-built *gamme* (hut) was torched along with every permanent home as the Nazis retreated from Russia's oldest border in 1944, leaving land bare and people cold and defenceless but ready to reclaim their land and their lives. And they survived – here at the top of the inhabited world where Europe becomes Asia in a clasp of peninsular arms, and the ever-widening Barents Sea keeps frozen motherlands apart.

'Would you like more coffee?'

The reality is yes. The answer must be no, unless I want to hyperventilate all morning and feel vaguely anxious all day. I have no idea what Swedes, Finns and Norwegians do to coffee. But when they come to Britain, they must feel they're drinking water.

'Have you been to Hammerfest before?'

'No. First time. It's exciting.'

I'm talking nonsense now – subbing complex thoughts down to tourist-heavy cliché as the engine roar drowns all subtlety. But not all communication.

'It's my favourite trip too.'

We seem to exchange a conspiratorial smile. Why not. We are the only two people on this plane not sleeping or steering.

I point down theatrically. 'It's like I always imagined it.'

She smiles, collects my coffee cup and leaves me in a perfect and now perfectly validated state of wonderment.

This is North so far north it beggars belief. North so far north it relates only to the frozen Antarctic – its southern counterpoint, an entire planet away. And it's a land of contradiction. Hard winter ice creates permafrost which becomes soft ground in summer where houses, roads and machinery just sink. No winter light becomes all summer light to create the world's fastest breeding season for birds, insects, plants and primates. Liquid gas for heating is somehow extracted from frozen pockets beneath the Arctic seabed.

Hugh MacDiarmid would 'aye be whaur extremes meet' and settled in Shetland. Scotland's contradiction-loving bard stopped travelling too soon. Here in the Far North there is time and space to indulge eccentricity. Here the sun can roam or sleep as the mood takes her, curling up inside caverns of mountain cloud or blazing in an endless day over sea haar and island-fringed fjord. It's a land of light without heat, in more ways than one. Cold and bright or cold and dark, the Arctic world seems clear, clean and rational.

At 7am with Hammerfest in sight, at long last... I fall asleep.

Inger Lise Mathisen is waiting at the airport. With long, auburn hair and gentle colourings she looks every inch a Celt (though I discover she is all Norwegian and part Sami).

Clearly my desire to see round for a (short) March day has flummoxed everyone. Not least because it's Saturday and Norwegians don't do work on days off. Normally.

FIG 1.2 Finnmark from the air.

FIG 1.3 Inger Lise Mathisen in Hammerfest.

'I can show you the board room of Hammerfest Strøm, and the old river turbine and a model of the Snovit gas production project or we can go to the place the tidal turbine normally sits – though it's out of the water right now and pretty well invisible when it's in…'

I feel like Wallander the Swedish detective unpacking a particularly complicated case. I've no idea what I want to know about the world's northernmost town. I just want to be in it.

Hammerfest is studded with claims to fame. It installed the first street lighting in Northern Europe in 1897 – for decades they changed broken lightbulbs in winter by climbing from top windows across the banked-up snow, to reach lamp posts. The company progressed from river hydros to tidal turbines. Meanwhile Statoil built Snøvit, the world's most northern liquefied petroleum gas plant by the harbour where the world's largest fish have been caught for centuries.

Inger Lise mistakes my momentary silence for lack of interest.

'We could always visit a friend downtown for coffee?' She scans my face carefully for signs of enthusiasm. 'Or we could take the snowmobiles and try to go up to our huts.'

I almost grab her.

'You've got a hut? You've got snowmobiles?'

'Well yes, who doesn't?'

'Try the whole of Scotland.'

'Ah, but we have the same problem you have in Scotland. Not enough snow.'

This was a curious concept.

In the Arctic at a temperature of minus five there was no fresh snow. Or at least not enough to use the most exciting means of transport ever invented.

'Yes, the snow cover has been really patchy this year. We were all watching the children in Britain play in the snow but it looks like we won't be skiing at Easter. The thaw has already begun.'

Having stood on one frozen spot for ten minutes to take in the majestic vista surrounding Hammerfest from a viewpoint marked by a large plastic polar bear (not indigenous to Norway) I could testify everything was not thawing. There is no bad weather only bad clothing – how often had I bored everyone back home with that quintessentially Norwegian observation? Only to arrive in the world's northernmost town wearing thin soled boots that radiated a damp chill up my legs.

'So, we can't walk up to your *hytte*?'

'No, it would take hours and we would have to carry everything.'

'Everything?'

'Coffee, water for coffee, milk, food, matches...'

I hear Inger Lise but my mind is elsewhere.

It's luscious country. Green and deep. It's Friday at 8pm in August. Wee smirrs of heat-haze hover just above the road that heads north from Perth to Glenshee, Braemar, Balmoral and beyond. This fabulous walking country is empty, as it always is, because this is Scotland. The tourists have reached their self-catering cottages and hotels. The lairds and entourages are in their shooting lodges. Anywhere else, a road through such majestic mountain scenery, would still be full of life on a beautiful summer's evening. Hutters would be heading north after a week's work – most quitting an hour early to get up the road in good time. Anglers would be on the move, making for huts along the salmon-filled Don and Dee. But as usual I was almost alone on that four-hour drive from Glasgow to my own rented hut, tucked between two hillocks in an obscure Aberdeenshire glen. Luck helped me stumble across it. Luck – and curiosity.

Back in the '80s, working as a radio reporter at BBC Scotland in Glasgow, I was sent to work in Aberdeen for three months. I opted not to stay in Granite City (no offence) in the hope I could sample some craic in its rural hinterland instead. The only rentable house between Aberdeen and Inverness with an all-important landline in those pre-mobile days was Coldstriffen, located in Glen Buchat, 45 minutes west of Aberdeen. The owners of the nearby Kildrummy Castle Hotel had renovated the house, lived there for a while, but apparently got snowed in one bad winter and concluded that living six miles from their business wasn't wise. So, it was available to rent. The house itself was fine, the drive into Aberdeen scenic but Glen Buchat was the real discovery. Unusually fertile, with lime deposits supporting fields up to 1,200 feet, the glen once supported dozens of farms and hundreds of people, till decline and depopulation kicked in.

The eastern entry to the glen is still a single-track road, passing just above Glenbuchat Castle, built in 1590 for a member of the Gordon clan to mark his wedding, but now a ruin. I generally approached from neighbouring Strathdon to the south, branching off the main road at the intriguingly named Castle of Newe (given that extra 'e' by its owner Sir Charles Forbes in the 1820s to stop post going to Newcastle-upon-Tyne). Another single-track road twisted up through dense, dark forests stashed with

FIG 1.4 Glenbuchat and the bothy, 1990s.

deer, owls, a wildcat (okay, a large, powerful-looking tabby, miles from a house), brambles and mushrooms in the autumn and a permanent air of mystery.

Emerging from the forest, the road continued to climb past Eastertown. No houses marked this old 'ferm toun' when I first arrived, just a few collapsed ruins, corners of fields with clumps of rhubarb and other poignant markers of past use. After 16 years of summer picnics amidst the clearance ruins of Caithness, this landscape of eerie absence felt strangely familiar. The road led on through the pass known locally as the Deochry to the highest point of an elegant heathery shoulder, which stretched up to the graceful, conical dome of Ben Newe. Below, I could see the little church and graveyard of Glenbuchat, the cluster of houses tucked into the knobbly drumlin hills that partly block the glen and Coldstriffen itself, at the foot of the dark hill opposite.

This became my regular entrance to the Glen – a perverse 20-minute detour beyond the easier, castle-flanked route. And over three months, that oft repeated journey brought something else to my attention – sitting high above my temporary home, meeting my gaze at the same elevated height, a single, simple, two-windowed cottage without any visible track or signs of life.

Below, the Water of Buchat ran through the glen to meet the powerful, silent River Don, producing bright patches of yellow marsh flowers and verdant, sheltered nooks. Above, the sub-Munro foothills reached up into heather and moor land. But my mind was somewhere in between. Fascinated by this abandoned house.

After three months, I reluctantly returned to Glasgow. But that Hogmanay, I headed back with my obliging boyfriend, and hauled him up the hill to investigate. We set off from Coldstriffen in the snow to discover that the cottage is a lot easier to locate from the hill opposite than the road directly below. After 20 minutes' erratic ascent, and stumbling in the falling darkness between clumps of woodland, we spotted it above the highest field of neeps.

The stone-built cottage sat sheltered between two low hills. It looked abandoned, but the slates on the roof were impressively intact. Perhaps that was what made me knock. To our astonishment, the old wooden door opened. Thinking fast – it was January 1st after all – I produced a half bottle, wished our mystery host a guid New Year and after some doorstep hilarity about the unlikely nature of this first-foot, we went inside and sat down. When my eyes adjusted to the darkened room, lit only by some candles and the open fire, Alan Campbell (a lecturer in Anthropology) explained the house was called Drumnagarrow – (arguably) in Gaelic 'the little garden on the hill' or the little ridge of the horses (*Druim nan gearran*). I remember the luxurious comfort of those ancient deep brown, leather armchairs. How relaxed the mood as we talked and drank whisky – yet also how daring. Here we, complete strangers, enjoying easy companionship atop a strange hill, in the pitch dark and freezing weather outside – talking earnestly about land reform, barbed-wire fences, hares and Scotland's future. It shouldn't have been happening. None of us should have been there.

But we were.

That was 1985.

A year later, I got a call from Alan. He'd just bought another cottage, 20 miles further east at Corgarff and the little bothy on the hill in Glenbuchat was empty. If I didn't rent it, Drumnagarrow would fall to pieces. A mission, a reason and a prospect of wee adventures. As a young(ish) broadcaster, there was no option but to live in Glasgow. But that didn't mean I had to stay there at weekends too. Maybe this would be the ideal compromise.

So, I headed north the next weekend to meet the owner Sandy McRobert, a tall, slightly stooping, flat-cap-wearing fairmer who spoke broad Doric and assessed me carefully.

'Aye, mebbe we could dae wi your stock in the glen.'

Trying not to rise to the bait, I assured Sandy there was no way I'd be boosting the local population, but would appear at least once a month all-year-round. Clearly Sandy didn't believe me, but wasn't all that interested. Not while I was standing beside an unsouped-up, entirely normal Peugeot 205. Even though I couldn't supply the desired details about horse power or towing capacity, Sandy thought the car was a stoater, eminently capable of scaling the hill and a good sign. He'd nearly bought a Peugeot himself once, was put off by the French sounding name and had regretted it ever since. Of such strange coincidences are possibilities born.

We left The Special One in the farm yard and took a run up the hill in Sandy's battered old Land Rover, accompanied by three cowed looking collies. Drumnagarrow was in a pretty battered state too. Nothing more than an (occasional) trickle of water dripped from one tap in the corrugated-tin-clad kitchen, there was no toilet, no electricity, thus no fridge, lights or heating, and the gutter was half-hanging off too. There was a deep, wide fireplace in the main room, with a box room, containing a single bed with a very vintage mattress, a central empty room facing north which felt damp and another south-facing room, which also felt unaccountably cold. Old carpets, those fabulous old leather armchairs, assorted pots, pans and cutlery, a wood-splitting axe, a small outhouse for a chemical loo and a semi-demolished shed overgrown with nettles completed the package. There was no proper track up to the cottage or creature comforts within, except for one surprisingly ornate dark wooden dresser, a small rectangular mirror cunningly held to a rickety wooden frame with a bit of twisted wire and above the fireplace in the main room,

FIG 1.5 Drumnagarrow in 2018, after 15 years without a tenant.

an unsettling large, framed photograph of a standing man and seated woman in classic, stiff Victorian pose.

FIG 1.6 Mirror.

Her slightly greying hair was tightly coiled. He looked out unsmiling, one proprietorial hand on her rounded shoulder. Their demeanour was hardly welcoming. And to cap it all, someone had popped her eyes with a pen, so her unseeing stare travelled everywhere.

'Ye can aye tak it doon, ye ken – if she's upsetting ye.'

Sandy's words sounded sympathetic, but his tone was scathing.

I realised the grim-looking couple would have to stay. They were part of Drumnagarrow's past – a reality I didn't understand but simply had to accept. Otherwise I'd be forever on the back foot, 'editing' the place instead of living in it and placing doom-laden meanings on entirely innocent objects. After a few months, I'd likely be so familiar with the place, I'd not even see that picture.

'I'll take it.'

Sandy seemed highly amused at the idea of a woman trying to fend for herself halfway up a hill. So back down at Milton, standing by the Peugeot, the deal was done. The rent was £365 – one pound for each day of the year. And there were no further rules. Or help.

And actually, that was the way I wanted it.

Without electricity, running water or a flushing toilet, the smallest everyday tasks become difficult. Satisfyingly difficult. Find a box of matches in the dark if you haven't put it back in its proper spot earlier. You cannae. Leave a box of matches there for two weeks assuming it won't get damp. You dinnae. Start a fire without dry kindling or firelighters. It's not easy. Try to cook food once the gas bottle has run out and the nearest supplier is an hour's drive away. Crisps again. Discover a sheep has died in the lean-to shed containing the chemical toilet. Recover, then break the habit of a lifetime and ask for help, only to discover no local farmer will acknowledge this as his dead sheep. Gritted teeth.

Try over and over again to use a Tilley lamp properly, but reliably fill the room with thick black smoke instead. Annoying. Then stumble across a roup (farm sale) with a box of 900 candles plus a manual typewriter thrown in for a tenner and no other bidders.

Deep joy.

Over time, I became rather chuffed at my general handiness (Tilley lamps notwithstanding). I could chop wood, though occasionally it was easier to heave a log indoors and keep pushing it into the fire over the course of a few days. Messy, hard to light, and doubtless a fire hazard – but satisfying all the same. Arriving one night to a flooded floor in the main room, I fixed the collapsed pointing in the hardest to reach upper section of the gable-end wall the next morning, only to discover the hard way how quickly cement sets. There were near constant problems of dampness, partly explained by the discovery of rocks, pebbles and concrete poured down the chimney of the less-used south-facing room. Sandy professed he had no knowledge of how this happened but speculated it might have been 'tae keep the birds oot'.

A few days later, Angus from neighbouring Strathdon turned up to unblock the chimney, sent by Sandy. Unhooking a ladder from the top of his car, he nipped up onto the roof for a look.

I could hear the long, whistling intake of breath from down below.

'It's nae good, ye ken. Someone's ta'en a puckle o' stanes and chucked them doon wi cement.'

This much I already knew.

'Dae ye hae onything I can yaise tae bash it oot, like?'

A woman without a ladder was hardly likely to have a battering ram. But after a quick, gloved guddle amongst the nettles that swamped the derelict outhouse, Angus came back with a long iron post he'd twisted off a disintegrating bedstead. He climbed back onto the low roof, complimenting the perfect state of the slates, and sat down carefully with a stabilising leg on each side before lifting the iron post and stabbing it down into the chimney-pot, over and over again. I could hardly watch.

Ten minutes of precarious, high-energy pounding later, nothing had moved.

'Angus, it doesn't really matter. I hardly use this room anway.'
'That's because it's damp, quine. It'll a' start tae move soon.'
It didn't.
'Would you like to stop for a cup of tea, Angus?'
He wouldn't.

Hell may have no fury like a woman scorned. It also has no obsession like a man performing an impossible act of DIY. Angus was now bent over the chimney, his sandy hair blown in a wispy hoop over his head.

'Looks like a bit of rain!'
'Och that'll come tae nothing.'

Clearly, Angus wouldn't stop till the stones were dislodged, the pole was broken or he was knackered. So, I left him to it.

An hour later, a massive crash signalled success. Of a kind. The hearth in the spare room lay almost demolished by rocks which had cascaded suddenly from on high, followed by the pole which had been sharpened into a veritable javelin by hours of grinding.

FIG 1.7 Bothy looking south over Glenbuchat to Ben Newe.
Courtesy of Steve Cameron

Leaving me to haul the heavy, jagged lumps outside over the next few days, Angus dusted himself down, reloaded the ladder on top of his car and absolutely refused any kind of payment for his help.

'I was just being neighbourly, ken.'

Still, neighbourliness should not have to be its own reward. I realised the right thing to do was find out what Angus liked to drink at the local shop, buy large amounts and leave it on his doorstep. I also soon discovered that a truly impossible-to-dislodge blockage remained in the chimney, along with a spear-sized hole in the outer chimney wall, which meant the fire and thus the room were still unusable.

I closed the door to consider my next move and opened it two years later. Only to find that a bird had indeed got in and made a nest in the corner of the room.

I shut the door again and pondered the possibility that Sandy might actually be psychic.

So, with dampness now a fairly permanent problem, pillows and duvets had to be hauled up and down with each visit, often meaning several repeat journeys by foot. Without running water, hygiene was confined to enlivening cold washes.

I'll be honest. The only time my former husband Chris had second thoughts about the wisdom of getting hitched was climbing the hill to behold life in the bothy.

But to me any difficulties were minor, temporary and liberating. The men in my life have always been confident about practical tasks, competent with tools and fond of solving practical problems. So in the 'proper' world I was generally stopped from having a go. Even though trying, making mistakes and having a go to tackle things your own way is a delicious experience and an essential part of building confidence in your own capabilities. So at the hut, I 'fixed' things my own way, cobbled together solutions, held my ground, and eventually knew that ground fairly well. I gave myself permission to make a total mess of tasks I'm sure the average power tool-wielding man would have found straightforward. And loved it.

This weekend life of small unpredictable adventures was

precious beyond measure after working weeks full of constraint, convention and convenience, not to mention fairly unbending '80s gender stereotypes.

Nothing compared to the delight of arriving at the dead of night and waking up amidst the hills, buzzards, stoats, pheasants and mountains hares – way above the farms, tractors, fields, moors and houses of Donside. I loved the freedom to walk up to the strange tor-like extrusion known locally as the garnet stone – or up to the old pines, where capercaillie often skimmed the heather like low-flying turkeys.

From the house, I could see all the way south to Mount Keen in Deeside and sit outside for hours happed up in blankets watching the Northern Lights. I went to dances at Glenbuchat Hall, piping at the Lonach Games, enjoyed the craic at the Kildrummy Arms and got supplies of freshly laid eggs from the local shop.

I also learned about the house itself.

It seems Drumnagarrow was once the home of James Strachan, who was born two years before Culloden. That overwhelming defeat saw the glen's ownership transferred from Jacobite John Gordon to the Hanoverian supporting Earl of Fife. Strachan's son, also James, was born in 1783 and became a well-known fiddler held in high esteem by his famous Deeside contemporary, Scott Skinner whose composition the 'Fisher's Rant' was renamed 'Drumnagarry' in Strachan's honour.

FIG 1.8 Bothy, 2020.
Courtesy of Steve Cameron

James lived at Drumnagarrow for 40 years until 1821. His daughter Mary married William Hardie, a descendant of another fiddling master Peter Hardie of Dunkeld, himself a pupil of the famous Niel Gow. William and Mary had a family of 15 and their own son James became one of Scotland's most famous violin makers. In 1851, nine of them lived at Drumnagarrow, in 1918, there were just two occupants and the last recorded resident left in 1960.[1] Reconstruction of estate houses, cottages and steadings just before World War One meant my bothy was probably a different building to the one occupied by the Strachan and Hardie clans – though in the same patch. But I was intrigued to think such a strong musical gene had run through the place for more than a century.

That long reach of family tradition was a feature of my own childhood through long summer visits to Wick, where our arrival from Belfast would prompt the distribution of Callard & Bowser toffees by my grandfather, Magnus More (extracted from white quarter pound bags stashed round the front room) before the womenfolk pulled in for tea and lengthy, painstaking tributes to the Wickers who'd died since our last visit.

'Och, ye mind, Helen, at chap, e mannie Farquhar, he lived up by Houstons. Ye do mind. He wiz ages with oor Kathlyn.' And so, it would go on until some particular detail finally prompted a memory. 'Aye. I do mind mither. He was related to Wheecha,' the local nickname for an auld man who struggled with cancer. They don't mince words in Wick. But they do go on. As one sadly demised Wicker was conversationally laid to rest, the women would move relentlessly on to the next nearly forgotten soul, aided by more tea and local newspaper cuttings stored between pages of Nana's bible. If we were lucky, my brother Graeme and I would escape to the Old Man's Rest above Wick harbour with Granda More to watch the third or fourth *Boy Andrew* pull into port, under the watchful, assessing gaze of men who'd fished on the original or maybe the second boat of the same name. An occasional summer highlight was the Halkirk Highland Games where sons of previous champions dominated the heavyweight events, children of well-known piping families

carried on their parents' winning ways and every prize list began
with a local Caithness name.

Family was a form of currency in Wick and I rather admired
its non-negotiable reach, even though my own life was lived very
differently. Mum ventured far beyond Wick by marrying a Banffshire lad and would-be poet turned RAF pilot and then insurance
manager in the sobering wake of World War Two. They moved
first to Wolverhampton, then Belfast and finally Glasgow which
meant a life of mobility, ever-changing local accents and persis-
tent outsider status for all of us. So, the thought of that family
of 15, produced by the awesome Mary Strachan, was a kind of
anchor. A borrowed anchor, a substitute anchor even, but a
connection to a particular place that felt worth honouring.

Knowing all of this, and presuming that the grim-faced pair
in the portrait were also part of Drumnagarrow's long, living
tradition, it seemed important to keep the frame on the wall and
the house intact.

But it wasn't plain sailing. During the first tentative year of
rental, some events were profoundly unsettling. One spring afternoon I arrived after a winter's visiting gap, and immediately made
the fire. I started the usual process of unpacking pillows, duvet
covers, sheets and towels and heard a bang outside like the sound
of a car backfiring. Except 1,200 feet up Little Firbriggs Hill,
that was hardly likely. I went outside to investigate – saw nothing
– and came back to find myself standing on a dead mouse which
certainly hadn't been there before. I scooped it up, chucked it
out, washed my hands in the freezing water of the cattle trough
and went back inside to make up the bed in the box room. Shaking
out the duvet, the remains of a rabbit fell out. Clearly it had been
there awhile and something had eaten all the flesh, leaving just
fur and bones. Trawling my limited knowledge of cat and stoat
behaviour (this was the era before the internet and mobile phones),
I was still taking nature's little mysteries in my stride when there
was a deafening crash from the main room. That picture complete
with the unsmiling Victorian couple, heavy wooden frame and
glass had smashed down onto the stone hearth. Seconds later the
room was full of flies.

That was it. All the shrugged-off mysteries of the previous year rushed back into my mind. All the sensible explanations of strange moments suddenly collapsed. Clearly, the place was haunted and I was going to die. Heart pumping, mind racing, breath panting, my only thought was to get out.

With every step across the fields towards the car I could feel the approach of the mad axeman. Of course. He'd been living in the bothy for years and was suddenly homeless because I'd come along. Now he was hounding me out with a flurry of small, hard-to-explain incidents which had finally produced the desired vortex of sheer terror and immunity to rational thought.

Exactly where was the mad axeman staying now, out here on the cold hill? How could he have contrived to insert a mouse under my foot? Where had the flies come from? Why was I now looking under all the seats in the car?

It didn't matter. I was completely spooked and went off to stay with a friend in neighbouring Deeside.

After that, I found it hard to stay alone overnight at Drumnagarrow. But bit by bit I pieced together a possible explanation. The cord on the picture frame had been ripe and only needed the first real heat of the year from the fire to give way. House flies spend winter in a hibernation-like state, hidden away in cracks and crevices (like the back of picture frames). When temperatures climb in spring, they're ready to move – and the sudden crash of the picture woke them up with a bang. It took longer to figure out the rabbit and mouse – but the explanation soon presented itself in the shape of a stoat, scampering from the house, still partly clad in its white winter fur. Stoats like to coorie into beds, duvets and bring their meals with them. I had simply disturbed this chap en route to the bed we evidently shared. A forensic examination of the wood-panelled interior revealed no obvious entry points, but a look outside showed several scrapped-out holes. Once these were blocked with stones, the animal appearances stopped.

Slowly, slowly, the panic subsided. Completely.

A couple of years later, after patiently connecting each strange sound, disturbance and half-chewed deposit back to its inevitable animal source, the paralysing fear had evaporated. By then, if the mad axeman had appeared, I would not have moved a muscle.

After years of the townie's over-reaction to every non-existent threat, I had gone to the other extreme – generally unrufflable and very calm in natural surroundings.

I didn't find the reason for every strange occurrence at the hut, but I stopped needing to. It would be just another quirk of nature that I might eventually understand. But it wouldn't be a problem.

One night, after four years as an occasional occupant of Drumnagarrow, I was sitting outside, reading in the twilight and heard something move through the tangle of nettles, grass and tansy towards me. I finished the page I was reading, set the book down and quietly turned to look into the face of a small roe deer. We surveyed one another. There was no threat coming from me and no panic coming from her. After a few minutes, the deer strolled off. It was a perfect moment.

And there were lots of them.

Life at the bothy made me feel like Heidi, who opened her front door every week of my formative childhood years to reveal villages, houses, civilisation, responsibility and the demanding world of people all safely distant, down below. Heidi lived above and beyond. In this ramshackle bothy, so did I. Though I imagine our hill-top lives had very little else in common.

I'd guess the delicately plaited Swiss lass never took all her furniture outside and leaned it carefully again the gable wall to cement that large javelin-shaped hole in the chimney. I don't suppose she stumbled slightly upon descent causing a cascade of old wooden furniture, a bruised arm and (looking on the bright side) a plentiful supply of firewood. I don't imagine thereafter she looked fondly at the radio/cassette player damaged in the fall – which henceforth operated only as a radio – and smiled each time she remembered the gloriously eccentric reason for its limited functionality.

I'm guessing Heidi didn't spend five hours carefully unpicking (and then rebuilding) a dry stane dyke when her valiant Peugeot came to rest there, after failing to thrash its way up the snow-laden track one winter's day. And I don't imagine Heidi eventually dragged that poor, unloved, unclaimed dead sheep on an old plastic bag to the back of her stone bothy, setting fire to it with a sprinkling of paraffin, because the winter ground was too hard for a burial. Discovering the paraffin did no more than blacken the fleece, I'm almost certain she did not then build a proper fire on the singed, sheepy mass and watch it burn all night, taking care to sit upwind of the terrible smell. I'll wager she did not thereafter have a large black shadow on her back wall. I don't suppose Heidi relished being free to try daft things, make mistakes, chop, build, burn, play, mourn, cook, imagine, eat or drink what she wanted. I imagine Heidi got sensibly married and in the fullness of time had her plaits cut.

I know that neither she, nor any other sensible human being, would enjoy the perverse pleasures of weekends without creature comforts. At least, no sensible human being in Scotland.

'So, would you like us to just drive up the hill – as far as we can go in the snow and see the Sami huts right at the top?'

Inger Lise was smiling gamely. No words can express the delight of being completely understood by a flame-haired, young Nordic stranger.

CHAPTER TWO

Hammerfest

INGER LISE DRIVES, zig-zagging up the steep, snow-capped hills at the end of Europe. We slow down to investigate a traditional Sami *gamme* (turf-built hut), spot the river which first gave electric light to Hammerfest and slide onto the precariously iced-over viewpoint which leads the eye towards the sparkling-white island of Sørøya and beyond to the matter-of-fact enormity of the Arctic Ocean.

Later, back in the town, we nip into the town's main café to meet Inger Lise's mother-in-law – Bjøorg, Queen of the Hammerfest *hytte*.

Bjørg Larsen is now retired but was first a nurse and then a teacher. She's married to Ola, a fisherman and their daughter is local teacher, Mariann Svendsen. Her son is Christian, who would become Inger Lise's husband in 2015. With most of her relations elsewhere, the Larsen/Svendsens have been like a second family to Inger Lise, so their huts have become her huts too. And boy do they have huts.

FIG 2.1 Sami *gamme* above Hammerfest.

Bjørg is a warm, kindly woman who's keen to communicate, but has no English and since I had no Norwegian back then, Inger Lise has to perform a lot of patient translation. Bjørg lists the holiday homes her extended family owns (or part owns).

My jaw hits the ground.

There are seven.

I tell her back home we would call her the Queen. Inger Lise translates and Bjørg is not offended by the comparison. It takes a while to get the full picture, because the story of each holiday home so precisely maps the changing fortunes of the Larsen and Svendsen clans.

FIG 2.2 and 2.3 Ola and Bjørg Larsen.
Courtesy of Inger Lise Svendsen

Bjørg's great-grandfather, Svend Andersson lived in Isdalen – considered remote even by Hammerfest standards. He built his first house in the 1850s before moving to a larger one nearby in Sør-Tverrfjord, Loppa, which is 50 miles by sea, sailing direct from Hammerfest or a full day's travel using two ferries. Svend's son Henrik, was Bjørg's grandfather. He took over both houses, but they were burned to the ground by retreating German forces at the end of World War Two. Bjørg's father Hagbart was 28, when he married Marie in 1942 (she was one of 17 siblings) and they rebuilt the house in Loppa.

'The family put a roof over the foundations of Heimstad and lived in it with the animals while they built a *naust* (boathouse) and then the house. The hay for the animals was already eaten so there was no insulation and the winter was terribly cold.'

Nonetheless, the family survived and Heimstad became Bjørg's 'family home', shared with the rest of her siblings and Hytte Number One.

It is still umbilically connected to the whole family and symbolic of Finnmark's survival and reconstruction. So, when Bjørg's mum, Marie, moved to the bright lights of Hammerfest in 1980 to live with her children after Hagbart died, Heimstad was left uninhabited, but not sold.

Didn't Bjørg or her siblings ever think of putting it on the market?

'Never. There are too many memories. It's beautiful in the high mountains, but it has no economic value. If we sold, we would almost be giving it away. There were 200 people there when I was a girl. Now there are just seven. The whole area is my family. I'm related to almost everyone. So, no-one sells old houses in Loppa. We've kept Heimstad alive by sharing it. Everyone does their bit to maintain it.'

Luckily, Bjørg has four brothers and sisters complete with their own families, in-laws and children. So Heimstad has a small *hytte*-fixing battalion.

Not content with Hytte Number One though, the family then built a cabin next to it in 1995 for more sleeping space. After all, five families come back in rotation every summer and often together at Easter so 15 people can all be there at the same time.

So, the cabin beside Heimstad is *Hytte* Number Two.

I am so clearly taken aback at the idea of building a hut just to accommodate people a couple of times a year that Bjørg asks, via Inger Lise: 'Well where does your family go for Easter?'

Woops.

'We don't really tend to um, do Easter any more, it's um...'

'Well, where do you take guests to celebrate after a wedding?'

The awkwardness deepens.

'Ah well, we normally...'

Let's face it. We normally try to buy a bit of temporary connection with a random somewhere for special occasions, and generally fail. Weddings mean hiring the over-priced wing of an anonymous hotel, with guests forced into dresses a size too small and shoes a little too high-heeled. Once the drink flows and the dancing starts some guests will stay – but many leave after a decorous interval, uncomfortable at the prospect of enforced intimacy with relatives they hardly know. It's normal.

In Hammerfest, normal is different.

Folk in the extended Larsen/Svendsen clan marry in the early summer and then head to the double *hytte* at Loppa to relax, talk nonsense, fish, swat flies, walk, tell stories, reminisce, cook, drink and enjoy one another's company. There is no rental, no restriction, no bar licence, no tarmac and no rules. There is plenty of work beforehand to get the huts shipshape. But that's not work. It's a labour of love.

Hytte Number Three belongs to Bjørg's husband, Ola Larsen who comes from Akkerfjord on the island of Sørøya – ten miles by sea from Hammerfest. Ola moved to Hammerfest with his parents in the 1980s. He is one of five children who decided to keep their family house in Akkerfjord for much the same reasons as Bjørg's family. Now Ola uses it all-year-round to fish and even takes his own boat across in the summer when the Arctic seas are calmer.

Ola recently bought out his siblings to own the family home, and plans to rent it out to tourists. He's bought more land at Akkarfjord and now stays at a new *hytte* he's built there. *Hytte* Number Four.

The most frequently used holiday home for the Larsen/Svendsens though is *Hytte* Number Five. In 1984, Bjørg and Ola bought a hut in Trangedal more than an hour inland from Hammerfest for weekends away (it takes a full day in each direction to reach either family home, making them both unsuitable for short weekend trips). The couple had that *hytte* for three years but sold it 'because the children didn't want us to drive that far.'

So, between 1990 and 1994 they built their own *hytte* in Skaidi ('where rivers meet' in the Sami language) – an hour's drive

FIG 2.4 Ola's new *hytte* on Sørøya.
Courtesy of Inger Lise Svendsen

south of Hammerfest. The rent for the plot is 70 Norwegian
kroner (about £7 per annum) and they have a 100-year lease.
The hytte cost 2,000 NOK (£200) to register and was built using
dugnad (community help) from other hutters, who were mostly
also neighbours from Hammerfest. Ola and Bjørg carried the
building materials in from the nearest road, including the pine
wood panels.

Hytte Number Five.

In 1997 Mariann, Bjørg's daughter, built another *hytte* nearby because her mother's hut was too crowded.

Four people in one tiny room were like sardines. Often there were 14 people in seven beds and on sofas. It was good to be next door.

I think that's what you'd cry tactful.

There was no cost except the building materials, because Mariann's *hytte* is on her mother's plot.

Hytte Number Six.

Bjørg and Ola live in a flat in Hammerfest during the week. That could qualify as *Hytte* Number Seven, but let's not stretch the point. After their marriage in 2015, Inger Lise and Christian would strike out and buy a new *hytte* of their own. But when we first met, that all lay in the future.

No, the seventh hut isn't even in Norway. Bjørg's brother, Helge married a lassie from Croatia, so the Larsens bought and renovated an old cottage near Pula because they dislike being 'packaged like tourists' and grow grapes and olives there every summer.

Hytte Number Seven.

And which of all these (including their flats in Hammerfest) is the real home?

Mariann and Bjørg look at each other.

'Well, my old dog is buried at the *hytte*, not outside my flat in town,' offers Mariann. 'I might have to move my home for a job, or I might downsize, but I'll never move the hut.'

Bjørg thinks for a minute.

'Yes, the Skaidi *hytte* is probably the real home.'

So many options, so many ways to keep family members connected to their roots, their landscape and to one another. Such a constant, year-round connection with land and sea – especially through the long, dark winters of the barren Arctic. Such a variety of places to relax in and people to relax with. Such a guilt-free experience of holiday home ownership. Such a low-cost, low-impact source of joy. And such a sharp contrast with Scotland

FIG 2.5 Grave of Mariann's dog buried at her *hytte*.

and our thin, truncated experience of one another, our special occasions, shared leisure time, family connections and our own extraordinary land.

The still-short Arctic day is fading with apricot hues spilling across the snow as Inger Lise delivers me back to Hammerfest Airport. I feel strangely emotional and we hug.

As the plane gathers speed on the runway heading back to the balmy south, my mind is whirring.

Why could I not have been Norwegian?

I could have been brought up outdoors.

My family could have had a *hytte*.

I could have been considered normal.

I could never have known a deep-fried Mars Bar.

I could have been carried forward by a healthy herd.

I could have not wasted several years in pubs.

Maybe it's not too late.

Glancing down, I glimpse the tiny wooden huts of Skaidi amongst the stubble that passes for forest in this majestic tundra. The plane soars up into the mist and I know I'll be back.

CHAPTER THREE

Facts are chiels
that winna ding

IT'S HARD TO BELIEVE Scotland can be so very different from Norway in the way we spend leisure time – those moments that really define us. Our selves beyond work. So, after that memorable trip to Hammerfest, I embarked on a bit of research. Believe it, Norway and Scotland are poles apart – not just in hut ownership, but in every 'leisure asset' that helps people enjoy the Great Outdoors. Facts are chiels that winna ding and the statistics dinnae lie.

Starting with huts, there's an epic difference between Norway and Scotland.

In 2018, there were 463,812 holiday homes in Norway, amongst a population of 5.3 million people. Norwegians also owned 55,000 holiday homes abroad mostly in neighbouring countries, to the slight irritation of Swedes, whose King actually ruled Norway till 1905.[1] That means almost ten per cent of Norwegians own a holiday home or put differently, there's roughly one holiday home per 11 Norwegians.[2] Even if some families like the Svendsen/Larsens have several huts between them, that's a fairly equitable distribution. You could say, almost anyone who wants a *hytte* in Norway can find access to one. Pretty much.

In Scotland by contrast, there were just 29,929 holiday homes in 1999 and 25,700 in 2018.[3] That drop is largely explained by the start of council tax surcharges for second homes in 2013.[4] So, just half of one per cent of Scots has a second home today, meaning holiday home-owning here is indeed a minority, elitist pursuit. It's worth spelling out the scale of difference. Ten per cent of Norwegians own a holiday home compared with just half of one per cent of Scots.

The main reason for this huge discrepancy is the *kind* of holiday home that's typical in each country.

In Norway 93 per cent of second homes are purpose-built wooden *hytte* (self-built wooden huts) and just seven per cent are converted farmhouses and family homes like Heimstad.[5] In Scotland the proportions are almost exactly the other way around. Just two per cent of Scotland's second homes are wooden huts and 98 per cent are 'detatched homes or farmhouses used as holiday homes.'

This is the root of our second homes problem.

Norway and Scotland aren't that different in the number of 'proper houses' used as second homes (though over there, most still belong to local families like the Svendsen/Larsens who originally built them). But what really sets the North Sea cousins apart is the wildly differing number of purpose-built wooden huts.[6] Easy to build, additional to the existing housing stock, traditionally low-impact and generally located in forests, the humble weekend wooden hut has been the sustainable leisure goodie of choice in countries with democratic land ownership patterns. But sadly, that's not us. So, Table 3.1 shows the stark truth. Scotland's huts are a wee almost invisible skinty of ginger icing on Norway's large hytte cake – a miserable 0.14 per cent of her huts total.

Another big difference between the two countries is where holiday homes are located. In Scotland they are often found in

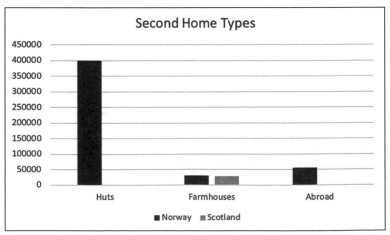

TABLE 3.1 Scotland and Norway – second home types.

the stunningly scenic Highlands and Islands which is a two-to six hour drive from the largest cities.[7] In Norway only 'family homes' (like Bjørg's house in Loppa) tend to be so remote. *Hytte* (93 per cent of the Norwegian second homes total) are used almost every weekend and generally lie within one hour's drive of the first home, so owners can get there on Friday nights. Proximity matters more than epic landscapes. If you want to enjoy every waking moment at the hytte, if life is a collection of everyday pleasures not very occasional special events, then you don't want to drive for hours, you just want to get to the *hytte* and start enjoying it.

According to *hytte* experts Dieter Müller and C. Michael Hall, 50 per cent of second home owners in Sweden live within 37 kilometres of their property and it's almost the same in the Czech Republic, because the primary requirement of a *hytte* is to be within reach.[8] That doesn't seem to be true of second homes in Scotland. Obviously, folk from a crofting background get land on the family croft, not anywhere else. Maybe people who can afford an expensive second home have more control over their time, and aren't restricted to quick weekend jaunts. But perhaps, the sheer impossibility of buying an affordable plot closer to cities encourages prospective second home buyers to try remote areas, where low wages block local competition for available houses and stunning landscapes justify the extra travel.

Whatever, this is one of the biggest differences between holiday homes in Scotland and Norway. For Norwegians, they are purpose-built, easy to access, frequently visited and surplus to local housing. For Scots they are distant, hard to access, rarely visited, stone-built detached homes and farmhouses, which could be occupied full-time by locals.

That's minimised in Norway (along with local resentment) by *boplikt* (the duty of residence) which stops owners of 'first' homes ever selling them as summerhouses.[9] Even where land is rented, there are friendly and sometimes familial connections between hutter and landlord and no loss of security of tenure just because hytte occupation is occasional. Hutters do pay local property taxes in Norway, but they are much lower than the Scottish council tax.

It's true that the construction of large, commercial hutting settlements at ski resorts like Trysil (Norway's 'Beverley Hills') has driven up carbon emissions (though improvements in electric car performance should help reduce that) and changed the face of the original, low-impact Norwegian hytte. Wooden huts need substantial maintenance or replacement every couple of decades, so the trend towards larger, higher spec hytte is bound to continue, unless planners intervene. with electricity and mod cons is bound to continue. For now though, 'hytte-palasser', grouped together like bungalows in remote cul-de-sacs, still appear to be in the minority. 62 per cent of Norwegian *hytte* are located individually and 38 per cent sit in clusters of ten or more huts.[10] So that's another important difference between the North Sea cousins. In Norway, *hytte* continue to be mostly scattered across woods, fjords, forests and lochs on private plots bought from local farmers – not located in camps or communities.

In Scotland, it's the reverse. Just 3.8 per cent of huts are found on individual plots, while 87 per cent are located on sites of ten or more.[11] So basically Scottish hutters get a plot on a fairly regulated site while Norwegian *hytte* owners get a walk on the wild side.

Income reveals another big difference. In Norway, the most affluent folk are likely to have a hut, in Scotland the least affluent tend to be hutters. Although Norwegians in every income bracket own *hytte*, rates of ownership are four times higher amongst top earners.[12]

So wealth, city-centre living and hut ownership all go together in Norway – but not here. A survey into the location and condition of Scottish huts was conducted for the Scottish Government in 1999, after Carbeth hutters pleaded for help to avoid eviction. Only a short summary of Hugh Gentleman's report into Scotland's 630 huts was made public, but the full survey, published after a Freedom of Information request to complete the PhD behind this book, revealed a very different income profile of Scottish hut owners:

> Site owners summarise occupiers as mainly older and retired
> people... from lower income groups, often with trade or
> other useful skills in building or maintaining their huts.[13]

Scottish hut owners also tend to rent their sites (82 per cent).[14]
While Norwegians tend to own them (80 per cent).[15] This distinction really matters. Tenants who are only temporary occupants of huts in Scotland forfeit almost all legal rights, whilst
tenants claiming full-time occupancy must pay a full (or double)
council tax. It's a choice between the devil and the deep blue sea
for Scottish hutters, and one that's peculiar to unreconstructed,
quasi-feudal Scotland. According to Professor Robert Rennie, a
legal adviser to the Scottish Government in 1999:

> For any private dwelling house to come under rent legisla-
> tion it must be the only or principal home of the tenant. My
> understanding is that the hutters do not use the huts as their
> principal dwellings and so are not covered by any of the
> security of tenure provisions.[16]

Since this ruling, around 200 hutters have been evicted across
Scotland without a legal leg to stand on, even though their rent
was up to date, their tenure was problem-free and their forebears
had built the huts they were forced to quit. You could call it a
modern-day clearance – though admittedly on a very small scale.
Carbeth is the largest remaining community, but only because
140 tenants went on rent strike for a decade before jointly taking
out a bank loan to buy their land for £1.75 million in 2013.[17]

Essentially, hutters in Scotland are vulnerable tenants with
no legal rights and next to no-one in authority on their side. And
they dare not fish or hunt on the laird's land – the freedoms that
are part and parcel of the whole *hytte* experience in Norway.

So why pour love, effort and money into huts, when you
could be out on a whim, almost any time? The fact that Scots
have persevered speaks volumes about the pent-up demand for
huts, and how quickly it might find expression again today, with
just a few of the supportive conditions enjoyed by the average
Norwegian.

Why does it matter? Because huts connect families. Bjorn Kaltenborn argues that second homes, inherited and passed on through generations, are the truly permanent homes in our lives, whilst our official primary residences are really just temporary shelters.[18] Research amongst Swedish summerhouse owners suggests the chance to spend quality time with family members is the number one attraction. Immersion in nature, relaxation, hunting, fishing and skiing always come second. Of course, there are *hytte* loners too. But generally, hutting across the Nordic nations is family-oriented and sociable. Probably a relief for folk who don't quite fancy dead sheep disposal as the price of having their ain wee but 'n' ben. In Scotland you must be dogged, eccentric and willing to tolerate all kinds of maddening difficulty to have a hut. In Norway, it's a normal, mainstream way of life where whole extended families spend the weekend together, with relatively little discomfort, uncertainty or constraint. Essentially, it's the emotional and social importance of the family hut that keeps hutters coming back, and not just in the Scandinavian countries:

> The cottage frequently becomes the home, the gathering place to which the far-flung family returns each year to renew contacts and once again experience the fundamental satisfactions of being part of something, the satisfactions of a family.[19]

There is relatively widespread ownership of second homes in Russia, the Czech Republic, Germany, Spain and France as well as many parts of North America and New Zealand – though nowhere are second homes as widespread as the Nordic countries.[20]

Country	Population (2006)	Second Homes	Population per second home
Denmark	5,427,400	202,500	27
Finland	5,255,600	450,600	12
Norway	4,640,200	379,200	12
Sweden	9,047,800	469,900	19
Nordic Countries	24,371,000	1,502,200	16

TABLE 3.2 Population and second homes in Nordic countries.

Yet it's not as if these countries have had holiday homes for centuries. Wealthy Norwegians did have fairly elegant second homes for much of the 19th century (just like wealthy Scots), but the big jump occurred when Norwegian workers were given a third week of paid holidays in the 1940s. This increased demand so much that in 1949 the Norwegian government had to ban *hytte* building because it was using up so many scarce raw materials.[21]

Another boom coincided with the post-war de-rationing of cars in 1960. Car numbers increased 12-fold between 1949 and 1974 and many Norwegians used them to build and visit second homes causing *hytte* numbers to double.[22] The point being that widespread *hytte* ownership in the Nordic countries is not ancient history – so the same transformation could happen here, if conditions were right. Perhaps though, mountain bothies, youth hostels and caravans took the place of the *hytte* here?

Brace yourselves.

Norwegians have more of all these things too.

The typical *hytte*-owning Norwegian *also* uses a DNT hut for cross-country skiing and long treks in the mountains. *Den Norske Turistforening* or DNT (Norwegian Trekking Association) was founded in 1868, owns 460 cabins and mountain huts throughout the country, has 240,000 members in 57 local member organisations and a Children's Trekking Club with 16,000 members under the age of 12.[23] It's big.

By contrast the Scottish Mountain Bothies Association (MBA) was founded almost a century later in 1965 and arose from the practice of secretly staying overnight in half-ruined labourers cottages after World War Two when the advent of jeeps, centralisation of farm production and eviction of tenant farmers emptied remote cottages – like Drumnagarrow.[24] Unlike the DNT, which owns all of its purpose-built mountain bothies, the MBA owns only one of the 83 bothies it maintains with the agreement of landowners. It's small.

Some DNT huts are more like mini-mountain hotels providing bed and breakfast – by contrast MBA huts are very basic, free to use and not bookable. The DNT has a quarter of a million

members. The MBA – staffed by volunteers who maintain the huts
– has just 3,600 – even though both countries have roughly the
same population. Yip. It is another world. And that's no reflec-
tion on the passion or commitment of Scots volunteers – it's what
happens when real enthusiasts cannot own and properly care for
the bothies they love.

Youth hostels have traditionally given Scots another route into
nature – in 2013 there were 70 hostels with 18,747 members. But
Norske Vandrerhjem (Norway's Hostel Association) has 77
hostels. Perhaps that's because mountains, rivers and lochs have
historically been easier to access in Norway than Scotland. The
Allmennsrett (right to roam) was codified into an Outdoor Recreation Act in 1957, and gave Norwegians the right to hike in mountains, camp overnight, cycle on tracks and ski in forests. It took
half a century longer for Scots to gain the same package of legal
access rights within the Land Reform (Scotland) Act 2003. But
rivers here are still generally owned and managed by riparian
owners and many are timeshared or let privately at exorbitant
rates, effectively excluding locals and the average local holiday
maker. Fish (and until 2003 even trees on crofts) still belong to the
landowner in Scotland, and although deer belong to no-one, the
right to hunt them is tightly controlled by landowners. That
contrasts with most of northern Europe, where hunting, controlled
by local municipalities, is an open and relatively classless activity.

This tale of everyday exclusion for Scots also extends to
forests – vital for hutting, since the vast majority of huts in
Northern Europe are located in woodlands not on open ground.

Some may feel this is where valid comparison with Scandinavia ends. Sweden and Finland are essentially one gigantic
forest, whilst Scotland has a more open landscape. Whether
that's natural or the result of land use is fiercely debated. But
there's no doubt we live at a 'wooded latitude.' As the Scottish
Government's Forest Strategy 2019-29 observes:

> Scotland's forest types are typical of those found in northern
> latitudes, including countries such as Canada and Finland.
> Without human intervention, it is likely that much of Scotland

would be covered by ... Scots pine and birch in the north and east, and oakwoods in the warm and wetter west.

So the big difference between Scotland and the Nordic nations is not so much latitude or the potential for forest cover but our old friend - ownership patterns (see Table 3.3). Almost 33 per cent of land in Norway is forested, with 171,000 owners. By contrast, only 18 per cent of land in Scotland is forested with a tiny number of forest owners. Research suggests one third is owned by the Scottish Government and managed by the Forestry Commission and 91 per cent of the rest is owned either by the large landed estates or by investment owners – half of whom are absentee owners and a third of whom live outside Scotland.[25] More than half of forest holdings in Scotland are over 50 hectares – across Europe only two per cent of holdings are this big. Veteran land researcher and Green MSP Andy Wightman concludes:

> Scotland has the most concentrated pattern of private forest ownership and the lowest proportion of the population involved in owning forests in Europe.[26] Unlike every other European country, local residents, councils, farmers and cooperatives have been almost completely excluded from forestry ownership here.

	Private forest (hectares)	No. of owners	Average size (hectares)	Population (million)	Percentage of forest owners
Finland	10,498,000	443,800	23.7	5.3	8.4
Norway	9,141,000	171,079	53.4	4.9	3.5
Slovakia	823,200	14,475	56.9	5.4	0.3
Sweden	17,916,200	268,235	66.8	9.1	2.9
Scotland	932,000	4,017	232.0	5.2	0.1

TABLE 3.3 Forestry owners in Scotland and Europe.

This has huge significance for hutting. In Norway, it's always been easy to discuss terms with small-scale, local forest owners. In Scotland, the majority are large, hard-to-reach companies and until recently, even the publicly owned Forestry Commission Scotland deterred public access and still forbids most overnight stays. The only dwellings within Forestry Commission forests are tied houses for forestry workers.

Exclusion from nature extends to inland and coastal waters too. Not only do most Norwegian families have access to a family hytte, a youth hostel, a DNT mountain hut, forests and rivers for fishing – many have a boat as well. Statistics suggest 600,000 boats (yachts, speedboats and rowing boats) were owned in the UK and Ireland in 2004. Impressive. But four times more boats were owned in Scandinavia and the Baltic States despite a combined population 50 per cent smaller than the British Isles.[27] In other words, there was one boat per 107 people in the UK and Ireland and one boat per 15 people in the Nordic and Baltic states. Given that Scotland has 31,460 lochs and a coastline that covers a third the circumference of the planet if laid out straight, that's a vast amount of river and sea we aren't exploring. Why not? Are Scots afraid of the water? Are boats too expensive? Or must feudalism, once again, take the lion's share of the blame?

Until 2018, half the Scottish foreshore and seabed were held by the Crown Estate, set up by King George III in 1760 and based at St James's Market, London SW1. Since then, the pin-striped gents at the Crown Estate Commission (CEC) have had the power to approve or reject local improvements (like constructing a small pier) in places they administer for the Crown but rarely visit. Just like feudal superiors, the Crown Estate could charge £1,000 to set down a mooring, without providing any service beyond the paperwork. The money raised didn't stay locally but was sent directly to the Treasury in London – for 250 years. Happily, CEC powers were devolved in 2017, and Crown Estate Scotland now sends its revenue surplus to the Scottish Government for public spending. But the pattern of remote authority over local decisions has not been broken.

Meanwhile, on lochs and rivers, fishing rights were (and mostly still are) owned by riparian (essentially feudal) landowners. Has that restricted the use of boats? It's hard to prove, but even harder to imagine this web of feudal restriction hasn't left an indelible mark. Has the average Scot ever expected to row, kayak, sail or boat through the most stunning loch and seascapes in the world? I doubt it.

It's much the same story with allotments, historically bedevilled by insecurity of tenure and unloved by the authorities because of their ramshackle appearance and admirably thrawn, hard to organise owners. Plots have generally been handed out during times of war, when growing vegetables was a praiseworthy and patriotic activity, but then taken back by local authority owners in peacetime on the grounds that housing for the many should not be blocked by allotments for the few.[28]

Allotments actually began in rural England, when landowners provided allotments to 'deserving' labourers, controlling their behaviour with 'gifts which might be ropes'.[29]

Land-based Scots already had some places to grow vegetables – farmers often gave workers 'potato ground', mining cottages usually had attached gardens and the pendicle system linked tenanted cottages with detached parcels of arable land. But, after the Allotments Act (1887), Scottish local authorities were required to provide allotments for the 'labouring population' if six or more ratepayers came forward with a request.[30] Very few councils did.

The first informal city plots were established during the early 1880s by the father of town planning, Patrick Geddes, whose Environment Society planted trees in the slums of Edinburgh's Old Town. His Open Spaces Committee found 76 open spaces 'awaiting reclamation' and redesigned these for communal cultivation.[31] The North British Railway Company followed, establishing 36 plots for staff on wasteland near Portobello in 1912.[32] One of the first self-organised groups to use the 1892 legislation was the Edinburgh Allotment Holders' Association. By 1916, 12 acres were managed as allotments under joint Corporation-Association control.

The situation was transformed by the need for self-sufficiency during World War One and the Cultivation of Land Order (1917).

By the war's end 3,400 allotment holders were cultivating 200 acres of former wasteland and parkland.[33] But once the national emergency had passed, house building became the priority and allotment holders faced dispossession. Edinburgh's Town Clerk described the dilemma:

> On the one hand, most allotment-holders have... found by experience the benefit of having a supply of fresh vegetables, and discovered the health [advantages] of this form of recreation. On the other hand, now the war is over... some owners of ground [wish to] have possession or a reasonable rent; and certain areas are urgently required for housing schemes and industrial development. It is extremely difficult to find other ground for allotment-holders who have to be dispossessed.[34]

But other cities managed. The same post-war housing pressure in Oslo did not result in allotment dispossession, even though Norwegian plots are generally larger than Scottish ones to accommodate the huts Norwegians automatically built. In Scotland by contrast, a prohibition on overnight stays was built into the 1902 legislation and remains there still – unique in Europe.[35] So, in Edinburgh, between 1920 and 1930 the number of allotment plots dropped back from 5,000 to 1,900.[36]

The decline in numbers was not just caused by land-hungry councils. The urban poor couldn't afford to buy seed and garden tools because of mass unemployment and the fear that allotment ownership would lead to the loss of unemployment benefit. There was also an aesthetic problem, all too familiar in the story of huts in Scotland: 'allotments can hardly fail to be a disfigurement of an open space such as the King's Parks.'[37]

In 1929, the Federation proposed a model allotment where owners would keep their plots – edged with stone or hedges – in a 'first-class condition'.[38] A communal hut with lockers would provide storage and preclude the need for 'unsightly erections.' A border of trees and flowering shrubs would give the site a pleasing appearance. As Caitlin DeSilvey notes:

FIG 3.1 Edinburgh's Warriston allotments (with tool sheds not huts), 1933.
Courtesy of University of Glasgow Archives & Special Collections,
Papers of Victor Douglas Eustace Webb, GB248 UGC222/1/3/1

With this proposal, the Federation tried to break out of a curious '*Catch-22* situation': insecurity of tenure led to plot vacancies. As a result, allotments presented a chaotic and unkempt face to the public. The public was then unlikely to support municipal investment to secure the continued presence of what they perceived as an 'eyesore'.[39]

Despite all their efforts, the proposal for model allotments was rejected.[40] By 1931 though, with unemployment reaching 27.7 per cent, the Scottish Allotment Scheme for the Unemployed (SASU) was devised as a means of encouraging the 'deserving poor'. Unemployed men got a discount on the cost of seeds, seed potatoes, fertilisers and tools and reduced rent on a plot.[41] By 1934, 74 arable acres – in Granton, Warriston, West Mains and Saughton – had been turned over to the scheme. A newspaper reporter visiting West Mains allotments found a large number of men busy at their plots:

If there was tragedy it was... seeing so many of what appeared to be the best type of worker without employment.

Something to occupy mind and muscle. This was better –
infinitely better – than walking the streets at a loose end.[42]

Still, the SASU scheme suffered from a lack of enthusiasm.
Doubtless unemployed but politically active Scots wanted more
than a vegetable patch. In July 1932, the Secretary of the Scottish
National Union of Allotment Holders (SNUAH) warned the Government that unemployed men were

> easy prey to Red and Communistic agitators and much insi-
> dious harm is being done in this direction against which the
> Allotment Movement could be a strong counteracting influ-
> ence if developed on scale.[43]

No-one listened, but the SASU scheme did introduce hundreds of
people to allotments, many of whom became the core of the 'Dig
for Victory' effort during World War Two. At the end of those
hostilities, the SNUAH did not wait for a declaration of peace. In
October 1944, it sent a circular letter to Town Clerks pressing
for security of tenure and stressing the allotment holders' contribution to the war effort. But once again, the need to build
houses trumped the recreational claims of allotment holders.
Food rationing ended in 1954, the advent of television, super-
markets and restaurants changed the way leisure time was being
spent and in 1957, all government support for the allotment
movement was ended.[44] During the 1960s, neglected sites were
seen as easy targets by developers. Low rents encouraged car
repair firms, garages and even sawmills to set up on old allotment
sites. By 1964, only 110 of the 170 acres listed in the 1953
Development Plan remained.[45] Meanwhile, plans to include
allotments in new housing schemes had 'not proved to be prac-
ticable'.[46] In 1965, the Secretary for the Edinburgh Federation
tried to re-label allotments as 'leisure gardens' on the grounds
that 'allotments' conjure up 'a wrong impression upon people
[who] immediately think of some piece of ground strewn with
broken down huts and uncultivated plots' and suggested better
facilities would 'attract and encourage the right type of person
to our allotment areas'. Higher costs would also filter out 'unde-

sirable elements'.[47] A month later, the Superintendent of Parks proposed 'large centres in the Green Belt' to replace the 'unsightly allotments' springing up in city parks.[48] The Corporation proposed three permanent centres in Edinburgh's green belt where displaced allotment holders could take advantage of improved facilities while children played on nearby grass lawns.[49] It never happened. The City Chamberlain expressed concern that the 'necessarily high rent' to cover the development 'would dissuade all but the most enthusiastic or affluent allotment holders.'[50] So poor workers were 'undesirable elements' but wealthier ones weren't worth catering for. A bit of a Catch-22.

The eco-consciousness of the 1970s coaxed a new generation into allotment gardening and by 1976, enthusiasts had rented each of Edinburgh's 1,020 allotment plots, with 300 people on the waiting list. Meanwhile in Denmark, a new law in 2007 stipulated there should be ten gardens per 100 flats without a private garden. So today Copenhagen (with a population roughly similar to Edinburgh's) has 17,000 plots while Edinburgh has just 1,300.

But yes, it's true that Scotland, with 6,300 individual plots, does have more allotment sites than Norway, with 3,000. That's mostly because urban Norwegians still own land and small farms and spend most of their spare time at the family *hytte*. In more urbanised Germany and Denmark, there's a higher proportion of allotments than both rural Norway and urbanised Scotland.

So the allotment is most definitely not the Scottish *hytte*. Neither is the caravan. Despite the plethora of huts, boats, youth hostels, mountain bothies and allotments in Norway, there are actually more caravans too. About 250,000 Norwegians own a mobile home (100,000 of them registered) on 800 sites.[51] There are even caravan sites in the Arctic – with attached huts. By comparison there are 34,116 pitches on 318 Scottish Caravan and Camping Forum member holiday parks in Scotland.[52]

Shamefully, 4,547 Scottish households were living perma-nently in caravans in the 2001 Census, backed up by a local authority survey in 2007.[53] So for some Scots, the caravan is no

FIG 3.2 Caravans in the snow near Alta, Norway.

substitute *hytte* – it is their static, poorly equipped and hard to heat first home. And that's the final important factor in Scotland's low rate of hut and second home ownership – the fact so many folk traditionally rented their first home.

The average Oslo citizen in the 1920s was a quasi-owner in a local housing cooperative financed by *Husbanken* (the National Housing Bank). Flats in block housing were privately but collectively owned by occupants; sale prices were fixed by the authorities and flats were 'bought' via waiting lists. By the 1970s almost all Norwegians were living in affordable homes, almost eight out of ten Norwegian households were homeowners and anxieties about basic living standards had mostly been removed.[54] But the blocks were featureless and identical. Perhaps this stoked the appetite for a *hytte* outside the city that would be less controlled and regimented and – since it was hard to alter or improve the flats – use up spare cash.

By contrast, the average Glasgow citizen in the 1920s was a public sector tenant with recent experience of the utterly grim conditions that prevailed during the Victorian era, in the private sector. The 1861 Census found that a third of 'houses' in Glasgow consisted of one room roughly 14 by 11 feet in size (the 'single end') inhabited by five people. Overcrowding was epic. People slept like sardines in rooms without furniture or sanitation and worked every day for ten to 12 hours without time off.[55] Hygiene suffered, disease was endemic and life was simply a grim struggle for survival. Dr James B Russell – Glasgow's pioneering Medical Officer – penned this haunting description of children who died young in 1888:

> Their little bodies are laid out on a table or a dresser so as to be somewhat out of the way of their brothers and sisters who play, sleep and eat in their ghastly company. One in five of all who are born there [in Glasgow's overcrowded slums] never see the end of their first year.[56]

Council housing came to the rescue at the end of World War One. Of the houses built in Scotland between 1919 and 1939, 67 per cent were in the public sector, compared to just 26 per cent in England. But there was a crucial difference between Scotland and the very similar municipal housing drive in Norway. Residents in Scotland were tenants, not cooperative owners.

In 1971, 70 per cent of Scottish households were public sector tenants compared to just 49 per cent of households in England and perhaps just 5 per cent in Norway.[57] And that meant Scottish workers were constrained in ways that Norwegians in self-built rural houses and cooperatively owned flats were not.

In Scotland, a council flat meant little control over décor, location, repairs, surroundings or neighbours. A private flat meant a six-month lease with equally little control. And in the countryside, it was also Hobson's Choice – a tied house (on a peppercorn rent with probable eviction at the end of the job) or a tenant farmhouse with equally little say or security.[58]

The widespread incidence of tenancy as opposed to home ownership in Scotland may have had an important impact on the development of hutting. Spanish researchers believe the propensity to have a second home is greater if the first home is owned and doesn't place a lifelong, regular strain on family finances. At some point the mortgage on a purchased home is paid up and cash is available for other projects, whereas tenants have a constant and never-ending need for cash.[59] This could be another factor behind low numbers of huts and second homes in Scotland which had the lowest home ownership rates in Europe till 1993, while Norway has long had one of the highest.[60]

In summary, Norwegians, with the highest levels of GDP in the world, choose to spend summers and weekends in boats and basic wooden huts, like most other countries at a wooded latitude, while Scots, with lower levels of disposable income, apparently don't.

Some will doubtless suggest Scots simply lost the appetite for life on the land, after being emotionally and physically 'locked out' for generations. But Hugh Gentleman's 1999 research suggests that's not true – or at least not the full picture. His report found that most of the 62 communal hut sites located across Scotland were just like sites across Norway and Europe – they began between the wars fuelled by a collapse in land values, legislative limits to the working day, increased holiday entitlement and the growth of outdoor activities encouraged by socialist and trade union movements and emboldened by returning soldiers determined to create a land truly fit for heroes.

Gentleman's research shows that Scottish hutting communities were set up during the interwar period, but unlike their Nordic counterparts, they failed to thrive, survive or attract investment from their private owners, support from the authorities or participation by Scotland's middle classes. Thus, hutting in Scotland rapidly became a pursuit for the eccentric few, a precarious way to spend time and money, a collective rather than an individual family activity and a marker of poverty – with hutters vulnerable to arbitrary removal, rent rises and gentrification.

How was this situation allowed to develop?

Pondering all of this in 2010, I knew the answer lay in Scotland not Norway, but with so many crazy rules and norms accepted here because they've 'ae been', I needed help to get going – inspiration from a country where hutting is joyfully ubiquitous and normal; some actual surprise about Scotland's hut-free landscape instead of the usual shrug of shoulders. Okay, it was an excuse to get back to Norway. I took it.

CHAPTER FOUR

Oslo fjord's *hytte* heaven

I STARTED BY searching Norway's National Library online. I had no real idea what I was looking for. But within an hour I'd found it. Three *hytte* islands, just 15 minutes by ferry from Oslo's Vippetangen pier and covered with small, self-built wooden huts and given to *barnerike* ('child-rich') families from the poor east end of the city in 1922 – the very same year huts began at Carbeth, north of Glasgow. It was an astonishing coincidence. North Sea twins. I flipped through the academic paper by Norwegian ethnologists, Ingun Grimstad Klepp and Inger Johanne Lyngø with mounting excitement and Google Translate, finding hints that the early experience of Lindøya hutters hadn't exactly been easy.[1] That seemed puzzling given their continuing existence and the ubiquitous nature of huts in Norway today. So, what changed? And more to the point, why didn't it change in Scotland too?

By January 2011, with a smattering of Norwegian and an invitation to stay with a Scots friend based in Oslo, I felt the overwhelming urge to head east for a recce. Agreed, dreich January might not be the ideal month to encounter Norwegians enjoying their island *hytte*. But I'd always rather savoured the dark, difficult winter months in Drumnagarrow. Besides I'd read accounts of composer Edvard Grieg picking his way along snow-covered scree to reach his cabin at Ullensvang in Hardanger.[2] So clearly bad weather was no obstacle to the hardiest hutters. Essentially, I was itching to be off.

So, I took the very late but only direct Scottish flight to Oslo, arriving in an empty, snow-covered, city centre just before 1am. Expecting some hassle as a lone female traveller or a tram timetable that somehow didn't operate on a Sunday night, I was relieved to find neither. Trams were working exactly as advertised and I managed not to get caught out by the curious foible of selling tickets via Narvesen and 7-Eleven corner shops.

Mercifully, one was still open in Oslo Central station, though it did seem strange to have an eye wateringly expensive ticketless journey from the airport, only to have a shop assistant print a physical paper ticket at the other end.

A quick walk from the tram stop at Adamstuen brought me to the elegant looking tenement where my friend Sarah lived in the ground floor flat. She'd left the side door open and I slipped in as instructed without waking the household. Thankfully, as a fellow Scot, she was familiar with that anti-social and knackering 1am arrival.

Needless to say, I found banks of ticket machines at Oslo S just behind the Narvesen shop the next day and bought a three-day Oslo travel pass which let me hop between trams, trains, buses and – unbelievably – the number 92 ferry to Lindøya.

Result.

So, travel pass in pocket, clad in a Michelin Man super-padded jacket and insulated fur-lined boots (learning from Hammerfest), I embarked on the combination of tram, walking and bus that took me to a suspiciously queue-free Vippetangen pier. The boat turned up as timetabled (eventually I would overcome this enduring doubt) and within minutes I was gliding towards Lindøya. The only snag – pretty much nobody else was. I was finding out the hard way that hutting on the *hytte* islands is strictly seasonal (May till October by law) and the trip offered only tantalising glimpses of brightly coloured, snow-topped and evidently empty wooden huts with no openings for comradely chat. Frustrating.

There was also no need to queue for the number 60 bus back into Oslo. Hardly anyone was waiting in the snow, except a young couple with their daughter, clutching skis and ski poles, overflowing canvas shopping bags and a large black binbag. The make do and mend nature of their baggage looked more Scottish than Norwegian. The bus wheeled into the turning circle beside empty piers that would be packed with sky-scraping cruise liners all summer long. The doors swung open.

It was my only chance to connect.

'Would you like a hand with the bag?'

'Yes thanks. Can you take the ski poles?'

FIG 4.1 Lindøya in winter.

There was no note of surprise in Maria's voice. Like she got offers of help from complete strangers every day.

I wondered how bold I could be.

Given the low odds of meeting any other *hytte* dwellers from Lindøya till the summer – very.

'Were you on the ferry from the islands?'

I knew she was.

'Yes – were you over there too?'

Her English was almost perfect.

I'd been on the top deck of the boat for half an hour in the biting cold. Despite all the thermal gear, my chin was frozen solid and I didn't have the energy to be evasive.

'Yes, I was upstairs taking photos – I'm actually doing research on huts because in Scotland we don't really have them.'

Even in hyper-chatty Scotland, such an irrelevant and unbidden conversational blurt would seem a tad over-zealous. But the astonishingly frank conversation ran on apace.

'Really – we have a *hytte* over there. Well, it belongs to my father. Well, to his new wife. Well, to her father really.'

Gosh.

'You can email me about it if you like.'

I glowed involuntarily with all the delicate, hesitant excitement of someone who had just been propositioned. If only I could find a pen. And get my frozen hand to work. To write down their email address. Before they got off the bus. Maria's partner scrambled in his pocket.

'Here's a pen. I'm Fredrik.'

'Hi. I'm Lesley.'

This was quite surreal.

I scribbled down the email addresses of Fredrik and Maria and sighed with relief when their details were safely transcribed onto the back of a receipt in large frozen baby writing. They started scrambling for their bags at the Nationaltheatret stop in the city centre. What next?

'Would you like to come for a coffee – we're meeting friends.'

And just like that, my afternoon and Fredrik's hutting experience began to unfurl.

Lindøya (don't pronounce the d) was first camped on by working people from Oslo in the 1920s. The authorities allowed them to build huts the size of their tents. As a result, most are just one large room. There's no running water in winter. The pipes are drained at summer's end to avoid ice damage later. So only a handful of people use them in winter – and they boil snow for water. The majority of hutters have always been working-class socialists from Oslo – many are still printmakers.

The island is only one mile by half a mile and people pick mushrooms in the summer and get involved in all sorts of communal events like mini-golf. Fredrik – a poet – goes out to write and tends to stay inside the cabin without socialising. This is not what you're meant to do, he confides.

Even a hut lover like myself can't quite see how anyone can find seclusion on a tiny island with 300 huts – especially at the height of summer when everyone's outdoors along with friends and extended family.

'That's why I use other huts as well.'

Fredrik recounts a stay in his own *hytte* – a very basic house on the south coast, on an island five hours travel from Oslo. This is more like it.

An old local man asked me how long I planned to stay. It was October and I said I would stay till my birthday in July. He said if I survived January, he would bake me some bread.

On the first day of February there was a nail hammered into the door with a bag containing two loaves.

Hardy is *hardfør* in Norwegian – not so different a word. But Norwegian hardiness runs on fairly epic lines compared to our own. That's what makes their *hytte* culture so fascinating. Despite their willingness to cross-country ski *en famille* in sub-zero temperatures just because it's Sunday, most Norwegians (ultra-tough cookies excepted) are relatively soft when it comes to their *hytte*. Not for them the makeshift water trough shared with cows, the telegraph pole pushed into the fire, or indeed any open fire at all (too wasteful of heat compared to a central log-burning stove). Norwegians *hytte* are generally reachable and function properly, because in sub-Arctic climes they must and because they mostly accommodate families with children, not eccentric loners (though before any complain, there are a fair few of them as well).

A university professor once told me a *hytte* helped rescue the relationship with his children after divorce.

'I bought the *hytte* deliberately to win back my children. They came every summer for the whole six weeks of the summer.'

'Did they like it or come out of obligation?'

'I asked them recently. They said the *hytte* gave them a normal childhood. For a guilty absent dad, you can't imagine how important that was for me to hear. My daughter learned to swim down at the beach there – I could leave her even when she was just seven because there were so many teenage girls around. She loved it. It was unbelievably beautiful. The hut is basic. We have to walk or ski up for half an hour. That's the trouble with these new fancy condo *hytte* – they may have roads up but if the roads dip, the cars get stuck. It's easier to use the old paths and just carry the stuff up.'

That's true enough. Eventually I did the same at Drumnagarrow, humping everything up with a stoic donkeyness only I would ever appreciate.

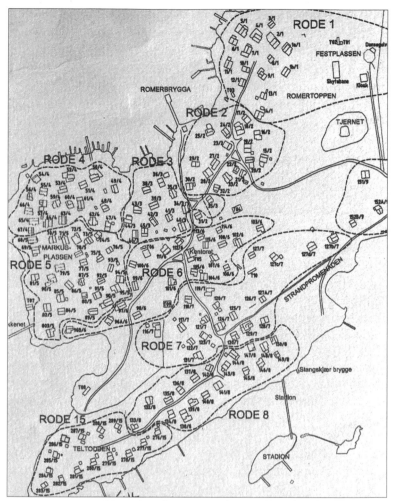

FIG 4.2 Map of Lindøya East *roder* (neighbourhoods).
Courtesy: Lindøya Vel

'So, will you come back to Lindøya in the summer?'
Maria brought me back to earth with a bang.
'Of course.'
'Then you must visit Tutta Normann. She knows everything about the island. Say Holger's daughter sent you. Take our map. She's got hut number 280.'

It was an unusual way to start academic research – with a slightly coffee stained map, the name of a stranger and a *hytte* number. Still, as a journalist I've started out with a lot less. And the direct approach appealed – I was being passed with care and precision, from person to person, like a weird, ethnological relay race. Tempting as it was to try and find the mysterious Tutta Normann sooner, I could sense that wasn't the way to do it. I needed to wait till the summer.

And I needed to make this love affair with other people's huts a bit more official. I spent a pointless six months trying to enrol for a PhD at the University of Aberdeen which ended with the Admissions Secretary rejecting me on the grounds I had no fluent Nordic language or history degree. This left me a tad despondent about the merits of academia.

But a chance encounter with a clutch of eminent historians at a slightly drunken dinner on Skye changed the course of events yet again. A meeting to discuss the future of the modern clan, hosted by the head of Clan Donald had produced an impressive turnout of Scotland's top academics, along with a few land reform types like myself for grit in the oyster purposes. As the drink flowed and other conversational topics were exhausted, the puzzle of Scotland's missing huts somehow bubbled up and the learned consensus was that it was indeed worth exploring properly. History Professor Allan Macinnes volunteered his services as PhD supervisor and since I suddenly had a lot of time on my hands after being dumped by BBC Radio Scotland, there was no reason not to throw myself wholeheartedly into this new endeavour. I enrolled at the University of Strathclyde, attended Norwegian classes, applied for a research grant from the Norwegian Government and won funding to stay in student accommodation at Oslo University for three months in the summer of 2011. I nearly wrote glorious summer, because the weather was indeed fabulous. But the visit began just weeks after Anders Breivik's attempt to change Norwegian society forever by killing 77 people – most of them teenagers.

Speaking on the steps of Oslo Cathedral immediately afterwards, without body armour or security guards, Prime Minister

Jens Stoltenberg had insisted there would be no War on Terror:

> No-one can bomb us to be quiet. No-one can ever scare us
> from being Norway. Our answer to violence is more democ-
> racy, more openness, and more humanity.

I arrived a fortnight later on a day of torrential mid-summer rain,
as 32 of Breivik's victims were laid to rest and a massive, silent
crowd with red roses lined the streets outside the Cathedral.

Stoltenberg reflected the public mood with a short, emotional
tribute to one young victim: 'Monica is dead. Even the roses are
crying.'

That set the tone for Norway's raw but dignified response.

As the days passed, it was clear the whole population shared
their Prime Minister's determined outlook. I was using a library
just one street from the location of Breivik's car bomb. Across
Youngstorget, the bomb-blasted government building was visibly
shattered and partly covered in tarpaulin. But folk at the Worker's
History Library didn't search bags, ask for ID or restrict entry.
Hostility, fear and mutual suspicion were simply not being allowed
to take root.

Of course, there were big questions to answer. Why were Oslo
police so slow to respond? How could a civilian have assembled
such a lethal arsenal of weapons?

That discussion continued for the duration of my study visit
and beyond. But it quickly became evident that Anders Breivik's
atrocity hadn't set Norway on edge. If anything, there was a
conscious effort to be more welcoming and helpful.

So, 2011 became an unexpectedly good time to be a visitor
at Oslo University. A room sitting unused in the Centre for
Archaeology was given to me for the summer.

Since Norwegians are generally at their desks by 8am, lunch
breaks are taken early and in shifts – 11.30am for the archaeol-
ogists and 12 noon for the smaller band of historians. The small,
bright dining kitchen was empty save for the coffee machine,
microwave, a cupboard with a ceiling-high stash of around 50
individual crispbread packets and a wiry band of Viking long-

ship experts consuming the most meagre-looking packed lunches I've ever seen, along with black coffee strong enough to rot the table. There was no canteen, no nearby takeaway shops and no way to redeem yourself in the eyes of colleagues if you failed to prepare a *matpakke* (packed lunch) before heading out. I realised instantly that my Mars Bar stash must hereafter stay completely concealed.

With seven mature researchers in the student house, we had to organise shifts to reach the tiny fridge behind the breakfast table (though happily the tall people were allowed to bag the top shelves). It took a few weeks to get my inner clock adjusted to rise at 6am, make the packed lunch, have breakfast, appear 'at the office' by 8am and thus be ready for lunch four hours later and slightly dozy by 3pm.

But even though I could now enjoy crispbread, say 'can I have a bag please' in Norwegian and get online in every part of Oslo University, I couldn't get any phone or email response from Anne-Marie (Tutta) Normann.

Clearly if I was to meet the Chair of Lindøya *Vel* (the hutters' association), I would have to get back on the number 92 ferry (now heaving with visitors, walkers, hut owners and tourists), bring the map, find the hoose and breenge in.

FIG 4.3 Ferry queue for the *hytte* islands in Oslo.

Even with prominently displayed numbers on each colourfully painted wooden house, I needed several stops for directions and a few about turns before I was standing on a small peninsula, with yachts sweeping past on one side and a huge ocean-going steamer ploughing through glistening seas on the other. Tempting as it was to just stand in the sun, offending no-one, invading no-one's privacy, risking no awkward rebuttal, surveying the sink fitted to the outside of the neighbouring house and conjuring up the bliss of outdoor dish-washing, I took a deep breath and went in. Happily, the jungle drums had been working:

'Ah, you are the Scottish woman who met Maria in the winter, doing research about our island. Come in, sit down. Ola, get her a drink. (The embarrassment of being a non-drinking Scot again.) Really? Well you won't mind if we have another two large gin and tonics!'

It all proved easier than I expected.

Tutta and Ola were helpful, playful and astonishingly willing to spend hours speaking English, since my Norwegian still wasn't good enough for any detailed discussion. Tutta handed me a '90s booklet published to mark the 75th anniversary of the hutters' organisation (Lindøya Vel), with a short history of their island. That prompted a week of painfully slow translation and a wheen of trips to the archives sprinkled around Oslo to find documents that might back up, contradict or (mercy) help me

FIG 4.4 Tutta and Ola Normann in their Lindøya *hytte*.

piece together an explanation as to why their little hutting revolution had been able to succeed.

Unquestionably the most memorable visit was to the Riksarkivet (state archive) perched right at the top of the tram line to Sognsvann. After spending some time with highly amused but extremely patient library staff to explain what I was after, I produced my passport and the letter from Oslo University, stashed my bag and laptop, snapped on a pair of blue elastic disposable gloves and sat in the calm, airy, wood-panelled reading room waiting for the selected pre-war Department of Agriculture papers to arrive.

After waiting for 20 minutes, flanked by proper researchers (I felt) who could speak actual Norwegian (presumably), the amused librarian emerged carrying a labelled cardboard box which he set down with an encouraging smile, but without any hectoring instructions about precious document handling.

'You just need to sign here.'

Øivind (from his name badge) was still smiling as he walked back to the main desk – but I was grinning ear to ear like a Cheshire Cat. At last.

I opened the notebook, put on my specs, removed the flimsy carton lid and carefully took out the first set of papers from 1915. They were in Danish. And the second set. And the third.

For some reason, I exploded with laughter. Not a single person stirred.

Of course. Norwegian civil servants had spoken Danish their whole working lives, despite union with Sweden for almost a century. So, they'd clearly taken time to make the leap into Norwegian and in 1915, even though the country had been independent for a decade, four variations of the Mither Tongue were battling it out to become the new national language (in the end they chose two), so officialdom stubbornly stuck to Danish. Overcoming any temptation to feel cruelly cheated by learning the wrong language for two years, I focused on the fact that one flimsy cardboard box had been a revelation. Its contents showed how Norwegian culture had been completely excised from official business in the days of devolution under Danish and Swedish control. No wonder the choice of official language provoked more debate than the idea of independence itself, when the time came in 1905. There was something almost beautiful about this accidental discovery.

And completely maddening.

Still, I could see obvious similarities with Norwegian, was able to reflect that languages are indeed dialects with armies (or at least independent governments) and resolved to pay more attention to detail before horsing off to learn a language the next time.

Next time.

As if.

But back to the story. Over the course of several visits, Tutta's family history unfolded along with the history of her precious island *hytte*.

Tutta's grandfather, Hilmar, was the son of Fritz Albert Kristiansen who moved to Oslo in the late 19th century from a tiny village, Blankvåndsbråten, in the Nordmarke, a huge area of privately-owned forest north of Oslo. His elder brother had inherited their father's farm and there wasn't enough room or food for both of them and their future families. So, Fritz Albert headed 20 kilometres south, changing his surname to Kristiansen,

FIG 4.5 Hilmar and Maria Kristiansen.
Courtesy of Tutta Normann

reflecting his new location as was the custom (a small clue about the enduring importance of place in Norway). Oslo was known as Kristiania till 1927 because the Danish King Christian IV rebuilt part of the town after a fire and renamed it after himself. Anyway, Fritz Albert Kristiansen got a job in Oslo collecting rubbish and married but died young from tuberculosis.

Hilmar was one of four sons. He became a tradesman, putting copper on the roofs of churches and houses and married Maria who was a tailor. The family lived in east end, working-class Grünerløkka in a one bedroom flat. With two incomes and (unusually) just two children – Lcif (Tutta's dad) and Synnøva (her aunt) – Hilmar was able to afford a small rowing boat which he kept at the busy mouth of the Akerselva (the Aker river), just 200 metres away. That boat was his pride and joy. Tutta believes Hilmar first saw the tents on the east of Lindøya, while he was out rowing and was so taken by the sight of this beautiful and slightly more private part of the island, that he waited ten years after the initial share out of land, until the peninsula's private owner died – an elderly lady without children, who left her land to the government. After his long wait, Hilmar was allocated hut site 280 on Teltodden and finally got cracking with a carpenter using 'good' wood instead of the usual packing crates liberated from workplaces. As a result, Tutta tells me proudly, her grandfather's hut is the only one on Lindøya that hasn't had to be rebuilt. But there was certainly hard graft. Tutta's father Leif spent a summer rowing soil out to the island to clothe the bare rock – when he was just 12 years old. Islanders are reluctant to say where the soil came from but thousands of tonnes were rowed out in the early years and soil is still imported every year to replace what's been washed away.

Hilmar and Tutta obviously had a close bond. They used to walk every Sunday from his city-flat through the city to the Hotel Bristol where she would get an ice cream and he would have a half pint of beer and a glass of port wine. They would wander back for their tea, meeting 'cousins' en route – Hilmar often said he had 200 cousins around the city. Strange that such a charming, gregarious man of habit would wait ten uncertain

years for the chance to rent one of the most isolated hut sites on
Lindøya. It's so hard to know what really motivates people.

FIG 4.6 Boats at Akerselva.

But one thing's clear. In
the 1920s, as Hilmar walked
to the mouth of the Aker River
to reach his rowing boat and
the freedom of the fjord, he
was passing a much easier
leisure choice in the shape of
newly-created *kolonihager*
(allotment gardens). If Tutta's
grandad just wanted a hut
and a small patch of land
without hours of rowing first,
he could simply have applied
for one of these. New allotment plots did dry up in the
1920s, so maybe he simply
missed out. Perhaps though
Hilmar wanted a greater

degree of separation from the authorities, the city and even the
Workers' Movement than a city hut could provide.

Growing vegetables in a plot surrounded by block housing
and three-metre high fences didn't appeal to Hilmar Kristiansen.
But that's not to say he was uninterested in growing plants. In
her research, the ethnologist Ingun Grimstad Klepp examined
the near obsessive interest in flower rather than vegetable
growing amongst the earliest settlers on Lindøya. She thinks it
was an attempt by hutters to show they enjoyed the same 'social
goods' as the middle classes with their upmarket second homes
on the Nesodden peninsula nearby.[3] Indeed Tutta recalls that her
grandfather became interested in growing flowers once he finally
got his plot and a boat-load of topsoil in 1932.

> Hilmar said he didn't have 'green fingers' and the truth was
> he could afford to pay other people to get their fingers dirty
> growing vegetables. He wanted to spend his spare time in

his boat and on the island outside the city – not on his hands and knees inside it.[4]

Tutta's husband Ola shares Hilmar's dislike for regimentation. His family did have a plot with a *hytte* at the Sagene *kolonihager* and lived there all summer, but Ola disliked the constant need to lock and unlock gates and the unnaturally long, straight roads.

Lindøya feels like you have left the city – Sagene did not.[5]

Unsurprisingly then, it was Tutta rather than her father Leif who finally took over the *hytte* from Hilmar in 1982 paying 50,000 NOK (roughly £5,000) split evenly between her grandfather and two sisters Eva and Reidun. That doesn't mean the wider family don't still visit. Ola recalls one memorable weekend when 16 relatives, bidie-ins and children were all squeezed in.

But large, extended, visiting families are normal on Lindøya and Hilmar's descendants are actually dwarfed by the neighbouring Bergum clan.

Liv Vargmo's grandfather Gullbrand Bergum had a thriving second-hand goods business, a rowing boat and 13 children when he first rowed over to Lindøya in 1916. At first, he stayed in a tent, then got a hut site in 1922. Liv's mother's family also have *hytte* on Lindøya and her husband Bjørn comes from the neighbouring *hytte* island of Nakholmen. In fact, amongst Gullbrand's

FIG 4.7 Tutta and Ola Normann outside their *hytte*.
Courtesy: Al McMaster

18 grand-children, all but one has access to an island *hytte* today. Why does this matter? Because each Lindøya *hytte* represents a family, knitted together and reconstituted over the generations in a way that's quite unremarkable to Norwegians yet quite unknown to Scots. On Lindøya there is a currency – it is family, not cash.

CHAPTER FIVE
Lindøya and the land-grabbers

WHAT MADE THE hutters of Lindøya so successful? Were they simply more tenacious than Scots who fought for huts but were soon huckled off, evicted or gentrified?

Were the Norwegians just smarter, better organised, luckier?

Or did they do almost exactly the same as Carbeth hutters, against the backdrop of a profoundly different democratic landscape?

One thing's for sure. The hardy souls who rowed across from Oslo for a few days' relaxation on the islands of inner Oslo fjord had no easy time of it – at first.

Lindøya's early history gave no hint of the unconventional land-use that would later develop there. In 1147 Cistercian monks arrived on neighbouring Hovedøya (the 'main' island), built a monastery and expanded their power base to include Lindøya. That turned out to be a lucky move for 20th century hutters. By the time of the Norwegian Reformation in 1532,

FIG 5.1 Piers on Lindøya with Oslo in the background.

Church-owned properties like Lindøya had been transferred to
the Danish King and then after 1814, to the Norwegian State.
So, by the 20th century, the inner fjord islands were owned by a
relatively benign Norwegian Government – not the Church, the
kommune (council) or private owners. That was a crucial factor
in the *hytte* battles that would follow and a massive difference
from privately-owned Carbeth.[1]

During the early 19th century Lindøya was hardly used except
by elite sports clubs.[2] From 1856 though, evening parties gave
Lindøya a reputation for being noisy and rowdy, and social gatherings were banned in 1859. The dramatist, Henrik Ibsen (no less)
composed a song for the last party.[3] Lindøya had nearly been
taken over by the intelligentsia and party people. Soon though,
against all odds, the island would become the workers' preserve.

From 1905, workers from Oslo's East End rowed out to
Lindøya and stayed for the summer in tents to escape their dark,
overcrowded tenement city flats.[4] These rower/campers were
called the *landliggerne* ('those who lie on the land') and included
folk like Brødkjorer (Bread Delivery Man) Olsen, Saddler Larsen,
Kino-Jonsen and Parafin Hansen. Some became legendary characters on the island – all became massive irritants to the middle
classes sailing past Lindøya to reach their own second homes. (See
Figure 4.1.)[5] Affluent citizens complained of the 'monstrous
noise from vile hobos' across the fjord in *negrelandsbyen* ('negro
villages'). Contemporary writer Johan Borgen criticised their
hysterical reaction:

> The first small cottages sprang up on Nakholmen and Lindøya
> to the indignation of the city fathers when they entered the
> morning fjord boat from their own country houses and sailed
> past. They wrote in the newspaper and asked on the train
> if these people had no shame in life, these people who came
> and destroyed the pristine nature – as they sat on the deck
> with their prejudices and privileges.[6]

Borgen was from the same class as the 'indignant city fathers',
but had a different perspective on island life. His grandfather HP
Borgen had a summerhouse on the fashionable island of Sjursøya

– considered by many to be the pearl of inner Oslo fjord (Figure 5.2)[7] Indeed Borgen's 1933 book *Barndommens rike* (The Kingdom of Childhood) describes his idyllic experiences there.[8]

But Oslo *kommune* (council) bought Sjursøya in 1921 and a few years later demolished the houses and levelled the island – removing 1 million cubic metres of earth and rocks. Indeed,

FIG 5.2 Sjursøya – pre-demolition, 1924.
Courtesy: Anders Beer Wilse

FIG 5.3 Sjursøya – post-demolition, 1933.
Courtesy: Ketil Blom Haugstulen

many of the original *hytte* on Lindøya were made from wood 'recycled' from the wreckage of Sjursøya. By 1933 the island was a featureless, concrete peninsula covered with oil tanks.⁹

The *kommune*'s destructive action on Sjursøya – justified in the name of job creation and port expansion – created influential opponents of further island 'improvement'. The *landliggerne* of Lindøya had won some unlikely allies. And they would need them.

> Between 1915 and 1922 more and more tent-people occupied the island. Their behaviour came in for every kind of criticism – they went to the toilet in the forest, drank, fought and danced throughout the night.¹⁰

Lindøya rapidly acquired a bad reputation in upmarket Oslo, but more and more families from the industrial east side were rowing across every weekend from early spring to late autumn and setting up tents in the same place, year after year. Often mothers and children would go for the whole school summer holiday, with the men working through the week and arriving on Saturdays 'with all the equipment they needed for a weekend – food, drink and an accordion.'¹¹ To be honest, it sounded like a gigantic, outdoor Eigg ceilidh.

FIG 5.4 Summer life on Lindøya by J Boes, 1920.

But, the *landliggerne* were not the only people with their eyes on Lindøya. Around 1907 the state received applications from the city's wealthier citizens asking to lease land for summer homes. These were rebuffed, perhaps because their houses would be permanent unlike the humble and eminently moveable tents of the *landliggerne*. A newspaper reported;

> The revenue the state gets at these sites is so small as to be of negligible importance compared with the glory of Lindøya for hundreds perhaps thousands of Oslo's poor who have sanctuary there.[12]

A more serious threat arose in 1910 when neighbouring Hovedøya was set to become a massive museum and commercial hub – one of two locations shortlisted as a venue for Norway's centenary celebrations in 1914. A bridge to Lindøya and Nakholmen would connect them with Hovedøya's new leisure space, and individual wooden huts weren't part of the plan. But after four years of debate, a cheaper venue in Oslo was chosen.

In 1914, the Norwegian Air Sailing Association applied for permission to construct Oslo's first airstrip – a seaplane harbour – on Lindøya. Large chunks of land were dynamited away – but it was located on neighbouring Gressholmen instead and the dynamited area was used instead as a storage yard for boats by the *Akerselvens Båtforening* (Aker River Boat Club).[13] This would create some useful and well-organised allies for Lindøya's hutters.

Still, the rejection of one proposal just heralded the arrival of another. In 1915, the Oslo Port Authority announced a competition to find the 'contemporary face of the future' for the city's harbour. Its own preference was to convert the Oslo fjord islands into a giant pier with a bridge and train from the mainland to relieve the volume of freight transport in Oslo.[14] But another option was chosen.

Perhaps there was not the political will (or cash) to develop the islands of inner Oslo fjord before World War One. Perhaps the need for green, open spaces for Oslo citizens, would easily defeat development arguments every time. But perhaps the state showed tolerance towards the *landliggerne* on Lindøya because

FIG 5.5 'Contemporary face of the future', Oslo Port Plan.

every other island in Oslo fjord was even more seriously out of bounds.

Nakholmen is the smallest of Lindøya's island neighbours and lies slightly further away from Oslo. The Forestry Directorate managed both islands for the State and created new plantations of pine and fir trees on Lindøya and Nakholmen in 1904. After this it was forbidden to land on either island to protect the saplings. Warning signs were erected and guards on Nakholmen included a woman called Miss Fritz who 'went about with a revolver, a large police badge clearly visible on her chest and a dog that was bad with people.'[15]

Regular visitors had their own rowing boats or 21-foot *snekke* (motorboats). But it was one thing to have the freedom to set sail for Nakholmen – quite another to have anywhere to land. According to Nils Zapffe (later a Lindøya hutter):

> The island had three so-called permanent 'residents'. Access to Nakholmen for other mortals was strictly prohibited. Sometimes people who were unfamiliar with the arrangement came ashore to make coffee, have some food and rest after a tiring trip on the fjord. But they wouldn't rest long before the officer was on hand with his four-legged guards, and coffee boiling and thoughts of siesta had gone. The officer would demand names, and in a grim voice, with meaningful side glances at the dogs, tell visitors to remove themselves

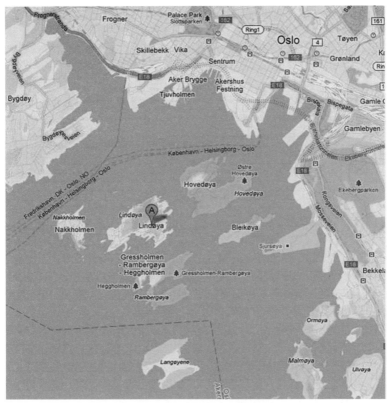

FIG 5.6 Map of Oslo fjord islands.

as soon as possible. Attempts at debate were useless; it was simply a matter of leaving. The state's island of Nakholmen was forbidden territory.[16]

It sounds like parts of the Highlands and Islands to this very day. State-owned Hovedøya was similarly out of bounds. After a cholera epidemic in Oslo in 1850, the western-most tip was used as a quarantine station for yellow fever, plague, cholera and typhoid. And the rest of the island was a military base.

Lindøya's eastern island neighbour was equally difficult. Tiny Bleikøya had one of the oldest functioning farms in southern

Norway and a sanatorium for children with scrofulous (a form of tuberculosis) which remained in operation until 1926 when it was moved to the mainland, creating a vacancy soon filled by the new hutters' organisation.[17]

Heggholmen – naturally conjoined to Gressholmen and Rambergøya – was effectively closed by the construction of a soap factory there in 1909.[18] As Clean Air regulations pushed chemical industries out of central Oslo, more islands became industrial locations. Indeed, Shell bought nearby Skjareholmen and evicted 30 *hytte* owners from the tiny skerry island in 1954. The hutters burned all the huts as they left in protest, presaging the action of despairing hutters in Galloway, half a century later.[19]

The most shocking industrial transformation was Langøyene – two separate islands until Oslo *kommune* bought them in 1902 and started dumping household waste between them in the vain hope the rubbish would sink. Instead the current brought all the debris back into Oslo and onto beaches of the inner fjord islands. The *kommune* then resorted to sinking five ships on the south side of the bay to interrupt the currents, was duly fined 200 million NOK – but kept on dumping.[20] North and South Langøy soon became one single, rubbish-connected island.

But islanders are nothing if not adaptable. In 1920 there were 18 houses, 155 inhabitants and a school with 30 pupils on Langøyene. Even surrounded by rubbish, people stayed – one local man cultivated flowers using the heat generated by the layers of decaying matter.[21] But even if the locals could stand the stench and flies, neighbours could not. In letters to the *Nordstrands Blad* newspaper in 1946, men on the nearby island of Ulvøya complained they couldn't see the pattern on their carpets or shave properly because mirrors were covered with flies: 'We wish that if a nuclear bomb falls, it should be on Langøyene and nowhere else in the world.'[22]

The dumping did finally stop in 1951 when Oslo *kommune* announced it would transform Langøyene into a camping and swimming centre, summarily evicted the 100-odd remaining residents and moved them to new block housing in Oslo. A hundred years of habitation on Langøyene ended almost overnight.[23]

The sudden changes on Langøyene and Sjursøya demonstrated how quickly islands could be destroyed and their people removed by an unsympathetic municipal landowner. So, it was all the more astonishing that three islands on Oslo's doorstep became permanent leisure havens for the city's poorest people. But they did, partly because forestry (the landowning function of their Government owners) was fairly compatible with sport and leisure but mostly because well-organised, defiant workers simply grabbed the land and presented the state with a fait accompli.

The impetus for change began with the boat men. When the *Akerselvens Båtforening* (Aker River Boat Club) was formed in 1918, members like Gullbrand Bergum and probably Hilmar Kristiansen moored their rowing boats at the mouth of the *Akerselva* (Aker River). Congestion meant the club was forced to move twice ending up in the old (failed) Lindøya seaplane base in 1924. Since members of the *Akerselvens Båtforening* (ABF) were mostly young men with lots of children, living in blocks of flats in East Oslo, it's likely many qualified for huts and also became Lindøya's hutting pioneers. Members of the ABF certainly intervened at pivotal moments. They sent a letter to the Ministry of Agriculture in 1919, identifying Lindøya as the last point of public access on the fjord islands and urged the authorities to let it remain open to the city population on grounds of health and leisure.[24] It was good timing. That very year, new laws had been passed in the *Storting* (Norwegian Parliament) which limited the working day to eight hours and (uniquely in Europe) gave each worker a daily entitlement to eight hours sleep and eight hours leisure as well.

Suddenly it was very hard for the state to look heavy-handed with leisure-loving, island campers. But since Lindøya was by then the only publicly accessible island, it soon became overrun.[25] There was neither running water nor a toilet on the island. Boat owners brought their own water, but people gave grim accounts about Lindøya: 'a semi-civilised camping place'.[26] One man recalled that in the years before huts were built, the newspapers' view of Lindøya was so negative, he couldn't let school friends know where he'd spent the summer.[27] In 1921 the Health Visitor from Aker Council made an equally damning indictment of conditions:

It appears in fact that the whole forest is practically a latrine.
It was almost impossible to go there. Similarly, there were
rubbish heaps everywhere. Since the state is the owner they
must answer for sanitary malpractice if duties are not imposed
on the individual plot owner.[28]

Meanwhile, the type of accommodation used on Lindøya was
becoming more permanent. A tent during dry, sunny weather might
be pleasant enough, but an outsider brushing by in wet weather
could soak everyone and everything inside. So, people started
building *lemmehytte* (jointed cabins, – part tent, part hut – which
hung together by means of hooks and were dismantled every
autumn. The base was about 2.5 by 3.5 metres and the walls inside
were papered with newspaper.[29] Adding 'rooms' in adjoining
tents, like kitchen and bedroom tents, extended these makeshift
homes – astonishingly, the very same transformation was also
underway one thousand miles west at Carbeth.

But complaints about behaviour on Lindøya were still pouring
in.[30] Drink was one of the biggest problems. The authorities
suspected the island was an active centre for smugglers trying to
break the newly-established policy of prohibition. Wartime food
shortages and high prices had prompted an outcry about precious grain being used in alcohol production. So in 1917 the state
had imposed partial prohibition, and in 1919 the Norwegian

FIG 5.7 *Teltodden* 1920s (tent valley) with a mix of tents and huts.
Courtesy: Lindøya Vel

people voted for a total ban on alcoholic spirits.[31] It remained in place until 1926.[32] In 1921 prohibition was one of the biggest issues dividing political parties and Lindøya was right in the middle of the smuggling zone.

Bootlegging boats were visited by small boats using the island as cover. Indeed, part of Lindøya became known as Dunderdalen (home brew valley).

Meanwhile, Lindøya's own records suggest that complaints about hygiene were not exaggerated.

Some of the first visitors were 'less good items', who caused complete disarray and disorder. Out here they found a haven where the city's law and order did not rule. Lindøya was a

FIG 5.8 Dunderdalen, 1918.
Courtesy: Lindøya Vel

popular destination for 'weary workers from Kristiania', and for families who were not well off enough to buy land and build cabins.[33]

The absence of water was a big problem. Supplies had to be carried from the city or the 'Monk's Well' on neighbouring Hovedøya.[34] The sole private well on Lindøya gave water only to permanent residents. Teltodden (the tent peninsula with Tutta and Ola's hytte) had two toilets where hutters paid a warden to use the facilities. Refuse collectors emptied the WCs at night using a handcart and the 'material' was taken in a rowing boat far out to sea and dropped overboard. The poor water quality of inner Oslo fjord was already a worry without this extra contribution by campers. It all intensified pressure on the state to act.[35] But the civil servant responsible for the island, Forestry Director Kjell Sørhus concluded that bans and heavy-handedness deterred only law-abiding folk and were completely ignored by the 'lawless' *landliggerne*.

> Ever since I came into office Lindøya has been a difficult child. It has been argued that no-one should be putting up new homes there. The consequence of the ban has been that decent people are kept away, while those with questionable exist-ences have taken up residence and are now building cabins happily enough without permission.[36]

Sørhus also believed the absence of drinking water was encour-aging the wholesale importation of beer – so he investigated the possibility of drilling boreholes for water.[37]

After all, the Norwegian state really only had two options. Ban the party people or give them a reason to settle down. It chose the latter option.

Over the winter of 1921–22, *Vaktsjef* (warden) Erichsen started measuring out plots before the expected influx at Easter. Huts would be divided into six *roder* (hut groups) and the inhabitants of each would share responsibility for maintaining order in their patch (there were finally 15 *roder*). When groups arrived to camp, they would be assigned plots, if they accepted the safety regulations. In 1931, the remaining 19 tent-dwellers (including Tutta's patient grandfather Hilmar) were given permission to build huts on Teltodden.

At long last, the conversion from chaotic tents to orderly huts was complete. But the new arrangements were not generous or long-term. In April 1922, the Department of Agriculture issued 'permits', not leases, which gave each cabin owner the right 'to erect a summer cottage,' but winter use between October and May was expressly forbidden.[39] Each plot was leased for ten kroner (£1) per year and building had to start within a month of the notice being issued. A maximum ground size and height for cabins was given which remained unchanged until the 1980s.[40] The landscape round each house was not to be changed, flower-beds should not spread more than 1.5 metres from the cabin, hutters must share and service blocks of toilets, fences were forbidden and cabins had to be torn down at a month's notice if the state needed the land. The cabins had to be painted dark green, light green or brown, so as not to stand out in the land-scape. Lots of restrictions – but at last a small part of Oslo's East End population had its own little bit of heaven.[41]

A few months after permits were issued on Lindøya, Sørhus's successor as Forestry Director proposed that Nakholmen and Bleikøya should also be sub-divided into cabin sites (180 on Nakholmen and 100 on Bleikøya), with a statement 'cunningly placed into the State Budget in 1923.'[42] There was considerable objection to Jelstrup's proposal, but it was finally adopted and at Easter 1923, the eastern part of Nakholmen was turned into plots arranged in six self-organising *roder*.[43] According to Oddmund Østebø, current leader of Nakholmen Vel, Jelstrup simply wanted to get ahead of the next inevitable 'landgrab' and make sure huts were laid out in an orderly manner to offer a contrast with Lindøya's scattered and 'untidy' appearance.[44] And another land-grab was considered inevitable, because the conversion from tents to huts on Lindøya had been such a success. In his account of the transition Director Sørhus said:

There are few things I have been dealing with since I came
12 years ago as deputy director, which have given so much
pleasure as the enterprise on these islands. It has been more
successful than we dared hope for. It is a pleasure to see how
nice the houses look with flowers etc [and] gratifying to see
how much improvement there has been since the cottage
settlement came.[45]

Public opinion also seemed mollified by the transition:

It must be remembered there is a humanitarian initiative
going on here. With very little funding, a healthy and cheap
summer residence by the sea has been obtained on Lindøya
for hundreds of East End residents. This is more important
for the health of the whole society and common people than
all the words, phrases and immature plans... from those who
call themselves friends of the common folk.[46]

Proactively organising new huts on Bleikøya and Nakholmen
had another advantage – it would let the government choose
who became new *hytte* owners. According to Tutta Normann:

The first hut sites on Lindøya could only be given to people
who'd already visited in tents. But on the other islands the
state began with a clean sheet.

Plots were advertised in Oslo newspapers – though the first huts
were probably snaffled up through word of mouth contact with
Lindøya hutters at workplaces in east Oslo. The hut plots were
assigned by lottery ticket – often after an interview with the
vaktsjef (warden) on Nakholmen. There was greater uniformity
in housing type compared to the 'mottled tangle' of Lindøya.
And on Nakholmen no tents were allowed.[47]

Still, there was fierce criticism of the huts' visual impact on
the sail into Oslo from newspapers like *Tidens Tegn*.[48] The habit
of the Norwegian middle classes was to escape the sights and
smells of the city whenever possible and the sight of the fjord
and its undeveloped islands was, for many, their compensation
for life in the 'un-natural' city.

FIG 5.9 Nakholmen.

In the eyes of many shepherds of the nation, the city was the
site of the mob, alienation, wealth, capitalism, bureaucracy,
centralisation, organised seduction, noise, traffic and foreigners who wanted to impose control. The effect of their
anti-urban propaganda was that in the 19th century the city
was morally expelled from Norway. In fact, it was not part
of Norway at all, but a displaced fragment of Denmark or
Europe.[49]

According to the architect Eyvind Alnæs, a prime mover in the
Oslofjordens Friluftsråd (Oslofjord Outdoor Recreation Society)
vibrant use of the fjord was 'a reaction to backyard-Oslo... a
force of nature breaking free'.[50] Middle-class, emotional connections to the idea of pristine, uninhabited fjord islands were strong,
so the newly-established Lindøya *Vel* decided to go on a charm

offensive. Chief amongst its detractors was Oslo's Mayor, Jacob Wilhelm Rode Heiberg who had initially pronounced:

> We find these villages spoil the whole experience of sailing into Kristiania – they are really an act of vandalism.[51]

So, the *Vel* Directors together with the Forest Director invited Heiberg for a visit. The bold move was a great success. A joint press release sent out afterwards said:

> Mayor Heiberg visited the summer huts on Lindøya and expressed praise for what had been accomplished. The Chief of Police at Aker and the Health Authorities also praised conditions this summer.[52]

The islanders had won over their sternest municipal critics – but while they were winning the battle, hutters were also losing the war.

In 1923, the same year Nakholmen and Bleikøya were divided up, Asker and Oslo *kommune* bought the island of Langåra for 120,000 kroner to prevent an eruption of private hut building there. Several thousand people use the island every summer but no permanent huts have ever been allowed and since 1993 visitors have only been able to camp for two nights at a time.[53] In 1924, the *Jernbanens Båtforening* (Railworkers' Boat Club) organised a petition to stop the creation of any more *hytte* islands.[54] The newly 'civilised' *landliggerne* had managed to unite left and right against the prospect of more family huts for low income families. That's how much fear and dread the Lindøya hutters manged to generate in just one year, simply by getting the same leisure opportunities as the Norwegian middle classes.

The hutters realised they would face a constant battle to keep their huts on Lindøya. They held a press conference and conducted island tours which prompted influential and strongly supportive magazine articles.[55] During the tours, visitors were told how the islanders' own organisation helped maintain those all-important standards of order and decency. The Lindøya *Vel* (Association) was the hub around which everything else turned. Formed at a meeting of all new hut owners in July 1922, the *vel* was a fairly common structure for managing voluntary organisations at the time –the *Akerselvens Båtforening* was also run by a *vel* and had suggested precisely this organisational structure for Lindøya.[56] It was good advice.

The first Directors were elected in July 1922 and immediately became the sole channel for communication between hutters and the authorities, acting like a mini-island parliament to connect hutters, head off problems and prevent islanders from being individually picked on or targeted. The *Vel* collected rent and created regulations governing hedge height, rubbish collection, water supply and social activities.[57] The long list of sub-committees hints at the blizzard of voluntary activity undertaken by islanders.[58] *Vel* officials also lobbied Oslo *kommune* to supply electricity and water – after several decades these services arrived via subsea pipelines in 1954 and 1960.

Conscious that tracks and paths had to be built between all 300 huts, the newly formed *Vel* delegated work to the 15 *roder* (small neighbourhoods) (Figure 4.2) with 8–10 huts apiece, and stipulated that the job of *rodemester* (head of the *roder*) be rotated annually amongst members. This highly delegated organisation impressed visitors. Contemporary commentators observed that something revolutionary, pioneering and genuinely socialist was happening on Lindøya through the exercise of self-discipline and camaraderie. Johan Borgen's vivid descriptions of life on Lindøya had a big impact too – especially since few citizens took up the islanders' invitation to come and witness the 'social experiment' first-hand for themselves:

> This was a landscape where force was an unknown phenomenon. This was the first socialist state. Here there was no speculation with property… This is more than an idyll. This is a social and aesthetic initiative that has succeeded to perfection.[59]

Contemporary writers suggest reality was less than idyllic because 'some guard commanders became little Kings' and Lindøya may have appeared like a 'socialist state' because the huts were closely packed together and boundary fences were banned.[60] But Borgen was more interested in the way island life was shaped by human values, in contrast to the industrialisation that dominated the city.

The islanders were allowed to build bathing areas, diving boards and small piers, a small sports arena and a football ground – but not a dance floor, village hall or restaurant. Sport was an integral part of 'decency' but socialising evidently was not. The ghost of 'Party Island' had not quite been laid to rest. A joint hutting islands' newspaper *Øy og vi* (*The island and us*) began in 1928 and in 1929 a joint *Vel* between the three islands was formed. A women's association was formed in 1925, a Youth organisation in 1927 and Nakholmen soon followed.[61] Since the 1920s dozens of societies have been formed, fallen into abeyance and re-formed.

Lindøya *Vel* joined the newly formed *Oslofjordens friluftsråd* (Society for Outdoor Living in Oslo Fjord) in 1933 – another clever move. Although the Society opposed hut sites on other islands to protect public access rights, it was persuaded not to campaign against existing huts on Lindøya, Bleikøya and Nakholmen.[62]

But despite the islanders' success at rebutting early threats to their summer huts, it still seemed unlikely the 'social experiment' would last. The islanders' great protectors in the Forestry Directorate retired, permits were not converted into formal leases and were never renewed for longer than one year at a time. Since many hut owners also rented their flats in Oslo in the '20s and '30s, they owned no assets against which they could borrow. So living conditions were very basic and it took decades for standard amenities to be fitted. As Tutta Normann put it: 'Our parents and grandparents lived with the constant fear of eviction until 1981.' Tensions naturally developed over the effective removal of three islands from civic planning and control. Campaigners from all sides of the political divide wanted to open up beaches, fjords and the *Marka fjell* (high moorland) for public access. Yet, three islands existed that could neither be opened up for universal access nor closed down for industrial development. It's testimony to the organisation and persuasive skills of the islanders that not a single alternative use for Lindøya,

Nakholmen and Bleikøya got the go-ahead over half a century.
Though many, many tried.

The first of many alternative land-use proposals was an open-
air swimming pool in 1923. That was built on Hovedøya instead.
In 1932, a version of the earlier Freeport was proposed at Oslo
Chamber of Commerce, using Hovedøya, Lindøya, Nakholmen
and the other fjord islands to extend Oslo's industrial base.[63] *Øy
og vi* commented:

> No political party in Oslo would dare take responsibility
> for the destruction of the islands in this way.

Within a year the plan was shelved.

Wartime brought development to a halt, but the next ambi-
tious plan arrived in 1960 – a fjord-based international airport
whose main runway would be built on top of Gressholmen,
Rambergøya, Langøyene and Husbergøya. The islands would
be levelled down to a height of two metres above sea level and
Lindøya would become a large car park, providing a 'natural
screen' against the sight and sound of the aircraft in Oslo. All the
hytte would have to go, but the island would somehow 'still be
the city's most valuable "lungs" in the summer'.[64] After a year
of consideration, the plan was abandoned and the international
airport was finally built (amidst much controversy) on a green-
field site at Gardermøen.

In 1967, another port redevelopment was proposed complete
with bridges, tunnels, and a Tivoli Gardens in the style of rival
Nordic capitals Copenhagen and Stockholm. Once again it involved the removal of all huts in Lindøya and Nakholmen. Once
again it was rejected.

Then, in 1981, 40-year leases were handed out to *hytte* owners.
It was a clear sign that the islanders had finally seen off every
challenge and alternative use for the islands. Since then the
kommune's energy has been focused on strict enforcement of
rules about *hytte* renovation (regarded as pointless red tape by
islanders) and forcing the removal of sheds, hammocks and flow-
er-pots which make public areas round the huts look private.

But these are small aggravations. Essentially the islanders have won – paying only peppercorn rents since 1922.[65]

So almost the only challenge the hytte islanders now face is themselves. In the 'old days', inheritance problems were resolved by the person most likely to use the hytte buying out brothers and sisters. Since prices have rocketed to several million kroner, such 'sibling buyout' is often impossible, so, the *hytte* must be shared and that can be hard – the season for legal occupation lasts just 20 weeks and the tiny cabins often have just one bedroom. If one sibling wants to cash in on high property prices, even a *hytte* owned by a long-established island 'dynasty' may have to be sold to keep the family peace. In this way the 'East Side' character of the *hytte* colony is being slowly diluted. The *roder* system helps keep gentrification at bay – once every few years, even consultants and professors must take their turn as *rodemester*, collecting fees and organising hedge cutting, fire safety, beer nights and a team for mini-golf. Indeed in 2017, more than a hundred hutters went together to Malta for a holiday playing mini-golf in the sun. So, the island hasn't been overwhelmed with Norwegian yuppies – not yet. Now that the 'old enemy' of

FIG 5.10 Lindøya *hytte*.

the *kommune* has been defeated, the future of Lindøya really depends on whether hutters can resist the temptation to sell to the highest bidder. True – some huts are reportedly sold for around 4.8 million NOK (£440,000) and have become the subject of tut-tutting headlines in Oslo. But it's more telling that only a handful ever come onto the market despite the life-changing prices on offer – testimony to the enduring value placed on these huts by descendants of the original hutters.[66]

The final change in their favour happened in 2011. The Land Regulations Act gave folk leasing land for holiday homes the right to buy after 30 years at 40 per cent of the plot's commercial value. So, if they wanted, Lindøya hutters could completely guarantee their future by buying their plots of land. In fact, only 13 out of 300 islanders have done that.[67] Perhaps it's foolhardy for hutters to ignore such an opportunity. Perhaps though, the *landliggerne*'s descendants know that it's politically impossible for any arm of government to dislodge them, now that *hytte*-owning has become a standard and essential part of Norwegian life. There's strength in numbers.

Yet the massive increase in huts occurred not within organ-ised hutting communities like Lindøya, but on individual plots located here, there and everywhere, principally away from these contested and highly sought-after island locations near Oslo. Such rare flat spaces in a country of fjords would always be wanted for other civic uses or general public access. Once cars were de-rationed after World War Two, when incomes rose and workers won more time off, Norwegians built huts on individ-ual plots far beyond the original interwar sites on the islands of Oslo fjord. For Scots though, this move from contested camps on city margins to secure individual hut sites in the countryside proved nigh on impossible. Scottish hutters simply couldn't follow where Norway led.

So was the Norwegian state involved in a social experiment to 'civilise' its rowdier citizens by giving them huts in 1922? If so, it seemed to succeed. Mind you, providing basic facilities like running water and loos for campers might easily have 'civilised' them too. But it's unlikely the subsea pipelines from Oslo would have been laid without years of pressure from the Lindøya Vel, and it's unlikely that would have happened unless the first hutters felt a permanent sense of attachment to the island and its future.[68]

Perhaps though, the social experiment really related to the 1923 expansion of huts to Nakholmen and Bleikøya, where the class background of hutters was very consciously mixed to include professors and middle-class tenants. If that was designed to contradict the *Arbeiderbevegelsen* (workers' movement) which maintained the working-class should follow a separate leisure path, then it worked – up to a point. Because whichever social experiment the state was engaged in (and of course it could just as easily have had no plan beyond responding to a stealthy land-grab), it failed to set a trend. The example of Lindøya didn't persuade any other councils, trade unions or civic bodies to allo-cate valuable coastal land near major cities for workers' family huts. Instead, it alerted agencies to the possibility that general public access and other municipal or industrial uses could be jeopardised forever, if the *landliggerne* got even a temporary toehold on the land.

Essentially, in the quest to understand why Norwegians have half a million huts today, Lindøya is a bit of a (beautiful) red herring. The island isn't typical of the way modern *hytte* are organised or located. But its story (half a century of constant struggle) and its very failure to invite imitation demonstrates how vital it was that hutting could expand beyond contested island sites near Oslo to woodlands, fjords and fjell across the country. Lindøya's history also shows that life for hutters got easier and more secure as Norway itself became more equal and democratic as a society.

Sadly, those vital prerequisites for a hutting culture were completely missing in Scotland, especially in the all-important arena of landownership.

Hutting? The Scots never had a chance.

CHAPTER SIX

Landownership: Scotland's burden

'NORWAY IS A country of houses and cottages – but no castles', wrote Norwegian author Bjornstjerne Bjornson.[1] The contrast with castle-strewn Scotland could not be greater. Norway's land occupancy rights were mainly defined by ancient *Odal* (Udal) laws dating back to the late Viking age, in which absolute ownership was gained by living on the land for a number of generations. Just like early Celtic society in Scotland, written title deeds were rare, no feudal superiors existed and there were no obligations on peasant farmers/landowners except a duty to pay *skat* (tax) to the king.[2] Thereafter, Norway's sparse population made it hard for huge farms or feudal ownership to develop and social movements worked to preserve diverse land ownership as an important national characteristic. In Norway, maintaining the status quo had unusually progressive outcomes.[3]

In 1821 nobility was formally abolished, though current holders were allowed to keep titles for the rest of their lives. A great example for more noble-strewn neighbours, methinks.

Actually, most feudal titles had already disappeared by the 17th century, when church land was annexed by the King. He gave peasants the right to buy in a bid to stave off unrest, limited the amount a landowner could charge a new tenant farmer and capped the fee for renewing leases every three years, encouraging fewer but longer leases and more security.[4] It was 'radical beyond anything else in the age'.[5]

But Norwegian peasants didn't just become secure tenants with reasonable rents – many became outright owners of land. Crown land was almost completely sold off to meet war and other debts, and most was ultimately bought by farming tenants. In 1723 a law even required anyone selling a farm to give sitting tenants the first chance to buy (it took almost another three centuries for the same to be enacted in Scotland). These laws combined to make landowning less attractive as a speculative proposition and wealthy Norwegians started to invest in timber operations and shipbuilding instead.

I think that's what you'd cry an early 'win-win'.

As a result, the percentage of land owned by individual farming families steadily increased from 19 per cent in 1661 to 57 per cent in 1801, and 70 per cent in 1835.[6] Nearly 90 per cent of farmers owned their farms in 1929, and the proportion rose still further in 1939 and 1949.[7]

As historians Helvig and Johannessen put it:

> Norwegian agriculture was not calculated to develop a powerful ruling class but [to create] an equal and independent class of peasants, free from bonds of serfdom.[8]

It succeeded.

As a result, the 'landed' classes in Norway have always had a different look to the landed gentry of Scotland. Over there landowners are generally just farmers with local roots and large extended families – so much so that almost every Oslo family boosted rations during wartime with food from country cousins. Furthermore, virtually every Norwegian that owns land has built some kind of dwelling on it, be they *bønde*, (peasant farmers), *husmenn* (labourers who technically did not own land) or urban Norwegians with wooden cabins in *kolonihager* (urban allotment gardens) where they traditionally lived for the summer. Many industrial workers also had small farms – they could claim a government subsidy for each quarter of an acre cleared and take out loans at very low interest rates to build a house and a barn.[9] And that was all because the government actively wanted to keep people on the land – everywhere. As Nina Witoszek observes:

> What was significantly absent from the Norwegian countryside was the experience of serfdom and the dehumanising machinations of state bureaucracy and officialdom. What was present and unique in comparison with other peasant societies was the sense of individual rights and freedoms

fostered by the allodial [Udal] property system, free of any superior landlord.[10]

By contrast, the vast majority of Scots did not own the land they farmed. In 1874, when 75 per cent of Norwegian land was owned by tens of thousands of individual farming families, only 3.7 per cent of Scots owned any land at all and 96.1 per cent of the population were tenants.[11] According to the earliest Scottish Land Register, published that year, 92 per cent of Scotland's total acreage was owned by just 1,809 landowners.[12] Shockingly, those proportions are hardly different today.

We have David I (1124–53) to thank for imposing the system of feudal tenure in Scotland, creating a hierarchy of ownership. The Crown as ultimate feudal superior could grant land titles to selected nobles in return for military or other services. They would in turn grant sub-titles for other services and so a feudal pecking order was born. Each landowner was also a vassal to his own feudal superiors. Sometimes that meant contributing military service – far more often it meant paying feu duties. And that practice continued, unaltered for centuries. Until very recently, a family who owned a tenement flat in Glasgow, for example, might have to pay annual feu duty to the Church of Scotland; a farmer who owned his land might still have to pay the local laird for permission to build a new barn. It was generally money for old rope, and a perfectly legal way for landowners to act as unelected planning authorities. There was no telling when the performance of 'unauthorised' activities in your own house, on your own land might land you in trouble with a shadowy feudal superior.

I remember a night with very good friends the MacPhails during the run up to the historic Assynt Crofters land buyout in 1993 – father Pat, mother Madeline and daughter Issie were all involved. Pat was flipping through title deeds of the croft-house they had restored on land they owned and read aloud the conditions attached by their feudal superior. Some of the restrictions were cynically designed to trigger a cash payment for permission to change them, others just looked plain crazy to modern eyes, including a ban on storing whale oil on the premises. We all roared with laughter at that one, sitting cooried together round the open fire. Suddenly Pat snapped the book shut, stood up and went upstairs. It wasn't funny. The long reach of feudalism had shaped and restricted his family for generations, causing most to leave and the small townships of Assynt to teeter constantly on the brink of economic and demographic collapse – even now after three decades of community ownership.

Feudalism has been that corrosive and long-lasting a feature of Scottish life. Back in the 1600s, the Reformation was the first big, missed opportunity for change. King David had given large tracts of crown land to the Monasteries, so the Catholic Church owned a quarter of all land in Scotland and church revenues comprised half the national wealth.[13] John Knox called for this to be redistributed to fund relief of the poor, education and ministers' pay (like Norway). But church money had already 'fallen into' the hands of the nobility and was largely irrecoverable.[14] This bolstered the power of Scotland's feudal nobility and led to the practice of evicting 'improving' tenants to demand higher rent from new ones. In 1697 the commentator and Edinburgh printer James Donaldson observed:

> When a tenant makes any improvement of his ground the landlord obligeth him either to augment his rent or remove – it has become a proverb; 'bouch and sit – improve and flit'.[15]

Things got worse. Laws passed by the old Scottish Parliament prevented bankruptcy, absence or even lunacy from breaking up large estates. So, they were rarely sold and if they were, it was in transactions so large as to be beyond the reach of their tenants.

Until the mid-18th century, Earls and Barons also had the power to exercise local justice. So, Scotland's largest landowners were also landlords, employers and judges who could pronounce the death sentence on their tenants. This intolerable situation was one reason some prominent and progressive Scots actually supported Union with England in 1707. In 1706 Dr John Arbuthnot – a Scottish doctor, satirist and the inspiration for Swift's

Gulliver's Travels – wrote a spoof Sermon at the Mercat Cross, which suggested Union with England would be 'a liberating experience for the Scottish people promising independence from the petty tyranny of lairds'. Sir William Seton MP also argued that Union would neuter the feudal Scottish nobility, removing their institutional playground (the unicameral Scottish Parliament) and 'substituting an arena where the English Commons had consolidated their interests in a separate chamber'.[16]

Predictably though, after the Union with England, nothing much changed for the ordinary Scottish tenant. Article 20 of the Union with England Act guaranteed that all inherited positions in Scotland would continue as before. It took the Jacobite Rising of 1745–6 to convince the British Parliament of the threat posed by standing armies of Scottish nobles. In 1747, their legal powers were transferred to sheriffs appointed by the King, their power to demand military service was ended and no rights beyond land-lordship (collecting rents) accompanied new titles created after 1747. Scotland's vanquished landowning nobles threw themselves (or at least their factors) wholeheartedly into this new realm of supreme control. There were some honourable exceptions. Sir William Forbes laid out the village of New Pitsligo in 1783 and effectively handed control to his tenants:

> Before his death he had the satisfaction of seeing assembled on a spot which at his acquisition of the estate was a barren waste, a thriving population of three hundred souls, and several thousand acres smiling with cultivation which were formerly the abode only of the moor-fowl or the curlew.[17]

Without security though, even the most productive tenants were easily removed and soon, a combination of events created the economic excuse. Before the Napoleonic Wars blocked trade with the continent, many Highland crofters were moved to the coast to collect kelp, which produced an alkali for glass and soap manufacture. It was unpleasant work so, at the landowners' insistence, the Government passed the Ships' Passengers Act in 1802 to make emigration prohibitively expensive.[18] During the Napoleonic Wars though, demand for kelp plummeted and by

1815 it had been replaced in manufacturing processes. So large populations found themselves on infertile, coastal patches of land, deliberately designed to be too small to sustain a family. Then in 1846 the potato blight sweeping Ireland and Europe finally hit the Scottish Highlands prompting outbreaks of typhus and cholera. By 1846, at least three quarters of the entire crofting population of the Northwest Highlands and Hebrides were completely without food.[19] According to *The Economist*, the famine demonstrated not that the distribution of land was cruel and unfair but that

> the departure of the redundant part of the population is an indispensable preliminary to every kind of improvement.[20]

Between 1849 and 1851 about 2,000 people were forcibly shipped from South Uist and Barra to Quebec. Some embarked voluntarily, with a promise from Barra's owner, Lieutenant Colonel John Gordon of Cluny, that government agents would give them work and grant them land – though this generally failed to materialise:

> Those unwilling to accept the Colonel's promises found them-selves hunted – men were attacked and rendered senseless before they were thrown, arms bound onto waiting ships. Members of families were torn apart and put on ships with different destinations in the Americas.[21]

Accounts like this finally led to the Crofting Acts of 1886, which did at last give Highlanders security over small heritable plots of land, though quick-thinking Aberdonian landowners (including descendants of Sir William Forbes) successfully argued change should only apply in the 'crofting countries' visited by the evidence-gathering Napier Commission.[22] But the Crofting Acts had little impact on rural overcrowding because crofts were already packed with landless members of the crofter's extended family. Besides, the plots were too small to allow self-sufficiency and were located on the poorest land. In 1906 men from over-populated Barra and Mingulay seized land on neighbouring Vatersay, cleared by the owner Lady Gordon Cathcart to make way for a sheep farm. These 'Vatersay Raiders' were arrested, jailed in Edinburgh, but released after a public outcry. The island was bought by the state and 58 crofts created for its new inhabitants – a small triumph for direct action.[23] Land raids like Vatersay erupted across the Scottish Highlands, encouraged by the revolutionary mood in Ireland and Russia and prompted the creation of the Highland Land League as a political party in 1909.

In 1918, the League affiliated with the Labour Party in frustration over the slow progress of land reform. Their protests led to the Land Settlement (Scotland) Act 1919 which restricted compensation for landowners and created 4,584 new holdings (evenly split between the Highlands and Lowlands) before the outbreak of World War Two.[24] But bureaucracy, landowner intransigence and lack of funds meant this satisfied only a tiny fraction of the popular demand for land. From 1912 to 1943 the Department of Agriculture received 33,196 land applications of which just 8,207 were settled – a miserable 25 per cent success rate. 12,916 applications were withdrawn, and after 30 years, 12,073 remained 'outstanding'.[25] In 1922, depression began to bite and hopes of getting land started to evaporate:

> Thousands of men began to withdraw their applications for land and applied instead for passage on the emigrant ships. Almost all the 300 people from Lewis who boarded the *Metagama* [in 1923] were young men with an average age of 22, off to Ontario where they had each been offered 40 hectares of land. Another country held out the opportunity Scotland had promised but failed to provide.[26]

It's depressing to realise that 100 years later, roughly the same situation prevails.

Meanwhile in the Scottish Lowlands, tenants were fighting their own battles against a law of hypothec, which gave landlords security over their property and thus helped drive up rents.[27]

Tenant farmers were also hit by the growth of lowland sporting estates and the destruction of crops by the laird's 'protected' game. This led to the creation of the Scottish Farmers' Alliance and a defeat for landlord candidates in the 1865 and 1868 elections. The 1883 Agricultural Holdings Act (Scotland) finally gave tenants the right to compensation for improving land (150 years after Norway).[28] Before that, a complex system of tenancy, subtenancy, hinds (male agricultural workers), cotters, crofters and farm servants existed. Most permanent farm workers in Scotland were farm servants (rather than labourers) who were hired for a period of one year, if married, and six months if single. Married servants were paid almost entirely in kind, receiving oats, barley, the keep of a cow and ground for planting potatoes. So being unemployed in the country meant being homeless as well. Cottages surplus to requirements were pulled down, so unemployed farm workers had no alternative but to move out of the area to search for work. Yes, life on the land in Scotland was that unflinchingly harsh. It's what happens when just 4 per cent of people own any land at all. It's what happens when 92 per cent of Scotland is owned by just 1,809 people. It's what those statistics actually mean.

Single men (many bunked together in basic bothies) usually left for the cities when they married because of the scarcity of family cottages.[29] Scarcity, in this vast, empty country. Married men slept rough around the farm or boarded in the farmhouse. With the commercialisation of agriculture, farmworkers slept in bothies, often two to a bed for warmth. Some married ploughmen lived in cottages attached to the farm. But these were like gold dust, so, marriage and children generally meant dislocation, upheaval and the end of life on the land for many country people. Some married farm workers opted to stay in the bothies of unmarried men, living apart from their own families in nearby towns and villages. A survey in Aberdeenshire showed almost half of married men lived like this in 1893 and only saw their families once a fortnight.[30] This is not ancient history. A few years later both my grandmothers were born. This kind of cruelty existed only a few generations ago.

Women fared worse. Since so much of the new industry in Scotland recruited men for heavy labour and lack of housing meant a constant haemorrhage of families, single women had to fill the labour gap on the land. Borders farmers in the 19th century required all male agricultural workers to provide female farm labour (bondagers) to work in the fields on half male pay as part of their bonds of employment. Sue Glover's tremendous play *Bondagers*, first performed in 1991, described the women's plight. One reviewer of the play wrote:

> The women fantasise about a life with no leaking roofs, only kind men around them and summers that last all year long. They cling to the idea of emigrating to Canada, though none know anything about the place. The reality is one of brutal hardship, the dread of winter and unwanted sexual advances from men.[31]

This system of bondage continued in the Scottish Borders until World War Two. Yes, that's right. In the 1930s, Scottish women were living in conditions of virtual slavery on the land. In rural Norway, though life was incredibly hard, forced labour was unheard of, for one simple reason – almost all farmers owned their own land.

The situation did improve slightly during the interwar period because of direct action and political pressure, as 'one misfortune piled on top of another' for Scotland's landed classes.[32] Death duties were imposed for the first time in 1904, prompting land sales, especially if an owner's death was followed by that of his heir and the 1919 budget raised death duties to 40 per cent on estates of £2 million and over. As Tom Devine notes, almost one in five of the landed gentry who served in World War One was killed in action, prompting the belief that 'the Feudal System had vanished in blood and fire and the landed classes were consumed'.[33] Meanwhile, income tax and local rates also rose steeply. New taxes on land were levied, including a surcharge on unearned income from rents in 1907. The Marquess of Aberdeen, for example, paid £800 in annual estate taxes in 1870 but £19,000 in 1920.[34] At last, Britain seemed to be getting serious about land reform and taxing unearned wealth. Income from landownership fell by a quarter between the mid-1870s and

1910. Aristocratic candidates in Scotland were rejected in the first election after the war and anti-landlord sentiments were stoked by polemical works like *Our Scots Noble Families* written by journalist and future Secretary of State for Scotland, Tom Johnston.[35]

> Today in Scotland our artisans and peasants appear to believe that these ancient noble families hold their privileges and lands at the behest of Divine Providence. The first step in reform… is to destroy those superstitions. Show the people that our old nobility is not noble; that its lands are stolen lands – stolen either by force or fraud. So long as half a dozen families own one half of Scotland, so long will countless families own none of it.

As a result of this 'perfect storm', one fifth of Scotland changed hands in three extraordinary years between 1918 and 1921, as large landowners sold up:

> A veritable social revolution was underway as former tenant farmers bought up land from the great proprietors on a remarkable scale. In 1914 only 11 per cent of Scottish farmland was owner-occupied, but by 1930 the figure had climbed to over 30 per cent. The very basis of landlord power seemed to be crumbling.[36]

But it didn't. Landowners sold marginal land and the odd castle, put the money in stocks and shares and maintained their core landholdings. After the late 1930s, land sales declined and land reform vanished off the political agenda.

> The depopulation of the countryside, the dominance of urban issues in a highly urbanised society and the crisis in Scottish industry all marginalised the land issue for over a generation.[37]

In the post-1945 period, the tax burden on landowners declined, sporting rates were abolished by John Major's government and subsidies for agriculture and forestry helped land prices recover from £60 an acre in 1945 to £2,000 an acre in the early 1980s. Now, landowners also receive subsidies for wind power, community buyouts and reafforestation. That's truly ironic, since Scotland's forests failed to be replanted or protected from sheep and deer – on their watch.

So, dependency, dislocation, insecurity and an inability to complain are all built into the Scottish rural experience – in stark contrast with Norway. It was (and still is) common for Norwegians to combine farming with work in industry or shops. In 1939 almost as many folk were part-time farmers as full-time. In 1984, even after a century of urbanisation, one in 15 Norwegians owned some land – often the site of the family home or weekend *hytte*.[38]

In Scotland such precise statistics are still hard to obtain. In 2013 only 57 per cent of land titles covering a quarter of Scotland had even been entered on the Scottish Land Register.[39] It may take another 40 years before 80 per cent of titles are recorded.[40] This is the enduring nature of landowner power in Scotland, unchanged by recent 'landmark' pieces of Land Reform legislation.

> It is claimed that currently 432 private land owners own 50 per cent of the private land in rural Scotland... so this means that half of a fundamental resource for the country is owned by 0.008 per cent of the population. As a measure of inequality in a modern democracy, this is exceptional and in need of explanation.[41]

Actually, things have got worse since Andy Wightman made that calculation. In 1970 Scotland's private land was owned by an estimated 1,750 individuals, with 1,000 plus acres apiece. In 2012 that number was even smaller, with just 1,550 people.[42]

Landownership in Scotland today is probably an even more elite club than it was in 1872.[43] Community land buyouts notwithstanding, that's a pitiful record. And it could be otherwise. Restrictions on who can buy productive land, legal changes to let all children inherit land, proper business rates or better, a new land tax could all be established right now, by the Scottish Government using the powers of devolution. Indeed, nationalisation of land for housing – or for huts – is also perfectly possible. The European Convention on Human Rights, Article One, Protocol One, does prohibit 'the confiscation of private property' but makes an exception for confiscation in the public interest, subject to 'the general principles of international law'. International law, in the shape of United Nations Resolution 1803, asserts that such nationalisation is legal if compensation is paid, and subsequent debate established that compensation need only be 'fair' and not full market value.

So, essentially the Scottish Government could take land into public ownership if it's in the public interest and fair compensation is paid. Why then is next to nothing being done?

It's fairly simple. Scots have been programmed by a long, inherited experience of dispossession to expect nothing. No land and no change. Politicians are included (with a few noble exceptions). And if they haven't chosen to shift that chronic imbalance of power to help permanent residents build affordable first homes in their own, native communities (and they haven't) why would they change things to suit occasional, holiday home owners? In the context of Scotland's uniquely harsh land heritage, the very idea of ordinary punters owning wee weekend huts seems almost offensively ridiculous.

How very dare they.

But like canaries down a coalmine, the presence or absence of huts tells us a lot about a country. It reveals whether physical assets have been shared out fairly and whether landownership patterns have boosted or hobbled the nation's emerging democracy. Once again, Norway and Scotland have very different stories to tell.

CHAPTER SEVEN

The wonders of the
Peasant Parliament

DRAMATICALLY DIFFERENT patterns of landownership sent
Scotland and Norway on very different democratic paths in the
early 19th century. In most European countries, the first voters
owned land. Widespread landownership in Norway produced
one of Europe's widest electorates in 1814, while concentrated
landownership in Scotland produced one of the narrowest. These
differences essentially shaped the kind of democracy each
stateless nation could become:

> Norway became a rapidly developing, consensus-oriented
> and egalitarian nation state, where democratisation ran
> parallel with the pursuit of national autonomy. Its cousin
> meanwhile... was characterised by adversarial politics and
> sharp social inequalities and saw its national aspirations
> run awry.[1]

Norway's democratic transformation was rooted in the events
of 17 May 1814 and the defiant publication of a constitution
which gave ordinary people the vote a century ahead of Scotland
and decades before most of Europe. Norway had grown in population and prosperity under 400 years of Danish rule but
remained marginalised as a supplier of raw materials while
Denmark became an integral part of the European economy.
That might sound familiar. In the late 1780s, protests broke out
in Norway's southern counties, against monopolies awarded to
some towns, sawmills, mines and ironworks which forced farmers
to buy expensive and low quality goods and get low prices for
timber and their own labour.[2] A radical farmers' leader and lay
preacher, Hans Nielsen Hauge, encouraged *bønde* (peasants) to
start rural enterprises in competition to these privileged towns.
Independent mills, shipyards, paper mills, textile industries and

printing houses were set up, strengthening the confidence and organisation of farmers and encouraging their involvement in local and national politics.[3] Thus the Norwegian *bønde* had already become folk heroes in the years leading to dissolution of the union with Denmark in 1814.

The Danes had made a grave mistake by deciding to support Napoleon. The British Royal Navy blocked all Norwegian ports from 1808, leaving Norway to run itself for several years. This prompted the creation of an independence movement in 1809 and when its goal was finally realised a century later, Britain became the first major power to recognise Norwegian independence.

But back to 1814. After Bonaparte's defeat, King Frederick VI of Denmark was forced to sign the Treaty of Kiel, giving Norway to the King of Sweden. For several glorious months however, the Norwegians scented freedom. Rallied by their own Prince Christian Frederik, 112 representatives of the Norwegian nation met at the Eidsvoll ironworks near Oslo and published a liberal constitution which established a national *Storting* (parliament), outlawed new nobility and extended the vote to male civil servants, urban property owners and farmers over 25 who owned their own land.[4] Overnight almost half (45 per cent) of all eligible Norwegian men were given the right to vote – a dramatic change made possible only because tens of thousands of men owned land in Norway.[5]

The 'Great' Reform Act of 1832 also gave the vote to male property owners, but that same measure in Britain only increased the electorate to 5.8 per cent of the male population in England and Wales and a pitiful 2.5 per cent in Scotland.[6] The twin nations were already set on very different democratic paths, thanks to their very different systems of landownership.

Armed with their new constitution, the Norwegians hoped to re-establish themselves quickly as an independent country, but the Swedes invaded in August 1814, backed by the crippling British naval blockade of Norwegian ports. They forced union upon the newly-created Parliament and the abdication of Christian Frederik. But this was only a personal union of Crowns under the Swedish King, so the Norwegian Constitution survived intact, prompting immediate and radical changes in the way Norway was governed.[7] Norway maintained its own constitution, ministries, legislature, laws, financial system, courts, army and navy so that Norwegian systems began to diverge further from Swedish norms, almost immediately.. The decision to enfranchise all male landowners had empowered Norwegian citizens in a way still foreign elsewhere.[8] In Sweden, the King could legislate with an absolute veto, but in Norway he could only suspend parliamentary decisions. For half a century these two systems ground away at one another – and in each battle the Norwegians emerged victorious.

In 1833, Norway's peasant farmers achieved a majority over officials and civil servants in parliament, earning it the nickname *Bønde-Stortinget* (Peasant Parliament).[9] The word *bønde* in Norwegian carries none of the negative associations of the English word 'peasant', which for those of a certain age immediately conjures up a world of Monty Pythonesque feudal subjugation. Instead, the *bønde* 'filled the role of 'heroes' in the years leading up to dissolution with Denmark, according to Professor John Bryden, because of their organised opposition to Danish rule.[10] One immediate outcome of 'peasant' domination was the establishment of local self government in 1837, which decreed that Norwegians had the right to govern themselves in geographically limited areas via *kommuner* (elected municipal councils). This Act acted as a brake against centralisation in Norway for almost two centuries:[11]

> This was the means by which the peasants successfully resisted centralised planning and the transfer of fishing rights to capitalist interests, and promoted concession laws and other progressive measures in the field of natural resources and land.[12]

In 1898 all men above the age of 25 got the vote and in 1918, independence brought universal suffrage for men and women.

But before that, the Norwegians had won their final battle with the Swedish King by declaring independence in June 1905, after a dispute about consular representation. The Swedish Riksdag decided not to invade but to negotiate separation, so long as Norwegian people backed independence. In August 1905 a referendum was held with 368,211 votes in favour of separation and just 184 against.[13] The King of Sweden stood his troops down.

What produced that overwhelming Yes vote? After all, upon independence Norway promptly became Europe's second poorest state. What really frayed the Union of Crowns with Sweden was Norway's dynamic democracy, born at Eidsvoll and strengthened by a Peasants' Parliament, made possible by widespread landownership. All of this helped carry the Norwegian people over the line.

Independence though, brought a new democratic challenge. Much of the newly expanded electorate backed the *Arbeiderpartiet* (Labour Party) but the electoral system discriminated against them. With 29 per cent of the vote, *Venstre* (the Liberal Party) had won 51 seats. With 31 per cent the *Arbeiderpartiet* had won just 18.

The Labour Party decided to confront the issue head-on. A resolution carried at the Labour Party conference of 1918 reserved the right to lead a revolution of the masses, in the Russian style, if the party couldn't achieve a majority by peaceful means.[14] It was a potent threat since neighbouring Finland was being consumed by civil war after declaring independence from Russia the year before.[15] In 1919 the *Arbeiderpartiet* upped the ante by joining Comintern – the only mainstream European Labour Party to align with the international federation led by the Soviet Communist Party. The threat of revolution prompted an immediate act of conciliation by Norway's non-socialist parties. In 1919 the *Storting* approved the use of proportional representation in national elections (80 years before Scotland) and limited the working day to eight hours (with excess work paid as overtime). The same year, 115,000 industrial workers in Norway gained the legal right to a week's paid annual holiday.

The *Arbeiderpartiet* (Labour Party) naturally benefited from all this and led a minority government in 1935 (after reunifying with the breakaway Social Democratic Labour Party). Thus started one of the longest periods of control by a political party in European history – Labour has led the Norwegian government for all but 16 years since 1935, and its outlook quickly reshaped the new state.[16]

> Planning was a central instrument in state economic policies, and sectors like agriculture, fishing, and transportation were all strongly state regulated. Markets were to be guided, private solutions were eschewed, and the chances for 'opting out' were restricted.[17]

Although it was a social democratic not a communist party, Labour's long custodianship of Norwegian democracy normalised regulation, planning and constraints on private ownership. According to Professor John Bryden:

> The idea that the market is embedded in society and its institutions... is perhaps best exemplified by the Norwegian approach. This idea is precisely the opposite of neo-liberals who believe that society, if it exists at all, should be embedded in the market.[18]

I wonder where he was thinking about.

Scotland

Scotland had no seismic democratic event like 1814, no new written constitution to defend, no broadly-based electorate, no representative national parliament, no slow progression towards independence and no subsequent period of national reassessment and growth.

Matti Goksøyr suggests there was renewed democratic activity in early 20th century Norway connected to the process of shaping its newly-established independent state. He contends that national identity is never static and so new generations, classes and ethnicities had to be won over to the project of building an independent country:

> After independence was won the task was to make it truly national – not just the property of the middle classes. The search for national identity that had been so clear in the

period 1880–1905 was, in the inter-war years, succeeded by
a concern to consolidate that identity by integrating ever-
larger sections of the population into a common culture
that functioned at a popular level.[19]

The move to give island hutting sites to Oslo workers in 1922
fits with this final phase of Norwegian nation-building, by integrating the poorest sections of the population into the common
culture of *friluftsliv* (the freedom of outdoor life) and consolida-
ting Norway's national identity as a more egalitarian society than
either Sweden or Denmark, with a more distinctively rural
'common culture'.

Scotland's democratic journey was rather different:

While Norway in 1814 moved from colonial status under
Denmark to a personal union with Sweden, Scotland went
in the opposite direction; from a personal union with
England and Wales (dating from 1603) to incorporation in
the union of Great Britain.[20]

The Reform Acts of 1832, 1868 and 1884 did widen the criteria for
political citizenship. But even after the 1885 reforms, only 40 per
cent of the adult male population of Scotland could vote and Scotland's tenant farmers were still subject to landlord pressure until the
secret ballot was introduced in 1874.

While Norway was preparing for independence, Scotland's
biggest constitutional development was the creation in 1885 of
a Scottish Secretary within the British government. Until devolution and the restoration of a Scottish Parliament in 1999, Scottish democracy was largely shaped by English MPs and the House
of Lords, which defended the interests of the Scottish landowning classes, by delaying the end of primogeniture for 38 years
after its abolition in England and the establishment of National
Parks for half a century after their introduction in England.

Another significant contrast with Norway was the frailty of
political connections between urban and rural workers:

> A progressive rural/urban alliance was the chief promoter
> of [Norway's] twin ambitions of democratic empowerment
> and national sovereignty. A similar movement never obtained
> a sufficient foothold in Scotland, a stagnation which can be
> attributed to institutional features such as electoral disen-
> franchisement and weak local government as well as cultural
> features such as the internal religious conflicts within the
> working class.[21]

The dual processes of urbanisation and industrialisation pulled
rural Scots and impoverished Catholic Irish workers into Glasgow,
transplanting languages, religious loyalties and cultural rivalries
which still exist to this day. Instead of helping to create a unified
working-class with a shared experience of loss, Ireland and the
Highlands and Islands provided large and often competing 'reserve
armies of labour' which helped keep wages in industrial Scotland
persistently lower than in England.[22]

Scotland's town–country divide has long been formidable.
It was soon formalised by holiday apartheid.

CHAPTER EIGHT

The search for the Land of Beyond

YOU MIGHT THINK the way we spend our leisure time as visitors, tourists, ramblers, walkers and participants in sport has little connection with our democratic traditions. But nothing in the life of a nation escapes the defaults, behaviours and expectations created by its governance systems. A thin democracy like Britain's produces elitism at almost every turn. A vibrant democracy like Norway's propels the idea of equality (even if not always fully achieved) into every aspect of public life. It was inevitable then, that sport became a pivotal part of Constitution Day held every 17 May to celebrate Norway's 1814 constitution and to protect its distinctive values from watering down by the Swedish King. Indeed, organisers consciously encouraged participants away from the elitist 'British pastime model' of sport towards a more practical, purposeful sense of activity.[1] The *Centralforeningen for Udbredelse af Legemsøvelser og Vaabenbrug* (Central Association for the Spread of Physical Exercise and the Practice of Arms) developed a national ideology explicitly designed 'to confront British thinking'.[2] The aim was to make sport serve higher purposes than mere socialising or competition for its own sake. Norwegian sport was concerned with the concept of *idræt* – a hard word to translate but more like activity than rule-bound games. Rowing boats (of the type used by Lindøya's first hutting settlers) had a particular significance in this nation-building context.[3] According to Constitution Day rowers in Bergen:

> The British way of rowing, less rational (and) involving crafts only suited to shallow waters and competition, is doomed… our fraternities are too much adapted to the people's and nature's practical requirements.[4]

A similar rejection of colonial sporting priorities occurred in Ireland after indepedence, when rugby union was excluded from the Tailteann Games – an Irish sporting and cultural festival held in the interwar years – because the Irish Rugby Football Union was seen as 'undemocratic and almost un-Irish'.[5]

The man who most powerfully articulated Norway's alternative conception of sport and developed the connection between activity, nature and Norwegian national identity was Fridtjof Nansen – scientist, sportsman, explorer, writer and humanist:

> I tell you, deliverance will not come from the rushing, noisy centres of civilisation. It will come from the lonely places.[6]

His book describing his expedition across Greenland on skis in 1889 was published simultaneously in English and German and the impact on public opinion of his triumphant return from presumed death after a bid to reach the North Pole a decade later is hard to exaggerate.[7] Nansen considered hiking, fishing, hunting and especially skiing to be mainstays of *friluftsliv*, a word first used in print by the writer Henrik Ibsen in 1859 to describe a state in which recreation, rejuvenation and the restoration of balance are achieved through immersion in nature.[8] Today *friluftsliv* is more easily achieved by living in town during the week and escaping to a *hytte* for weekends. But more than a century ago Nansen was encouraging Norwegians to reject Danish and British hierarchies of sport and instead embrace *idræt*:

> Skiing is the most national of all Norwegian sports. Nothing teaches the quality of dexterity and resourcefulness, calls for decision and resolution, like skiing. Can there be anything more beautiful and noble than the northern winter landscape when the snow lies foot-deep, like a soft white mantle over wood and hill?

Nansen so disliked the British conception of sport that he urged all Norwegians to 'detest sport and record-breaking'. A contemporary magazine even remarked that sport was just 'degenerate' *idræt*.[9] In 1926 Nansen was elected Rector of St Andrews University, the first foreigner to hold the position. His inaugural address was a rousing tribute to the friluftsliv ideal, which reportedly moved many students to tears:

> We all have a Land of Beyond to seek in our life – what more can we ask? Our part is to find the trail that leads to it. A long trail, a hard trail, maybe; but the call comes to us, and we have to go. Rooted deep in the nature of every one of us is the spirit of adventure, the call of the wild – vibrating under all our actions, making life deeper and higher and nobler.[10]

At a more prosaic level, leisure in Norway was also shaped by the country's patchwork of small landowners. Norwegian farms were more like small villages than single-family concerns with a cluster of smaller dwellings around the main farmhouse. The *bønde* who owned his land, generally gave or sold land to labourers, creating a network of people able to bequeath land and farmhouses to children and happy to hunt, fish, walk and ski together – in contrast to feudal Scotland.[11] There was also the tradition of the *skyss*, whereby farmers could provide transport for passing government officials in lieu of tax.[12] When officials appeared at a country inn, the farmer on the duty rota had to appear within a couple of hours and let them drive his horse and cart to the next appointed handover stop. This created an early habit of depending on farmers for tourism and travel – a habit which naturally expanded into the provision of small-scale tourism and *hytte* building in the high pastures once guaranteed leisure time was won by workers in 1919.

Throughout this nation-building period, many writers sought to valorise everything connected with nature in a bid to emphasise points of distinction between Norway and Sweden.[13] Norway's political leaders decided the 'real' character of its nation could be found not in industry or urban life, but in the inland valleys – as far away as possible from the influence of 'Mother' Denmark. High art – literature, music and painting in the 19th century may have been produced in Oslo but was often inspired by life in rural areas.

Miroslav Hroch suggests there was a three-stage evolution of nationalism in Norway.[14] The first phase consisted of a mostly cultural, literary and 'folkloric' focus on national identity by a narrow intellectual elite. A second phase of 'patriotic agitation' dominated the years 1814–40 and the third stage, in the last half of the 19th century, focused on expressive nationalism and popular movements. There was growing demand for written Norwegian in schools, wild, inhospitable looking mountains became national images and Norway's 'mountain home' provided inspiration for paintings, music and poetry – not principally for incoming visitors but for Norwegians themselves.

Their heroes were people like Nansen, Roald Amundsen and later Thor Heyerdahl who challenged the forces of nature by skiing to the poles or crossing the oceans on wooden rafts. Yet, despite the daring and classically masculine nature of their famous feats of physical endurance, these exceptional explorers all acknowledged the importance of rural origins and country childhoods, shaped by women.

Women and children were responsible for taking cows to the high pastures and lived all summer in the *seter* (summer farm or shieling). Berry picking, moss gathering and mushroom picking also went on with the aim of filleting nature – selectively foraging every last usable thing it could safely provide. Thus, the culture of the high mountain life was not exclusively masculine (as it has tended to be in hut and shelter-free Scotland, despite the best efforts of writers like Jessie Kesson and Nan Shepherd). *Koselig* (cosy) features softened the bleakness of Norway's mountain surroundings and this seems to have been important in creating almost universally warm, fond memories of childhood in the fjords and fjell of Norway.[15] Writers like Ellen Rees suggest modern Norwegian cultural identity is still based on literary works located in this liminal zone between wild country and tamed country – between the *hytte* and the *seter*.[16] Indeed, the first *hytte* owned by the Norwegian DNT Mountain Cabin Association was a converted *seter*, though thereafter the rest were purpose-built.

Academic Nina Witoszek goes further and argues that Norwegians have no urban culture at all, and that everything praised, coveted and socially desirable lies in Norwegian nature.[17] She quotes the 19th century Romantic poet Henryk Wergeland (a frequent visitor to Lindøya) who said ironically:

> The Mountains are, in the last instance, our best Norwegians... So strong was the equation between nature and nationality that... the Norwegian patriots of the nineteenth century [regarded] the city as a parasitopolis despoiling native ground. Urban culture, associated with extra-terrestrial [ie Danish] clergy, bureaucracy and townsfolk, was alien to the folk spirit. It was nature not culture that was national.[18]

Witoszek believes the Norwegians were 'too worldly, pragmatic and Protestant to fully identify with rapture and the over-wrought aesthetics of excess.'

But independence campaigners did successfully deploy Norway's exceptional landscape to create a sense of distinctiveness that bolstered national confidence.

> Nature relieved the Norwegians from having to apologise for their lack of castles, cities, ruins and libraries. The vast reserves of mountain, fjords and forests functioned as castles and cathedrals. Nature became the sole expression of national heritage and the city as a symbol of progress and enlightenment – Wordsworth's 'place of wonder and obscure delight' – became something Norwegian patriots were inclined to disown.[19]

Does the stunning yet 'owned' landscape of Scotland have as bolstering an effect on the national confidence of Scots, I wonder. Or the equally 'owned' cityscapes of Georgian Edinburgh and mercantile Glasgow?

Certainly, for 20th century Norwegian nationalists, a home-grown and peasant-owned rural culture was at the centre of everything. One of the languages created upon independence, Nynorsk, was based on western dialects found 'in peasant cottages in our valleys and on our seashore' and was described by its supporters as 'true Norwegian speech.'[20]

This positive cultural association with all things rural was based on the hard fact that peasants and country dwellers had considerable political and social autonomy, compared to rural Scots. Until 1870, three quarters of Norwegians lived in rural areas with no native nobility.[21] The rest of the traditional ruling class was also generally absent from the country, since Danish bureaucrats lived in cities and forged closer ties with urban professionals than rural landowners. So, for Norwegian peasants the countryside was a relatively uncontested arena (though by no means an easy existence), while cities contained alien and uncontrollable influences.

Scotland

On this side of the North Sea, things were very different.

Scotland was central to the development of tourism in the western world and was becoming one of the most important new European destinations in the early 19th century. But not principally for Scots. MacLellan and Smith's comprehensive survey tracks the transformation of Scotland from a place with nothing to see before 1760 into the most fashionable holiday location for wealthy Europeans half a century later.[22] James Boswell reported that Voltaire looked amazed when he announced an intention to visit the Scottish Highlands, 'he looked at me as if I had talked of going to the North Pole.'[23] But as AV Seaton observes, that soon changed:

> In the eighteenth century, a forbidding wilderness was turned into a genteel pleasure ground, an alien and hostile race of people became an object of sentimental myth, and a climate regarded as brutish was transformed into an environment of grandeur – proof that tourism is about ideas and ideologies as much as amenity.[24]

In the wake of the Jacobites' defeat in 1746, those 'alien and hostile' people, Highland Scots, had their culture repressed and a sanitised version of it fed back to themselves and to foreign tourists. Wearing the plaid in the aftermath of Culloden was enough to get you killed, but a century later Sir Walter Scott and

Queen Victoria had safely reinvented the kilt.[25] The MacCrim-
mons's piping school closed in the 1770s when traditional
pipe-playing was banned, but piping was encouraged in Scottish
regiments of the British army.[26] As Calum MacLean observes in
The Highlands:

> The Hanoverian regime... formulated the brilliant policy of
> enlisting the 'secret enemy' to destroy him as cannon
> fodder. Highlanders were again dressed up in kilts and, by
> the ingenious use of names such as Cameron, Seaforth and
> Gordon; old loyalties were diverted into new channels.[27]

Meanwhile there were (at least) two versions of place names as
mapmakers found their way to the most distant parts of Scotland
and, without any Gaelic, invariably changed what they found.
The misnaming, loss of local meaning and resentment that
resulted mirrored the same heavy-handed process of map-mak-
ing in Ireland, later critiqued by playwright Brian Friel in his
play *Translations*. In Scottish dance, many of the enduringly
popular 'Highland Dances' like the Gay Gordons and Dashing
White Sergeant sprang from the English military barracks, not
Scotland's own indigenous traditions.[28] As the Englishman Edwin
Landseer painted the classic image of the Scottish Highlands,
The Monarch of the Glen in 1851, thousands of Scots were
being cleared from surrounding hillsides to make way for deer.
For any aspect of Highland culture – dress, piping, dance, speech
– at least two competing versions emerged. But after Culloden,
the British version became the safest to espouse and highbrow
English traditions the most profitable to learn. This meant
Scottish culture (until recently) was identified not as a source of
national strength but of confusion and weakness:

> Scottish culture is characterised as split, divided, deformed.
> This is a not unfamiliar view of Scottish culture, epitomised
> by Walter Scott, in which Scotland is divided between the
> 'heart' (representing the past, romance, 'civil society') and
> the 'head' (the present and future, reason, and by dint of
> that, the British state).[29]

Eventually the idealised view of the noble stag in an empty Highland landscape won out and became the defining depiction of rural Scotland for landowners, visitors and ultimately for many local people too.

Scotland first became popular with English visitors in the early 19th century because continental Europe was closed during the Napoleonic wars and developed a tourism industry faster than mountainous Wales thanks to Sir Walter Scott, whose novels helped reshape the image of rebellious Scots into something noble – but unthreatening. Under Scott's influence, the British royal family, led by George IV and then Queen Victoria, made the Scottish Highlands fashionable. By the 1820s local papers were commenting on the influx of tourists – 30,000 folk were said to have come to the Highlands after Scott published *The Lady of the Lake* in 1810 and established the vogue for cruising along Loch Katrine.[30] Forty years later, a railway through the Highlands was proposed with an expected 50,000 passengers a year.

> By the mid-19th century Scotland had virtually become an adventure park for those with the money or inclination to partake of its pleasures.[31]

Royal approval helped turn the Highlands into a playground for the rich. Prince Albert's construction of Balmoral as a holiday home in 1853 set the trend for other wealthy incomers and sporting estates soon proliferated. The typical field sports enthusiast was 'a self-made businessman or solicitor graduate educated at Harrow'.[32] But his transformation into an authentic Highland Laird required the construction of a Highland Shooting Lodge:

> Schlossy sporting lodges were little more than the self-indulgent holiday homes of those who had made a fortune in the new industries of Victorian Britain.[33]

Eric Simpson observes that the ideal Highland sporting estate was 'a man-made wilderness with plenty of deer to stalk and no crofters to bother the sporting tenants.'[34]

It's suggested the 'shooting box', used by English gentlemen during deer and grouse shooting was the first hut to be mentioned in Scottish literature, though in fact it was more often 'a small house or lodge'.[35] Perhaps anything less than a mini-Balmoral felt like a hut to its temporary occupants. But one thing's certain – local Scots were not the huntsmen. Not during daylight hours, anyway.

Deer, pheasant and grouse shooting was reserved for landowners and guests and the only involvement by locals tended to be poaching – vividly described in novels like Neil Gunn's *Highland River* – and the hard work of stalking, gralloching (disembowelling) and transporting the deer 'home', beating grouse for waiting shooters, carrying and providing refreshment, retrieving catches, and generally guiding and supporting paying guests who rarely possessed any hunting skills at all.[36] The near-total exclusion of locals caused great (if rarely expressed) resentment, until John McGrath's wildly popular *The Cheviot, the Stag and the Black Black Oil* delivered a biting 70s satire on upper-class domination, from the safety of the village hall stage.[37]

Local people were cleared to create these 'sporting estates' but that fact was swept under the carpet. Instead commentators insisted locals were grateful to see work and income flowing into their poverty-stricken glens. Might wealth, happiness and security have been increased further by the equitable distribution of land? The idea was never entertained. Lairds, their wealth, habits, outlooks and comforts fast became the lynchpins of Highland life. A *Sunday Mail* article in 1937 suggested that three quarters of folk in a typical Highland village depended on 'the streams of wealth released by rod and gun'. The author contrasts the income now derived from sporting estates with the meagre yield from farming in days gone by:

> Today the Highlander has a spotless white-walled cottage with four or more rooms, a garden and a good road and the benefit of a daily post and modern transport. How much of all this he owes to the grouse he, more than anyone, realises. It has paved the way to a new prosperity and a happier outlook on life.[38]

Whether locals actually felt happier being paid buttons to help southern visitors shoot grouse is highly debatable. Some left, some bit their lips and stayed, and some doubtless admired the class that had so skilfully woven its own history and values into Scotland's national narratives.

> The opening of great country houses to the public, mass tourism and the popular addiction to nostalgia have enabled aristocratic families to act as guardians of the nation's heritage and to personify symbols of an enduring link with the glories of Scotland's past.[39]

Thus land, nature, hunting, landscape and the outdoors all provoke mixed feelings amongst Scots in a way straight-talking, landowning Norwegians will probably never understand. But then again, why should they – neither do we.

From the start, the visitor to Highland Scotland was typically a member of the literate middle or upper classes and came from England, Germany or France, not Scotland. The domestic market only developed in the second half of the 19th century with the growth of cheap rail and steamer excursions which brought west coast seaside resorts within reach of urban workers for day trips and, after the Holidays with Pay Act of 1938, for longer stays in rented accommodation. This resulted in holiday apartheid as different parts of Scotland catered for different classes of tourist.[40] Incomer tourism created a demand for picturesque landscape which

> favoured roughness against smoothness, the ancient against the modern, the unimproved against the improved and the empty and desolate against the populated and the everyday.[41]

David Marshall observes:

> The picturesque represents a point of view that frames the world and turns nature into a series of living tableaux. It begins as an appreciation of natural beauty but ends by turning people into figures in a landscape or a painting.[42]

Indeed, this quest for shaped, 'picturesque' landscapes excluded
people so completely that landowners cleared labourers' cottages
and sometimes whole communities just to improve the view.
William Cobbett, on a tour of Scotland, was outraged that
Edinburgh – which he regarded as the finest city in the world –
was not surrounded by thriving agricultural villages because
aristocrats owned the estates and kept them empty, rural and
'unspoiled'.[43] Cobbett also raged against the Clearances:

> It may be quite proper to inquire into the means that were
> used to effect the clearing, for all that we have been told
> about [Scotland's] sterility has been either sheer falsehood
> or monstrous exaggeration.

The transformation of rural Scotland into a clutch of private
sporting estates created a template of easy exclusion and
throughout the 19th and 20th centuries, the level of farm and
estate tourism north of the border remained low compared to
England and Wales.[44]

> The aversion towards tourism by feudal sporting estate
> owners was reflected by others who viewed land primarily
> as a resource for making a living – farming, forestry and
> fishing interests and heavy industry like pulp mills, hydro
> power and (later) blanket forestry.[45]

Until the advent of going 'doon the watter', sea voyages, spas
and coastal resorts were no less exclusive. Steamers opened up
the Highlands and Islands for wealthy travellers with regular
summer trips from Glasgow to Fingal's Cave on Staffa. Felix
Mendelssohn's visit in 1829 and his Hebrides overture prompted
even more wealthy travellers to visit (like an earlier and more
highbrow *Outlander* effect). Oban, was nicknamed 'the Charing
Cross of the Highlands' and became an important western
resort. A succession of steamers plied a new route via the Clyde
and the Crinan Canal (opened in 1801), to Fort William and
Inverness (via the Caledonian Canal which opened in 1822).[46]
Perth and Inverness were connected to the railway network in
1863 and became especially busy in early August as the rich and

famous arrived with their servants for the grouse shooting season. So many visitors came from England that Episcopalian church services were held during the summer months and Highland Games were revived or invented for their benefit – Birnam and Ballater (1864), Aboyne (1867), Crieff (1870) and Oban (1873). But little of this was directed at the average holi-daymaking Scot.

Once railway lines were built to Greenock (1841) and Helensburgh (1858), the working classes were easily concen-trated elsewhere, heading to Dunoon and Rothesay for day trips and short summer holidays, though even these brief escapes were criticised because of overcrowding and 'immorality'. A feature in the *Scottish Temperance Review* 1850 observed:

> Hundreds of men and women lay in the woods and fields about Rothesay on the nights of Saturday and Sunday of the fair week. Lodgings were not to be had at any price. In one attic 15 males and females were accommodated.[47]

This kind of pressure (so similar to objections about Lindøya) prompted Parliament to pass the Forbes-Mackenzie Act of 1853, which prohibited the sale of alcohol on Sundays. But it didn't apply to steamers. Thus was born the working-class Scottish tradition of getting 'steaming' to go 'doon the watter' for holidays, while wealthier foreigners went more soberly 'up the glen'.

At first, the state's strategy was to ban or license undesirable alcohol-saturated activities. The Temperance (Scotland) Act 1913 gave communities the right to 'go dry' but prompted only a small number of local votes in 1920. Soon though, the sheer volume of 'rough' activity, participation by the middle classes and the pres-sure on police and court time all combined to force a change of approach in the form of the Betting and Lotteries Act 1934, which legalised betting at licensed racecourse and greyhound tracks:

> With this surrender the strategy changed. When ice cream shops first appeared in the 1900s, the state's instinct was to suppress and control. But they became tolerable compared to billiard halls, and both were preferable to worse forms

of youth culture, leading to state support of billiards in
youth clubs. Voluntary was better than commercial, but
commercial was better than illegal and rough.[48]

Perhaps this change in official attitudes explains the 'tolerance'
shown by some councils towards the hutting communities
springing up around Scotland during the interwar years – especially Bruce's Camps at Seton Sands.

In Norway and Sweden, similar worries about the siren
attractions of 'the street' prompted churches, trade unions and
governments to urge construction of self-built family huts.[49] But
not in Scotland. There was deep official unease about the prospect of workers organising their own newly-acquired leisure
time. Instead, more voluntary and charitable sporting institu-
tions began life in turn of the century Scotland than anywhere
else in Europe (pro rata), with one shared mission – to organise
the leisure time of young people for them. Motives were mixed.
Some were doubtless as paternalistic as they sound to modern
ears, others aimed to extend a Christian upbringing to city children and some arose from the poor physical condition of Boer
War volunteers, which prompted the Scottish Education Department to recommend physical training programmes for all school
children in 1900. This was followed by a Royal Commission on
Physical Training in 1903, a Committee on Physical Deteriora-
tion in 1904, Syllabus of Physical Exercises in Public Elementary
Schools in 1905 and compulsory medical supervision of school-
children in the Education Act of 1908.[50]

Perhaps though, the cluster of outdoors organisations that
sprang up in turn of the century Scotland was an unconscious
act of compensation for children whose parents had been denied
any access to the land. Without the validating presence of the
great and good, groups of working-class boys and young men
from Scotland's cities simply wouldn't have been welcome to walk,
much less camp in most parts of feudal rural Scotland.

The Boys' Brigade – the world's first voluntary uniformed
organisation for boys – was founded in Glasgow by Sir William
Alexander Smith in 1883 to develop 'Christian manliness'

through gymnastics, summer camps and religious services. Smith introduced the concept of camping to allow boys and 'officers' to remain in contact over the summer break and his 1st Glasgow Company held its inaugural one-week camp at a hall in Tighnabruaich in 1886, before moving to camp in tents near Portavadie in the Kyles of Bute, a location that remained in use until 1974.[51]

In 1903 Robert Stephenson Smyth Baden-Powell returned from the Boer War and Smith encouraged him to develop citizenship training for boys based on his handbook for soldiers, *Aids to Scouting*. This was so popular (even published in Russia on the order of Tsar Nicolas) that in 1910 Baden-Powell retired to devote his life to the international Scout Movement, which, unlike the devout Boys Brigade, was a non-Christian organisation. Baden-Powell's Boy Scouts were in fact the only large uniformed youth organisation that refused to join the government's War Office Cadets scheme.[52]

These organisations built on the 'games' revolution devised by the Glasgow-born Hely Hutchinson Almond, headmaster of Loretto School in Musselburgh from 1862 to 1903, whose programme of education contained very specific ideas about healthy food, clothing, outdoor activity, fresh air and cold baths.[53] Another Scot, Archibald MacLaren, provided Almond with a set of physical exercises for his school and private boarding schools like Glenalmond, Merchiston and Fettes followed his lead either through direct contact or by employing ex-Lorettonians.[54]

The term Muscular Christianity was applied to Almond's outlook and Edinburgh Academy rector Robert Jameson Mackenzie helped spread his ideas to the state sector. This all doubtless helped produce generations of excellent sportsmen and women.[55] But it also strengthened the idea that children and young people needed structure and guidance to behave well in the countryside, not just easier access to land for walks or camping and hutting within their own families. In short, Scotland was no less outdoors-oriented than Norway during the early 20th century, but access was far more controlled and formally organised. Indeed, politicised workers in the west of Scotland soon created their own outdoors organisations in a mirror image of these Victorian structures.

Ironically, huts for working-class Scots finally came into their own during World War One. Obviously, soldiers used huts for sleeping, washing, storage and latrines. But YMCA branches fund-raised to provide special huts for relaxation and convalescence behind the front lines. For many soldiers, it may have been their first experience of a wee 'home from home'.

> The [YMCA huts] are like kitchen firesides set down at the Front at which our lads can rest and refresh themselves with a cup of tea or cocoa, a smoke and a sing-song. These huts of ours must be kept going, briskly and brightly. There must be no 'out' fires. We must keep the kettles singing and the loaf on the table.[56]

By 1918, 2,000 YMCA huts existed in every part of the combat zone, staffed by 200 Scottish Ministers. Free and Church of Scotland churches were paired so that one Minister could travel abroad.[57] By March 1918, huts and equipment worth £150,000 had been destroyed, but they were being replaced and fund-raising for 'civilian' huts continued beyond the Armistice.[58] After the war, many surplus huts were put up for sale. Dundee City Council, struggling to accommodate returning soldiers bought ex-army huts for accommodation.[59] Enterprising private landowners like William Bruce of Seton Sands saw their leisure potential.[60] This ad from the *Evening News* of 1924 offered, 'Officers' tents with floors to hire' suggesting a half-hut, half-tent construction like the *lemmehytter* being used on Lindøya a few years earlier.

> **HOLIDAY CAMPING.**
> **PORT SETON, Near Edinburgh.**
> Excelent sites adjoining Seton Sands; water on ground; Restaurant, Grocery Department; Ridge and Bell Tents with wood floors, for Hire; Dancing. BRUCE, Seton Mains, LONGNIDDRY.
> 'Phone 14.

FIG 8.1 Newspaper ad for tents with wooden floors at Seton Sands.
Courtesy: Edinburgh Evening News, *Wednesday 16 July 1924*

In parallel to all this was the fight for statutory holiday rights. The idea of paid holidays had not gained general acceptance in Britain before WW1. Employers rejected any suggestion they would improve productivity and unions, focused on the fight for basic industrial rights, dismissed the idea of paid leisure time as 'somewhat utopian'.[61] After the 1929 General Election, the new Labour government gave one week's paid holiday to nearly 100,000 workers in state-owned industries.[62] Unions and some unlikely newspaper groups pressed for more. The *Daily Express* ran a campaign in 1938 listing 24 nations that already provided annual paid holidays for all workers, including France, Finland, the USSR... and Norway.[63] Finally, the 1938 Holidays With Pay Act recommended a week's annual paid vacation for all full-time workers, but didn't make it compulsory – a pattern which would endure for the rest of the century. Nonetheless, this was a game-changing moment in the history of leisure in Britain, and produced panic amongst affluent Britons who feared their own favourite holiday escapes would soon be overrun. The government was ahead of them. The 1938 Act also recommended the immediate construction of large-scale holiday camps to accommodate workers and their families.[64] Councils responded by cutting local tax rates for commercial holiday camps and even considered building and running their own.[65] While the Norwegian and Swedish governments were financing mass *hytte* building campaigns, the British government favoured organised, regulated, commercial camps.

> Those concerned with the public spaces of the nation, including beaches, parks and resorts... claimed cultural custodianship of the landscape in the interwar years [and] constantly questioned the kind of public to be permitted and cultivated. The [1938] legislation deeply implicated the state in the construction of... commercial class-based sites of leisure.[66]

The new wave of working-class holiday-makers looked certain to expand the potential for 'vulgar behaviour and anti-citizenship'.[67] This prompted much anxious debate about overcrowding, 'cultural trespass' and rights of access to national space.[68] But a week after the publication of the Committee on Holidays With Pay report, entrepreneur Billy Butlin had solved the problem by opening a 'luxury' holiday camp at Clacton-on-Sea with accommodation for 2,000 people. He extended his original Skegness camp to cater for 4,500 guests a week and later, purchased a wartime, naval base near Ayr which he reopened as a holiday camp in 1947.[69]

Guests slept in individual 'chalets,' ate three daily hot meals, used childcare services and enjoyed a packed schedule of outdoor and indoor activities for an all-inclusive pre-paid price. It was

> an inexpensive holiday in which a wife can enjoy rest and recuperation and freedom from arduous household duties.[70]

By 1938 there were approximately two hundred holiday camps in Britain organised by unions, political groups and commercial operators including Butlin and Harry Warner who between them catered for 140,000 campers. This usefully diverted the working classes away from existing middle-class resorts and any temptation to make trips into the off-limits countryside by themselves.[71]

> The holiday camp expansion was driven partly by middle-class anxiety that droves of vacationing workers and their families would overwhelm the already congested seaside resorts along Britain's coast – the middle classes hoped holiday camps would provide contained and inexpensive pleasure for those unwelcome workers and their families.[72]

The outbreak of war interrupted full implementation of the 1938 legislation, and the cost of holidays still lay beyond most workers until labour shortages pushed up wages after World War Two. The Education Scotland Act of 1945 established plans for state-run 'camps, holiday classes, playing fields, play centres, gyms, swimming baths and other establishments... for recreation'.[73] But most of these failed to materialise. A Ministry of Education circular demonstrated the state had no confidence in the ability of workers to make good leisure choices if left to their own devices or the vagaries of the marketplace.

> Men and women do not as a rule make the best use of their leisure if the only facilities are those provided by commercial enterprise. The provision of communal facilities for the rational and enjoyable use of leisure is... a necessary part of the country's educational system.[74]

Of course, many urban Scots refused to be 'organised' and 'provided for' and simply walked or cycled out of the city and into the hills. The first climbing clubs were middle-class and exclusive. The Scottish Mountaineering Club was formed in 1889 and the Ladies Scottish Climbing Club in 1908. Hiking and cycling clubs for working people were quite separate:

> Some Glasgow shop workers toiling of necessity till late on Saturdays could count themselves fortunate if they caught the last train or bus out of the city. Many lived rough, finding primitive forms of shelter such as caves or overhanging boulders. Rough and ready howffs were made using old tarpaulin for roofing material. For these proletarian pioneers the campfire was at one and the same time a comradely expression of freedom and a practical necessity. 'We carried no tents,' said Jock Nimlin, one of the working-class trailblazers, 'and some of us carried no blankets or sleeping bags. It hardly seemed worthwhile as we had so little time for sleep.'[75]

Nimlin and his fellow 'Mountain Men' were hardy in the extreme. They caught the last bus or walked from Glasgow to Balloch, rowed up Loch Lomond to Tarbert, slept in a cave, rose the next day to climb the Arrochar Alps, did the same on Sunday, rowed back down the loch and walked into Glasgow having generally missed the last bus.[76] This herculean physical effort was then repeated the following weekend. Nimlin and his working-class colleagues used caves, bothies, self-built rooms beneath road bridges and even hollowed out trees for overnight shelter and were reportedly contemptuous of those using youth hostels or indoor accommodation.[77] Perhaps they were making a virtue of necessity and assumed that asking permission would only result in humiliating rejection. Perhaps life in the tough conditions of Glasgow bred a self-reliance which depended on never asking for help, especially from landowners. Evidently, 'Mountain Men' like Jock Nimlin, Tom Weir and Hamish MacInnes were keen to distinguish themselves from the soft, feather-bedded, deer-shooting elite whose louche enjoyment of the land was a world away from their own limited means. But, for tens of thousands of less hardy, Scots, it became simpler to accept that the land and countryside was out of bounds – either the private, guarded domain of the landed gentry or a physically demanding landscape suited only to the toughest men. As Katherine Haldane Grenier observes:

> Victorian men participated in a range of what William Hamilton Maxwell termed 'manly pastimes' in the Highlands: hunting, fishing, hiking, camping, climbing mountains. Renditions of parts of the Highlands, such as the Cuillin, as 'desolate', 'sterile', and 'inaccessible' implicitly elevated the achievements of those who went there.[78]

By contrast, Norway's early emphasis on huts as a place to stay in nature encouraged whole families to experience the Great Outdoors together, regardless of age, gender or physical ability.

The die was cast. Holidays for Scots would not be in DIY wooden huts, handed down over generations as individually owned second homes, but in rented, Butlin's style chalets, caravans, boarding houses and other 'packaged' holidays.[79]

Holidays on the land would be the preserve of incoming visitors, and their 'subjugating gaze' would change the image of Scotland beyond and even within the country itself:

> As the pace of economic and social transformation intensified in England, English tourists came to envision the north as a place immune to change and understood journeys there to be antidotes to the uncertainties of modern life. While praised as the home of preindustrial virtues, Scotland was also valuable as a place 'rooted in the past'. The rhetoric of tourism increasingly froze Scotland in time in the 19th century.[80]

As well as the vexed issues of where and how leisure for the masses should happen, there was also the basic issue of whether enough paid holiday was available to finance it. After the small advance of one week's paid leave in 1938, it wasn't until 1975 that a 40-hour week with 20 days' annual paid holiday was established (though still not enshrined in law).[81] Ten per cent of the Scottish workforce still received no paid holidays in 1995 but largely thanks to the European Working Time Directive, British workers have been entitled to 28 days of paid annual holiday since 2009.[82] In short, British workers have the longest working hours, the shortest statutory holidays, the strongest tendency towards packaged holidays and the smallest number of huts and holiday homes in Europe. Yet against this daunting backdrop, some Scots still managed to defy the odds, the social norms and political constraints to build huts. The largest hutting community is still thriving. And that is a minor miracle.

CHAPTER NINE

Carbeth and William Ferris: The rough diamonds

On 30 October 1999, Billy Coote and his partner Donna Russell, were at a Halloween dance enjoying themselves, oblivious to the fact their hut at Carbeth was being burned to the ground. They were devastated. Not only had the hut, built by Billy's father, been destroyed – their beloved dog Chips had been trapped inside and was burned alive.[1]

CHRIS BALLANCE, *The Fire That Never Went Out*, 2000

THIS TERRIBLE SCENE at Carbeth described levels of violence and confrontation no-one ever faced on Lindøya or the other *hytte* islands – not even in the bad old days of Miss Fritz and her unfriendly dog. The arson attacks shocked those who knew Carbeth as a peaceful place – a small landed estate with 340 acres of hilly, hummocky terrain, a farm, loch, forest, upland pasture, gardens, estate houses, offices, and, since the 1920s, hundreds of small, self-built wooden huts.[2] But in the run up to the millennium, it didn't look as if Scotland's oldest hutting community would reach its 100th birthday.

The landowner's decision to hike rents had prompted a rent strike lasting almost ten years, during which time hutters were taken to court by the estate, and huts belonging to leading strikers were mysteriously burned down. Hutter and poet Gerry Loose spoke for many when he wrote:

That was always the worry. You would be thinking: 'Will my hut still be standing or will someone think: this is a Bolshie wee bastard, let's teach him a lesson?'

Knowingly, or accidentally (well, he is a poet), Gerry's words precisely channelled the situation 70 years earlier, when anxiety

FIG 9.1 William Ferris.
Courtesy: Murray Ferris

about 'Bolshies' almost stopped Carbeth from developing huts in the first place. That they did, in the wake of the Bolshevik Revolution in Russia, was down to the persuasive powers of one man – William Ferris. Over his lifetime, this modest man from Govan – one of 11 children – either set up, or helped run the Camping Club of Great Britain and Ireland, the Scottish Council of Physical Recreation, the Scottish Rights of Way Society, the Scottish Camping Club and the Scottish Ramblers Federation as well as setting up the first Youth Hostel in Britain.[3] By all accounts, he was an extraordinary man:

> William Ferris reverenced his conscience as his chief tribunal. His kindliness, his integrity, his tolerance were manifestations of the fact that his supreme interest in life – in the

midst of a truly remarkable wide range of activities – was in his fellow men. This had its beginnings in the early days, when life was non-too easy; when there were handicaps to be overcome; when he was surrounded by the evidence of 'equal opportunities for every citizen' appearing little more than a high-sounding phrase instead of an inalienable right. It is not surprising that he identified himself with socialism.[4]

To be fair, the man Ferris won over was not your typical land-owner either. Born in 1894, Allan Barns-Graham Senior (ABG Senior) was a modest and artistic man – according to his grandson – who supported Home Rule for Scotland, and in this regard found a political meeting of minds with William Ferris.[5] ABG Senior's elder brother, Patrick, died after a skating accident and his younger brother, John, 'inherited the investments', went to New Zealand and prospered.[6] Allan followed his brother there and spent several years 'gaining practical experience of cooper-ative dairying.'[7] On return to Scotland he inherited Carbeth and ran the Stirlingshire estate as an experimental dairy farm, winning the Highland Society's Gold Medal in 1904. But he lived in St Andrews and didn't move permanently to Carbeth until 1924, by which time the hutters were ensconced, which suggests he was either intrigued by his new tenants or determined to lay down the law.

His grandson – the most recent private landowner – is also called Allan Barns-Graham. He suggests life at Carbeth House was spartan and his grandparents lived frugally, compared to more gentrified neighbours. ABG Senior didn't go for holidays or own a car. Carbeth House had no curtains and ABG Junior recalls that his grandmother boiled water before they drank it.

Locals had been using Carbeth for leisure pursuits since the 1830s when the loch first became a venue for curling matches. In 1868 Carbeth Curling Club persuaded tenants on both sides to flood the meadow to an agreed height between November and March, confirming that the area wasn't exactly prime agri-cultural land.[8] But it was wooded and close to Scotland's largest city. Already, some of the preconditions for hutting were in place.

Three miles over the hill at Strathblane, the construction of a water tunnel built in the 1850s brought an influx of workers, who stayed in the village and got jobs at a print works, owned by the local Coubrough family. It closed in 1898 leaving a large number of vacant cottages and a demolished factory whose bricks helped build at least six more homes. The village adapted to become a holiday retreat in the early 20th century and the Coubroughs were active in their support of youth movements and hosted scout rallies in the grounds of Blanefield House, giving hospitality to invalid soldiers during World War One.[9] Perhaps the regular presence of scouts and soldiers at this nearby 'holiday village' helped normalise the idea of hutters at neighbouring Carbeth – eventually.

Workers at the print works were expected to be punctual. Anyone late three times in a row had to pay a farthing into a tin, given to those on the Poor Roll, perhaps a template for the strict hutting rules deployed later by ABG Senior.[10] John Coubrough stayed in the village after the printworks closed and was known as 'Penny Jock' because of his involvement in the War Savings Movement. By a strange coincidence, the man who finally persuaded ABG Senior to have huts on his land saved money through just that scheme.[11]

William Ferris would have remained a name on a page had it not been for a stroke of luck. For years, I'd been following the trials of the Carbeth hutters and two of their number, Morven Gregor and Gerry Loose, were active in the Thousand Huts Campaign, which was launched in 2011 just before I headed off to Norway. I'd read enough bits of archive and the invaluable book written by fellow hutter Chris Ballance, to know William Ferris was largely responsible for getting hutting off the ground at Carbeth. But who was he? What motivated him? I could see he'd been in the Highland Cycling Battalion during the war, and later ran a clutch of Scottish and UK outdoor organisations. But calls and emails to them drew a blank. No-one had heard of him, which made me all the more curious.

After sessions in The Mitchell, Glasgow and Strathclyde University libraries, a meeting with Elspeth King (ex-People's

Palace curator extraordinaire), chats with archivists and an online surf of the National Cooperative Archive in Manchester, I was starting to despair. There was nothing. Or at least nothing I could find.

So I went back to basics and started flicking through the Glasgow phone book. If William Ferris had children, if they stayed in the Glasgow area and if they weren't ex-directory, it would just be a matter of time before I found them. How hard could this be? The answer was fairly hard, given the involvement of one Paul Ferris in the longest and most expensive trial in Scottish legal history (which I hasten to add, ended in his acquittal on all charges). After three bruising phone encounters with members of the extended Ferris clan (three down, 300 to go), I reconsidered my strategy. William Ferris had a stamp shop in West Nile Street between the wars. He helped set up the Ramblers Federation and the Citizen's Theatre and persuaded a reluctant landowner to embrace hutting. Where would the children of such a man live? I took a punt on Glasgow's West End. So, I scanned the directory for a Ferris with a 339 prefix, found one, called the number and found myself speaking to Murray Ferris, William's son, who was busy preparing to move house and leave Scotland.

Archive searches be damned. I'd found my man just in time and headed south a few days later to record a two-hour conversation with Murray in his lovely ground floor flat on one of those quiet, tree-lined terraces along Great Western Road. Happily, Murray had a mini-archive of newspaper cuttings about his dad and was able to bring the paperwork alive with his own vivid memories. He let me take some material, photocopied other documents and scanned most of the photos used here. Without this faithful custodianship of his dad's eventful life, we would all simply be none the wiser.[12] And the history of leisure in the west of Scotland would be missing an inspiring and formative influence.

William Ferris was born in Govan in 1894 – one of 11 children, only two of whom survived past the age of five. That tells its own story. He also seems to have been involved in two of the great socialist movements that swept the west of Scotland – the Socialist Sunday Schools and the Clarion Cyclists. Both are as unknown today as William Ferris himself.

Murray recalls that his father was a keen cyclist, who found a firm in Glasgow able to make bicycles with gears that could cope with the Scottish hills and paniers long enough to take tents, made by Blacks of Greenock, which were light enough for weekend jaunts.[13] Murray recalls going to David Rattray's workshop and showroom off Parliamentary Road in Glasgow as a boy to buy his own first grown-up bike with his dad: 'They couldn't do enough for us and I found out later that dad had lent the family a tent and equipment at a time when such things were like hens' teeth.'

The war brought those days of relatively carefree cycling to a temporary end. In 1914, Ferris signed up for the Highland

FIG 9.2 Cartoon captioned 'The Optimist'.
Courtesy: Murray Ferris

Cyclist Battalion (HCB) which provided mobile infantry, signals and scouting. By 1918 he was a sergeant, stationed at Ballinrobe in Ireland, and it was here that Ferris drafted the letters that eventually opened up hutting for hundreds of families at Carbeth. But in December 1918, just weeks after the Armistice, his letters had only one immediate aim – to get a hut at Carbeth for himself and his closest colleagues. A modest enough reward you'd think, for surviving a hideous war.

Ferris's plan was to write to ABG Senior to ask for land to build a hut. Realising rank and social class mattered when addressing a Scottish landowner, Ferris wrote first to an officer in the HCB – a Mr Hotchkiss – asking him to intervene on behalf of himself, Corporal Fraser, Sergeant McCallum, and two other colleagues Smith and Robertson. Ferris explained Craigallion near Carbeth 'was a favourite camping site' before the war and that 'our little camping club would like a 'club house' in the district for weekends after the war,' to be financed by £30 the men had put aside in War Savings Certificates.[14] In a fuller letter sent to Hotchkiss the same day, Ferris recollects that three of the group had met Barns-Graham, 'a friend of yours', on a pre-war cycling/camping trip, 'and your brother arranged a meeting when we were stationed at St Andrews.' Ferris makes the case for a humble hut with great skill, citing the men's war records and single-mindedness of purpose.

> We have always been optimists about seeing this war through – never once did we cease our contributions [to the War Savings Scheme]. Corporal Fraser went out with the big draft in 1916 and has since been twice wounded. The other member of our club has been through the Jutland battle and got wounded during his ship's hunt after the old German raider *Möwe*. He also got clear of Antwerp before the Bosch got in during 1914. We are all looking forward to the time when we may resume our peacetime outings.[15]

Astonishingly, given the power of their case and modest nature of their request, Barns-Graham turned them down, offering the chance to camp instead.[16] Nothing daunted, Ferris wrote again, this time directly to Barns-Graham in July 1919 after being demobbed. Again, he was refused. We don't have the landowner's letters, but Ferris's reply tried to tackle the apparent source of his anxiety – the state of revolutionary fervour in Scotland, two years after the Bolshevik Revolution and just months after Glasgow's first ever General Strike. Thanking Barns-Graham for sharing the thoughts of a 'Soldier', Ferris suggests the anonymous neighbour objecting to their presence should know about the 'Bolshies' before passing judgement:

> There are five of us and we have all served during the war. Robertson was in the RNVR (Royal Naval Reserve) at the outbreak of war and has Antwerp, Jutland and a broken leg as his war honours. Fraser joined when the Post Office allowed him (1915) and managed to have a few years 'holiday' in France where he collected a few wounded stripes until demobbed a few months ago. Smith visited Gallipoli, Egypt and France perhaps on 'bolshie' propaganda, but his three gold bars indicate he did not have it all his own way. McCallum and myself both joined voluntary in September 1914 and came with the others to enjoy the lovely district of Carbeth just a few weeks after being demobbed. I wish sincerely that such [neighbours] as 'A Soldier' would not hastily rush to conclusions.
>
> Yours Sincerely W Ferris 'one of the Bolshies'[17]

It seems extraordinary, but even this heartfelt letter didn't change ABG Senior's mind. Ferris however was determined. He took up the offer of camping along with many others. By the 1920s visitors to Carbeth were using tents with wooden floors, stored in a recreational hall – very like the *lemmehytte* (half-tent half-hut structures) on Lindøya.[18] And within a few years, the same transition to huts also took place.

Barns-Graham Jr insisted that his grandfather finally allowed huts to avoid the health and hygiene problems associated with camping (another echo of Lindøya), and to house homeless families after the Clydebank Blitz.[19] Some suggest ABG Senior ran

FIG 9.3 Layout of Carbeth with huts and Fellowship Camp.
Courtesy: Carbeth Archive

the estate 'on a non-profit-making basis', but his grandson believes
the huts might have been an important income source for his 'asset
rich but cash poor' grandfather – not just a philanthropic move.[20]

> He got £1k per annum from the huts (rent was £5/6 per hut)
> and he often used to say that was his only income. I think the
> bulk of their money came from his wife's side of the family.[21]

Either way, there were soon well over 200 huts. But despite all
his efforts, there wasn't one for William Ferris. According to his
son and ABG Junior, the landowner made it a condition of
allowing huts that William Ferris would do all the paperwork.
The combination of this, political activities, representation on
the boards of half a dozen outdoor organisations, keeping his
own business afloat and helping to start the Citizens Theatre,
meant Ferris had no time for a hut. Instead he made that possible

RULES AND CONDITIONS.

NOISES.
Disturbing noises of any sort, especially after 10 p.m., are not permitted, as they are not appreciated by neighbouring tenants on the estate, and take from the peace and rest which must be preserved. No noise or noisy games on Sunday. Football is prohibited.

FENCES.
No climbing over walls or fences or exceeding the camp boundaries laid down in your section. Tenants (or their visitors) breaking this rule will be requested to remove their hut.

TIMBER.
Timber must not be cut, dead wood or turf removed or camp fires made without written permission.

FIG 9.4 Rules and conditions at Carbeth Hill Camp.
Courtesy: Carbeth Archive

for hundreds of others by running the Hutters' Association and Swimming Pool Club from the stamp and bookshop he owned at West Nile Street in Glasgow between 1920 and 1943.

The hut sites marked out in 1922 were 60 feet square and the annual rent was £9 (much higher than rents on Lindøya), paid in two six monthly blocks, plus occupiers' rates. Just like the *landliggerne* on Lindøya, hutters at Carbeth were governed by strict Rules and Conditions which included a list of prohibited activities that might prompt intervention by the local Sanitary Inspector.[22]

Harbouring secret overnight visitors, for example, could 'endanger our scheme' and make tenants liable to prosecution for overcrowding under the Public Health and Housing Acts (Scotland) 1897–1937. Hutters were warned that unsightly buildings and rubbish would reduce the value of surrounding huts, so railway wagons, coaches, old tramcars and bus bodies were not allowed on the estate and applications to deploy them would be 'a waste of time.' Barns-Graham was worried about pollution of water supplies and, in yet another echo of Lindøya and Nakholmen, the provision of hut sites allowed him to ban 'insanitary camping'. Hutters were only allowed at weekends and owning dogs, playing football, climbing over walls and having overnight visitors were all forbidden.[23] Apparently, the landowner went around the site after the last bus each Sunday to check every chimney was cold, and each hut empty.[24] According to early hutters, ABG Senior behaved like 'a benevolent dictator'.[25]

Despite this heavy-handed approach, Ferris and Barns-Graham seem to have agreed on many things – up to a point – including the need for more sporting activity in Glasgow.[26] In 1920, Barns-Graham donated land in Cambuslang for an ex-Service Men's Club, two bowling greens and a cricket ground.[27] In 1930, unquestionably prompted by Ferris, the landowner financed and unveiled the first Right-of-Way Indication Boards in the West of Scotland, erected by the Federation of Ramblers, which William Ferris had just set up.[28] Remarkably, Ferris also established the first youth hostel in the whole of Britain at Kinlochard, as part of a group of Glaswegians called the Rucksack Club.[29] This offshoot of the Glasgow Ramblers' Association aimed to give members open-air holidays at minimum cost. Headed by Ferris, 40 men each bought a £1 share in the new company, purchased a road-mender's hut at Kinlochard and refurbished it to accommodate 12 people at a time. But without investors, the club hit financial trouble and decided to sell its hostels to the Scottish Youth Hostels Association in 1931.[30]

Meanwhile at Carbeth, the site continued to expand. In

FIG 9.5 Carbeth Swimming Pool, 1930s.
Courtesy: Murray Ferris

1929 the Carbeth Swimming Pool or Lido was opened and at a 1936 event there were 50 hut owners present.

In 1941 Clydebank Council asked permission to build 47 new huts for families made homeless in the Blitz, boosting numbers to 285 huts by 1947.[31] Barns-Graham's acceptance of these new hutters was somewhat grudging and the new arrivals found their rates bills had doubled, prompting an emotional appeal by William Ferris at Stirlingshire Valuation Appeal Court who argued it would be a 'hardship to force working people to give up alternative shelters, so valuable in wartime'. He concluded: 'Why should the [county] assessor have an adding machine where his heart should be?'[32] The assessor's response revealed the real source of the problem – Barns-Graham, who was demanding that new hutters pay his own rates and income tax bills. This was completely unreasonable but also, according to the Assessor, completely within his rights.

> There were only two remedies; an alteration of the law of Scotland or that the proprietor should delete from the agreement the extremely unusual provision that the tenants pay the proprietor's rates and income tax. He had never heard of such an agreement before.[33]

Blitz evacuees of primary age attended Craigton School about three miles away, travelling by bus in the morning and walking home.[34] Older children attended Balfron High School, though 60 children were still without a school place in 1941. There were two shops – one owned by a local man Jimmy Robertson – 'a legend who had an old bus with a tree growing out of the roof' – and the other by Barns-Graham. There were very few private cars and Alexander buses provided a special service into Glasgow 'lining up on a Sunday night' to take the hutters home.[35]

Conditions were pretty basic for the decanted Clydebank families. A journalist reported that a family of six was living in a hut 'like a kennel it was so small', a revelation that prompted Barns-Graham to order the family off his estate, though apparently he later relented.[36] Indeed, when he died in 1957, Allan Barns-Graham's will revealed a total change of heart towards

the hutters he once shunned, undoubtedly due to his long friendship with William Ferris. ABG Senior wrote: 'My estate of Carbeth
shall not be feued or leased in such a manner as to interfere with
the tenancies or rights of the original hutters.'[37] Barns-Graham
also instructed his heir to 'look after the hutters without remu-
neration.' Within a year though, the spirit of ABG senior's will
had been bent if not broken.

According to Carbeth hutter May MacGregor, ABG senior's
son and heir, Patrick doubled rents soon after inheriting Carbeth
estate in 1959, ostensibly to invest in mains water. May's husband
Bill started a tenants' association when water supplies failed to
materialise.[38] Patrick Barns-Graham took the couple to court and
won. They were evicted in May 1961 but in yet another ruling
where the judge clearly sympathised with the tenants, he ordered
no new huts could be built on their site. According to another
hutter, Netta Wallace, a neighbour was evicted around the same
time for merely cutting down a tree.[39] Patrick Barns-Graham
threatened to evict him and charge him £50 if the hut was not
demolished by the weekend. The neighbouring hutters deftly
dismantled the hut and recycled the wood into their own huts.

An undated letter (probably sent in 1962) offers an insight into
the lack of investment at Carbeth. Robert Maxwell Beveridge, a

FIG 9.6 Early hut, Carbeth.
Courtesy: Carbeth Archive

self-proclaimed 'founder' of the Carbeth Swimming and Athletic Club, writing from an address in Canada, recalled that his

> happy little group of hikers occasionally passed over the Blane valley and stopped for a swim in Carbeth Loch with the consent of its owner, Baron [sic] Graham who made us welcome to his home one Sunday afternoon to discuss the possibility of forming what is now the Carbeth Swimming Club.[40]

Once again, there is no reply in the Carbeth archive, but the next letter suggests Beveridge was informed that improvements did not occur because 'Scottish youth is no better than any other nationality regarding vandalism.' Beveridge commiserates and tells Patrick Barns-Graham that his hiking group was always willing to clear up the mess left by others – 'one reason your father and Mr Ferris allowed us free access to the estate.' He concludes that he 'expected to see great changes and improvements... but nothing much has changed in 40 years.'[41]

This pinpoints another difficulty facing Carbeth and all the other hutting sites in Scotland – a chronic lack of investment and improvement. The accounts of the Swimming Pool show it was clearly meant to be a business venture, but never made more than £150 profit. Ferris received ten per cent of the takings as Secretary and evidently became a keen swimmer as well as a cyclist.[42]

The biggest attendance at Carbeth Swimming Pool was in June 1940, when 1,054 visitors took to the waters (excluding members) because free access was given to anyone wearing the King's Uniform. Thereafter prices rose and, on each occasion, swimming numbers plummeted.[43] Tram services from Glasgow to Milngavie were axed in 1956 which must have further dented numbers coming to Carbeth. But Patrick Barns-Graham was reluctant to mention another factor – his own reluctance to provide decent standards of sanitation for the huts. In 1962 he did bring mains water to the estate and provided 17 standpipes for hutters.[44] But by then, the hutters of Lindøya already had piped water, flushing toilets and electricity.

Meanwhile, Ferris had been invited by Tom Johnston (then

Secretary of State) along with Dr TJ Honeyman (later Principal of Glasgow University) and Lord Bilsland (Chairman of the Scottish Council of Industry) to form the committee which set up the Scottish Tourist Board.[45] His son remembers that Ferris was on the board of so many outdoors organisations (at UK and Scottish levels) that meetings were arranged back to back in London, to make best use of his monthly visits

FIG 9.7 William Ferris by Carbeth
swimming pool.
Courtesy: Murray Ferris

FIG 9.8 Medals after Carbeth swimming gala.
Courtesy: Murray Ferris

there. Indeed, so prolific was Ferris in the sphere of outdoor sports that he was to have received a presentation marking 21 years as chairman of the Scottish Camping Club in 1963, when the biggest change in the fortunes of the Carbeth hutters occurred. William Ferris, their great protector, suddenly died. Delivering the tribute at his funeral, Tom Honeyman said:

> He had a natural faculty for sizing up an apparently compli-
> cated situation, extracting from it the important issues.
> Subtleties of debate and strange circuitous manipulations,
> he despised. He spoke his mind bluntly and his rich Glasgow
> accent – especially in London – could pierce any kind of
> sophisticated shield his opponents raised in defence. I once
> heard it said of him – and it was with affection – 'Ferris is
> a rough diamond.' Implicit in the description was recogni-
> tion of the jewel-like quality of his unswerving honesty. When
> he saw the right course, he followed it without a glance
> over his shoulder.

Ferris's funeral was not a Christian service because he was an agnostic. But apparently not an aggressive one. According to Honeyman:

> His attitude was more like one of a favourite character from
> a Shaw play: 'Well, sir, you never can tell.'

Indeed, Honeyman's fulsome and heartfelt eulogy passed on much helpful information about Ferris's early life (as a good funeral so often does). In addition to his energetic expansion of outdoor access, he was also passionately interested in the arts and a founding member of the Clarion Players. According to Honeyman:

> He never lost his admiration for the giants of the Fabian
> Society and treasured the memories of meetings, the notes,
> the postcards and the letters associated with the trials and
> rebuffs, common to all reform movements.

Ferris's involvement with the Clarion movement may place him at the centre of another version of Carbeth's origins – the Holiday Fellowship Camp and Association. This was established in 1923 by 'three fellow sergeants in the Highland Light Infantry'.[46] They rented a partly wooded area at Carbeth for a summer camp, close to a hut Clarion Scouts used to store bicycles with the encouragement of Allan Barns-Graham, as early as the 1890s.[47] The camp could be occupied between 1 July and 30 September each year and was praised as

> a very well-organised enterprise with its own elected executive committee and strict rules about membership and behaviour.[48]

By this account, each hutting area at Carbeth had a site warden tasked to ensure site rules were adhered to – a bit like the *roder* of Lindøya, although presumably not set up by the hutters themselves.[49]

Although the Clarion Scouts' use of Carbeth predates William Ferris's involvement, the competing versions of Carbeth's origins appear to be multiple versions of the same story. The establishment of the hutting community has also been ascribed to the wider outdoors movement and the Depression. Certainly, by the 1930s Carbeth had become a hub for climbers and cyclists en route to the Highlands:

> The unemployed from the shipyards of Scotstoun and Clydebank and climbers, many of them in the legendary Creag Dhu, all met at Craigallion Loch, a little south of the huts, where a fire was reputedly never allowed to go out, such was the coming and going of walkers, mountaineers and tramps.[50]

Amongst those who met at the campfire near Carbeth were

> adventurous spirits who went on to volunteer for the International Brigades, and used the site for training before sailing to Spain and the civil war.[51]

Before it was axed in 1956, the nearest tram station was relatively distant Milngavie. So, many of the first hutters had to walk to Carbeth, which might explain why so many came from Clydebank, walking over the Kilpatrick hills on an old right-of-way.[52]

Without the mediation of William Ferris, relations between the hutters and the newest generation of Barns-Grahams grew strained. In 1968, the Fellowship Camping Association disbanded and terminated its lease.[53] During the '70s and '80s the community struggled 'due to a general lack of care and maintenance.'[54] In 1972 the swimming pool closed, many huts were vandalised or became derelict and although the West Highland Way opened in 1980 and passed within yards of Carbeth, the site declined. On Lindøya by this stage, hutters had the security of 40 year leases. But in 1981, hutters at Carbeth had very little. Stirling Council did provide water to standpipes and collected rubbish, financed by rates the hutters had to pay. According to hutter Bill McQueen:

> On my site, the landlords have not spent a penny for 60 years. I am a retired clerk of works and maintenance officer. As far as repairs go, the site has to be seen to appreciate how much disrepair it is in at present. It is a disgrace.[55]

Matters came to a head in 1997, when Patrick Barns-Graham died and his son Allan (who'd taken over running Carbeth in the 1980s), decided to raise rents.[56] The remaining 150 hutters went on strike.[57] ABG Junior said charges had only risen by 26 per cent while the hutters said rent had at least doubled and more in some cases.[58] The result was a standoff, led by Tommy Kirkwood, a former shipyard worker, leading member of the hutters' association and director of the community company. His words echoed the defiance and the politics of William Ferris, some 80 years earlier:

> I don't think Barns-Graham realised that a lot of the people up here were very politically minded. I was a member of the Scottish Socialist Party, and there were people here from the Scottish Communists and the British Communist Party. They weren't likely to stand for being ordered around by a landlord.[59]

A bitter clash of wills followed. Hutters Bill and Margaret McQueen were taken to court. They appealed, but lost and couldn't pay costs. So Bill was made bankrupt at the age of 70 and their hut was one of many that mysteriously burned down.[60]

Discovering they had no rights as tenants because they were only temporary occupants of the huts (a legal distinction that doesn't seem to apply in any other jurisdiction), and because the 1907 Sheriff Court Act lets a landowner of leasehold property evict without reason and charge any rent he likes, hutter Chris Ballance and others petitioned the newly formed Scottish Parliament in 1999 for help. The hutters wanted a law change giving security of tenure and rent control to hutters, and this prompted the Scottish Parliament to commission the first ever survey of huts in Scotland, undertaken by a researcher, Hugh Gentleman.[61] Ballance (who served as a Green MSP between 2003 and 2007) told the committee Allan Barns-Graham Jr had wound up the original Trust around 1990, simply to get around the clause in his grandfather's will stipulating that Carbeth should not be feued or leased in any way that might interfere with the hutters' rights. Bill McQueen gave this evidence to the Justice Committee:

> We received two letters (in 1993), one in the morning post and the other in the afternoon. The first letter said great changes would be made to the Carbeth estate but we had to sign the new lease. The letter received in the afternoon post said our tenancies were terminated, so if we did not sign the new lease we would be evicted. We had no option; we either walked away from our huts or signed the lease.[62]

This had a dramatic impact on security of tenure at Carbeth. If hutters were unable to sell their huts to someone approved by the landlord within 40 days, he could take possession without compensation – even if hutters had undertaken decades of repairs and improvements and gathered generations of fond memories.[63] But the Justice Committee decided not to recommend any new legislation. After discovering there were only 600 huts in Scotland, the Scottish Executive apparently decided the hutters' problems were too limited to justify action.[64] Holyrood's Deputy Justice Minister wrote:

> The Executive's underlying position is that it would not be appropriate to seek to intervene in private negotiations

between landlord and tenants. We would be extremely reluctant to undertake anything to jeopardise the negotiations at Carbeth and therefore do not think rent control or compulsory arbitration would facilitate resolution at this stage.[65]

Well, well. Hugh Henry said the Gentleman research suggested dissatisfaction only existed in two of the 37 hutting sites, annual rolling leases without provision for rent review 'operate perfectly satisfactorily in many circumstances' and concluded that hopes of future protection for hutters 'do not make the terms of the original contract unfair'.[66] He also suggested legislation might prompt estate owners to 'terminate leases because of concerns about security of tenure or rent control... or even sell their estate.'[67]

As the Vice Chairman of the Carbeth Hutters said at the time: 'How pathetic... they can't legislate to protect hut owners. And we elected a Scottish Parliament to change outdated laws.'[68]

Perhaps a couple of hundred hutters didn't look that important to new MSPs who couldn't see these humble huts as historic landmarks – the culmination of a century-long effort to give working-class families a toehold on the land.

But while the new Scottish Parliament didn't help, the local council did. From 1998, the hutters had been trying to persuade Stirling Council to award the Carbeth huts conservation area status. In 2001 they succeeded when Stirling Council researcher Fiona Jamieson declared the huts to be 'unique in Scotland and significant in European terms.'[69] This persuaded the Council to designate each hut as a conservation area, effectively saving the lot of them, since no-one would buy land covered with huts they couldn't demolish. Ironically, it was precisely the makeshift and shabby appearance of their huts that finally saved Carbeth:[70]

The Huts represent a unique type of 'arcadia' from the 1930s and '40s and have a group value in their own right.[71] Being hand-made as opposed to constructed from ready-made factory components, the huts have a natural if sometimes rickety charm and piecemeal appearance, which sets them apart from modern chalet-type developments. They evince a back-to-basics ethic and magpie evolution. Only by maintaining the continuity in the scale and style of building and by ensuring replacement huts reflect the variety and individuality of their owners, can the character of the area be preserved. Individually they would not merit attention, but collectively they are of architectural and historic interest.[72]

Fiona Jamieson's decision to attach architectural and historic significance to the huts at Carbeth reversed half a century of planning hostility and political indifference and halted development plans by Allan Barns-Graham Junior. Huts were now protected against demolition, but bad feeling between landowner and hutters persisted and eight years of fruitless meetings between the two sides followed.[73]

Eventually, in 2009, something changed. The hutters say it happened after Barns-Graham remarried. The landowner himself praised the common sense of hutter, writer and artist, Gerry Loose, who 'mixed amiability with iron determination' and joined Barns-Graham for talks around his kitchen table in an echo of the earlier rapport between William Ferris and ABG Senior.[74]

In October 2009, the landowner suggested hutters could buy the site, and have a legal agreement to manage it while they raised the money. A price of £1.75 million was agreed which was finally paid in 2013 through a combination of grants, public

FIG 9.9 Carbeth hut, 2010.

FIG 9.10 Relaxing at Carbeth after the buyout.

donations and a sizeable commercial loan from Triodos Bank that's scheduled to be paid off in 2035.[75] After almost a century, the hutters had finally secured their modest wee cabins for their ancestors, in perpetuity.

How did Carbeth survive? By doing exactly the same as their counterparts on Lindøya. Finding an opportunity, digging in, organising well, staying optimistic and making clever alliances. But both sets of hutters also drew strength from the socialist movements sweeping Norway and the West of Scotland at the time. Movements which in Scotland at least, seem largely forgotten.

FIG 9.11 Another hut at Carbeth.

CHAPTER TEN

What will working people use their free time for?

GREAT CHARACTERS LIKE William Ferris aren't just born, they're made. And one thing that clearly shaped the founder of Carbeth in his journey through poverty, war and class prejudice was the wealth of cultural socialism surrounding him as a young man. Perhaps the earliest influence was the Socialist Sunday School movement (SSS), so confident in the West of Scotland in the early 20th century that it could produce an alternative ten socialist commandments and fill Queen's Park with members, banners and flags as recently as 1960. Yet like Ferris himself, the organisation remains a well-kept secret in the story of 20th century Scotland and the rise of self-taught, confident, socialist Clydesiders.

Keir Hardie effectively kick-started the Socialist Sunday School movement in Scotland in 1892 – the year before he became the first Chairman of the Independent Labour Party (ILP) – with a monthly column aimed at children in the *Labour Leader* newspaper which he owned and edited.[1] Hardie proposed the formation of a club called the Crusaders and by 1895 with a thousand children enrolled, he wrote to colleagues in Glasgow urging them to establish formal classes.[2] The ILP's trades union organiser Caroline Martyn called the class a Sunday school – she had a high church upbringing and worked on the *Christian Weekly* – and organised a meeting to form the Glasgow Socialist Sunday School. She became its secretary and the first openly-socialist Sunday school for children in the whole of Britain, opened in 1896.[3]

This constituted a challenge to middle-class liberal philanthropy, and an explicit rejection of the idea that working-class people were 'incapable of collective activity or self-governance'.[4] An array of adult educational and cultural enterprises had already sprung up with lectures, reading groups and classes on economics, history and politics. Socialist Sunday schools would imbue these same values in the minds of workers' children and combat the conformist influences of Christian churches:

> As the orthodox Sunday Schools serve as a recruiting ground for all creeds, so will the Socialist Sunday Schools become the chief recruiting ground for the adult Socialist organisations in the future.[5]

Weekly gatherings developed the habit of questioning amongst young people and the habit of activity.[6] The connections between religion and socialism in Scotland produced a Sunday School curriculum that portrayed socialism 'not only as a system of ethics but... a kind of agnostic religion'.[7]

Some Sunday Schools ran children's orchestras, encouraged choral singing and folk dancing and put on festivals of music and dancing to attract non-socialist audiences. They also organised country rambles using trams to get out of the cities. In 1909 the National Council of British Socialist Sunday Schools (NCBSSS) was formed with and *The Socialist Sunday School Song Book* was published by the Glasgow Clarion Federation.[8]

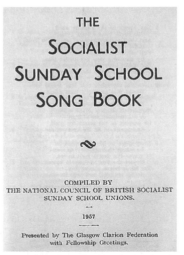

THE
SOCIALIST
SUNDAY SCHOOL
SONG BOOK

∾

COMPILED BY
THE NATIONAL COUNCIL OF BRITISH SOCIALIST
SUNDAY SCHOOL UNIONS.
--
1957

Presented by The Glasgow Clarion Federation
with Fellowship Greetings.

FIG 10.1 Socialist Sunday School song book.

The National Council also produced ten socialist commandments (later changed to precepts), which were recited by children and underpinned lessons. Consider these concise and beautifully constructed words. It's a shame they don't sit in every Scottish classroom today.

1. Love your schoolfellows, who will be your fellow-workmen in life.

2. Love learning which is the food of the mind; be as grateful to your teacher as to your parents.

3. Make every day holy by good and useful deeds and kindly actions.

4. Honour the good, be courteous to all, bow down to none.

5. Do not hate or speak evil of anyone. Do not be revengeful, but stand up for your rights and resist oppression.

6. Do not be cowardly. Be a friend to the weak, and love justice.

7. Remember that the good things of the earth are produced by labour. Whoever enjoys them without working for them is stealing the bread of the workers.

8. Observe and think in order to discover the truth. Do not believe what is contrary to reason, and never deceive yourself or others.

9. Do not think that those who love their own country must hate and despise other nations, or wish that, which is a remnant of barbarism.

10. Work for the day when all men and women will be free citizens of one fatherland, and live together as brothers and sisters in peace and righteousness.

William Ferris was the living embodiment of these precepts. Even though Murray cannot be certain his dad was a member (it all happened long, long before he came on the scene), Ferris Sr was the right age – a child in the 1900s, a teenager before World War One and a dad who took his own son to a Socialist Sunday school in Clydebank in the late '50s. According to Murray, his father also possessed many of the skills associated with sss membership, including the habit of taking minutes, even during youthful camping expeditions:

> I remember him saying he went out to Cadder Woods with friends when they were boys and took minutes of their informal meetings and produced a diary of their movements. They were very organised.[9]

That is quite a coincidence. Children were trained in Socialist Sunday Schools to become future leaders and undertake tasks like minuting meetings to acquire essential organisational skills.[10]

Murray also remembers seeing Paul Robeson, the African-American singer marching with the communist contingent at the Glasgow May Day rally in 1960.[11] The 10,000 strong crowd gathered in Queen's Park, along with hundreds of floats and banners created by sss branches to hear Robeson sing 'Loch Lomond'.[12] It must have been an extraordinary moment – yet it's all but vanished from Glasgow's story, along with those formidable Sunday Socialist organisers. Strange, when the west of Scotland effectively pioneered this part of the Labour movement.

In March 1901, the *Young Socialist* newspaper reported the existence of 15 sss schools: Bradford, Edinburgh, Halifax, Huddersfield and Paisley each had one, while Glasgow boasted six and London, four. Already Scotland had half the total.[13] By 1907 the UK total had quadrupled, with 13 in Glasgow, and a further four across Scotland, 18 in London, 13 in the Yorkshire District and 12 in Lancashire.[14] Still, almost a third of sss schools were in Scotland.

The Socialist Sunday schools organised monthly 'At Homes' to involve children in singing, musical performance and dancing, to 'encourage communal attitudes' and to provide relief from the drudgery of working-class life. Rambling and cycling were encouraged to develop an appreciation of nature and Esperanto was taught to demonstrate the new working-class culture of internationalism.[15] Another coincidence – Murray Ferris recalls that his father spoke Esperanto. The organisation of sss schools was democratic and non-hierarchical and girls were encouraged to be as vocal and questioning as boys. Essentially, members behaved quite differently to their conventional Sunday School counterparts, 'not least because [we] were taught to be independent and to respect but not bow down to others.'[16] There could be no better summary of William Ferris's direct, self-assured manner when he first proposed huts to Allan Barns-Graham.

So, it's probable the future founder of Carbeth attended a Socialist Sunday School. But it's certain he had a leading role in the Clarions, a movement based on Robert Blatchford's paper, *The Clarion*, which launched in 1891 and acted as 'a cultural support for socialists'.[17]

The sheer range and diversity of Clarion activity in Glasgow was demonstrated by one showcase event in 1939 at the McLellan Galleries, which featured Clarion Cyclists, Campers, Choir, Film Group, Scouts and Clarion Players who performed a new Bernard Shaw comedy and took up a collection to send food to members of the International Brigade in Spain.[18] Ferris ran the Glasgow Clarion Players which, in turn, helped set up the Citizens Theatre. Indeed a *Sunday Post* article recalled that Ferris spent 15 minutes chatting to George Bernard Shaw at the Malvern Festival, in his capacity as business manager of 'a club which stages sensational plays – some of them banned.'[19] But as well as trying to master the proselytising power of theatre, Clarion members also provided direct relief, setting up Cinderella Clubs (forerunners of foodbanks) to provide meals and entertainment for poor children.

Horse-drawn Clarion vans carried Clarion speakers, most of them women, around Britain to preach the principles of a socialist society, often accompanied by local cycling clubs. (see Figure 10.2). So, the Clarions encouraged a heady mix of activities that crossed easily between the arts and poverty alleviation to expeditions and mass cycling events.

Clarion Cycling began as a non-competitive pastime and a practical way to distribute socialist literature. But in Glasgow,

FIG 10.2 Women's Van built by Glasgow Clarions.

Clarion Cyclists soon added a 'racing' wing – only the second in Britain to hold time trials in 1900 on the concrete track at Celtic Park. Five years later the event was moved to Rangers' stadium and money raised through admission fees and programmes went to the Glasgow Clarion Cinderella Club for poor children.[20] Across on the east coast, the Clarion Home for Poor Children in Errol took groups of children from Dundee and Perth for weekly stays:

> While the newcomers were pale-faced and flaccid-looking
> – real town birds – the returning children were rosy and
> healthy-looking. Even a week makes a wonderful difference
> to the little ones.[21]

A week's holiday is still more than many inner-city kids get today. Connecting city children with the healing qualities of fresh air, country life and the great outdoors, became a distinctive feature of the Scottish Clarion movement after the Camping Section of the Clarion Field Club started activity on Arran in 1896.[22]

William Ferris sat at the apex of all these strands of socialist endeavour – a keen cyclist, a lover of drama, a father and a Clarion organiser. It seems likely that a Clarion Cycling outing provided Ferris with his first experience of Carbeth, since a size-

FIG 10.3 The Govan Clarion Cycling Club, *c.*1910.

able club was based in Govan, where his family lived. Involvement with the Clarion Cycling movement may also have motivated Ferris to join the Highland Cycling Battalion during the war.

> In the 20 years before the First World War a Clarion cyclist, was someone riding a machine with saddlebag crammed or carrier piled high with copies of [The Clarion], all of which would be sold or given away.[23]

Another description that would perfectly fit the the the young 'Optimist', William Ferris.

Cyclists these days are often dismissed as a bunch of self-regarding, uncommunicative, Tour-de-France strip-clad, lycra-wearing fanatics. But in the interwar period, before widespread car ownership, cyclists were pilgrims, agitators and activists. They were also some of the first workers to reconnect with the Scottish countryside and observe the massive gap between rural and urban lives. The founder of the first Clarion Cycling Club, Tom Groom said:

> the frequent contrasts a cyclist gets between the beauties of nature and the dirty squalor of towns makes him more anxious than ever to abolish the present system.[24]

Socialists in the temperance movement also believed cycling was a wholesome activity that could 'wean workers away from the dreaded intoxicant', and for obvious reasons, cyclists were strongly involved in the fight for a shorter working week.[25]

It's hard to prove that the connection between cycling and socialist activity in 1920s Scotland helped camping and hutting gather momentum. No archive of Clarion or SSS material exists in Scotland, and research about workers' political movements and living conditions tends to focus on working conditions and urban-based leisure pursuits. Nonetheless, a meeting of a thousand Clarion cyclists was organised by the Independent Labour Party in 1909 with delegations from Glasgow, Clydebank, Motherwell and Govan.[26] This massive event involved about 20 per cent of the ILP's UK membership. On one Saturday alone in the summer of 1910, ten Clarion races headed out of Glasgow in every direction.[27] It's hard to believe the young William Ferris wasn't racing in one of them.

The advent of war saw the *Clarion* paper lose support as many readers enlisted (though some like William Ferris maintained their cycling credentials by joining the Army Cyclist Corps).[28] But after the war, Clarion Cycling teams competed in the Workers' Olympiads in the 1920s and '30s and in 1930 the *Clarion Cyclist* newspaper attacked the biggest 'bourgeois' cycling organisation, the Cyclists' Touring Club (CTC) for 'glorifying capitalism'.

> It's our duty to build up the Clarion Cycling Club so that at least one sport will be under the control of the workers and thus cut out the harmful propaganda carried out... by such tools of the capitalists as the CTC.[29]

But despite the urge to create exclusively workers' sporting organisations (mirroring developments in Norway), cycling was no longer confined to socialists after the war. Costs had fallen and Scotland entered the 'Golden Age of Cycling', with crowded bicycle racks outside factories and 'bell-ringing torrents of cloth-capped workers' cycling out of factory gates at the end of shifts.[30] Exploring the countryside by bike became a popular leisure pursuit with 10 million regular cyclists in 1935, compared to just 2.5 million regular drivers.[31]

FIG 10.4 Cartoon from Clarion Cyclist, 1930.

The Woodcraft Folk, sponsored by the Cooperative movement, also had branches in Glasgow and the west of Scotland, and was formed as an alternative to the Boy Scouts.[32] Meetings were held weekly and Elfins (the youngest children) learned about outdoor activities sitting around a campfire, while Hardihoods (older children) went on outings where they met other groups and 'practised the ideals of cooperation'.[33]

All of these organisations, but particularly the SSS produced generations of young activists ready for more practical and militant socialism than the Labour Party or even the ILP was willing to offer. Many became involved in the rent strikes of World War One and the General Strike of January 1919 – itself the culmination of a campaign by the Clyde Workers' Committee (CWC) for a 40-hour week, so that work and wages could be shared with recently demobilised soldiers.[34] On 'Bloody Friday', 31 January 1919, tensions came to a head when 20,000– 60,000 demonstrators arrived in Glasgow's George Square to hear the Lord Provost deliver the government's response to the CWC's demands. Police charged unarmed demonstrators and the ex-servicemen in the crowd quickly retaliated. Fighting continued around the city centre for many hours and there were running battles between police and demonstrators in Townhead and Glasgow Green.[35] According to historian Richard Finlay:

> The Glasgow Herald estimated that the potential revolutionaries could call on the support of over 100,000 people. To the middle class the threat seemed real. After all there were militant workers going on strike and a mass movement had forced the government to intervene in the payment of rent, something the middle classes regarded as sacrosanct to the market. And the workers appeared to be led by committed socialists. The middle class took the leaders of the workers at their word and believed they were about to abolish the market and take over private property.[36]

In his memoir, strike leader Willie Gallacher said:

A rising was expected. A rising should have taken place. The workers were ready to effect it; the leadership had never thought of it.[37]

Nonetheless, this 'Scottish Bolshevik Revolution' (as the Secretary of State for Scotland described it) had varied impacts. The strike may have failed, but leaders like John Wheatley, Manny Shinwell and David Kirkwood became MPs in the 1922 General Election, when the Labour Party swept the board across the industrial central belt of Scotland.[38] All of this made the 'threat' posed by Socialist Sunday Schools a lot more visible. A meeting of Glasgow Presbytery in 1921 discussed a special report on Socialist Sunday Schools and criticised the local education authority for letting them use school premises 'without supervision' – even though just 4,000 children attended SSS while 120,000 attended church-run Sunday schools. SSS organisers were not cowed:

> Let the church condemn the system, which allows bad housing, insanitary conditions, rack rents, and a large proportion of our population existing below the subsistence level while the few revel in pomp and luxury. If the Church would only fulfil its mission, the function of Socialist Sunday Schools would cease.[39]

Heated exchanges culminated in the Seditious and Blasphemous Teaching to Children Bill introduced by Sir John Butcher in 1923 who told the Commons:

> Class-hatred, a rebel spirit, and hatred and disaffection against the King and Constitution are preached. Private property is anathematised as robbery, and owners of property are held up to execration as 'robbers and Judas Iscariots'. Revolution on the Russian model is glorified, and, to use their own language, 'Russia is the one bright spot.'[40]

Butcher's proposal was later talked out at the report stage.[41] But the controversy over Socialist Sunday Schools was reaching fever pitch, just as Allan Barns-Graham Senior was deciding whether to take a chance on the 'Bolshies' and open up his estate to working-class Glaswegians. All the more extraordinary then, that huts went ahead.

By 1930 there were only 52 affiliated Socialist Sunday Schools – half the membership of 1921. World War Two further disrupted the movement leaving it 'with little strength outside the West of Scotland where the rump lingered on as a symptom of social discontent.'[42] Or to put it another way, the sss shaped west of Scotland political thinking for almost 70 years.

But despite the epic organisational efforts of the Socialist Sunday Schools and the Clarion movement (and for that matter the ILP or Labour Party) none managed to achieve the lasting, historic compromise with capitalism reached in Norway during the same interwar period.

Norway

In 1919, as activists in Scotland joined the General Strike, Norwegian workers were already beneficiaries of the world's most progressive working hours legislation. The *åtte timer* (eight hours) law was unique, because it went further than simply legislating for a maximum eight hours at work – it created a legal right to a daily eight hours sleep and eight hours leisure as well.

This created an idea of time away from the confines of workplace much earlier than any other country. It was the result of a hard-fought campaign by the workers' movement, a Labour Party prepared to threaten revolution and traditional parties who quickly realised that compromise between labour and capital was preferable.

FIG 10.5 Banner demanding eight hours work, sleep and leisure.
Courtesy: Copenhagen Workers Museum

Hitherto, time 'off' in Norway was like time 'off' anywhere else. It rarely meant more than a few unpredictable hours away from work – for men, women and children.

Child labour in 19th century Norway was widespread – half the workers in tobacco and match factories in 1875 were under the age of 15.[43] New legislation set an age limit of 12 and restricted working hours for young people to ten hours a day.[44] But clearly not all these hours were spent working. Small breaks were so frequent that Sundt Brothers in Oslo mounted boards with nails on the walls of their mechanical workshop to stop workers leaning against them. Other companies removed the doors of toilets and made uncomfortable sloping seats, 'so people would not find the stay too pleasant.'[45] Absenteeism was high and some workers were gone for a quarter of the working day.[46] So, many employers were ready to reduce working hours in exchange for higher productivity, and some holiday deals were agreed with well-organised trade unions before the step-change of 1919.[47] That year, Norway also became the first country to give every industrial worker seven days paid holiday by law.[48] It would take a World War and another two decades before most Scottish workers got the same basic holiday entitlement.

Eight hours work, eight hours recreation, eight hours rest had been the Labour Movement's slogan since 1889 on both sides of the North Sea. Its realisation in Norway meant leisure became a state-sanctioned activity, and this had a profound impact on official attitudes and workers' lives:

> It was the end of having to get food taken to the factory where we lived as if we were in a prison camp and not released except to sleep.[49]

But the sudden arrival of statutory time for rest and sleep did prompt concern amongst Norwegian professionals. The journal *Sociale Meddelelser* published an article entitled 'What are working people going to use their free time for?'. It argued a 10–11 hour working day had been the norm for such a long time that workers couldn't possibly know how to use their free time properly.[50]

The *Arbeiderbevegelsen* (workers' movement), the fledgling Labour Party and trade unions however were all upbeat about the political possibilities that might arise from more time out of the workplace.

> The new free time would give workers... a chance to come into line with the other classes – to access welfare benefits, a universal human community and culture. Leisure was a prerequisite for building autonomy in the individual's life and the class as a whole. Workers organisations had to be created outside the spheres controlled by the bourgeoisie.[51]

Workers' sports clubs believed educational and sporting activity should be organised quite separately from 'bourgeois' or national teams (like campaigners against the CTC in Scotland).

The first workers' sports club in Norway, *Fagforeningernes* TIF (Unions' Gymnastics and Sports Association) was formed in 1916 and clashed with the official Norwegian Wrestling Federation when members were banned for taking part in a 'politicised' wrestling bout where the Internationale was played.[52] This incident spurred the creation of a new federation in 1924, *Arbeidernes Idrettsforbund* (Worker's Sports Federation), known as AIF, which immediately joined the Red Sport International and began forming clubs across the country. In 1925 it had 96 sports teams and a combined membership of 6,608. Originally dominated by communists, it was taken over by Labour-supporting candidates in 1927 and co-hosted the *Winter Spartakiad* (Workers' Olympiad) in 1928, doubtless attended by Clarion Cyclists from Glasgow.

> Red not national flags were used, the best athletes were awarded with diplomas, not medals, visiting athletes stayed mostly with local families, events were open to all-comers, emphasising the importance of mass participation rather than elites, women were included [unlike the Olympic Games at that time] and the Workers' Olympics included poetry, song, drama, artistic displays, pageantry and political debate.[53]

Indeed, Norway's *Arbeiderbevegelsen* (workers' movement) had developed far beyond the usual forums of party, trade union and cooperative enterprise. In the 1920s, workers' associations were set up for Esperanto speakers (just like the Socialist Sunday Schools in Scotland), abstainers, theatre-goers, hunting enthusiasts, adult learners, athletes, radio listeners, Christians, first aiders and children.[54]

> In Oslo one could live and die in the movement – there was even a workers' cooperative funeral service operating in the working-class town of Aker.[55]

According to Finn Moe, later a leading Norwegian figure in NATO:

> By creating our own culture, we are creating the world for ourselves, as the labour movement should be – a world that cannot help but stand in contrast to the bourgeois world, because it thinks and feels differently about things than all the inhabitants of castles do.[56]

But the growth of commercial recreational pursuits made the *Arbeiderbevegelsen* worry that its activists would be plucked from their class background by watching football, going to the cinema, dancehalls and even family huts, and that leaderless workers would 'prioritise the record player not the revolution.'[57] Time spent hanging around on the streets was feared as a source of distraction and 'contamination':

> Life on the street signalled abomination; urban conditions, dark nights, poor people, smoking, 'laddishness, drunkenness and growing lust' in the doorways, crime, vandalism, children's exploitation, movies, bazaars, lotteries and other temptations. The project to split off from civil society was also a desire to shut off capitalist mind pollution. It was a new form of bathing where one shed bourgeois contamination and dirt.[58]

Chief amongst worker activists was Martin Tranmæl, a hugely influential figure who worked in America as a painter in the first years of Norwegian independence and studied the organisation, theory and methods of the American Labour movement. From 1907 to 1911 he travelled round Europe and was imprisoned for political agitation after his return to Norway in 1915. Inspired by the Russian revolution in 1917, Tranmæl helped form the group that persuaded the Norwegian Labour Party to declare itself become a revolutionary party in 1918. He was also a great believer in the importance of *fritid* (free time) and *friluftsliv* (outdoor living) and when he became editor of *Arbeiderbladet* (the workers' paper) in 1921, circulation doubled.[59]

After a visit to England in 1910 Tranmæl wrote critically about workers' leisure habits:

> Their spiritual food was cheap, petty sensationalist magazines – they were gluttons for family scandals, betting and other sports-oriented idiocy. Did this not give the capitalist class good reason to feel safe?[60]

FIG 10.6 Newspaper ad for Martin Tranmæl meeting.

Maybe if he'd visited a Clarion or Socialist Sunday School meeting in Glasgow, Tranmæl might have felt more at home. Maybe. The Norwegians workers' movement was already one step ahead, providing collective leisure *hytte* for members with dormitories, bunks and shared kitchen and bathroom facilities.

Unions in Norway also provided *hytte* for occasional family holidays – 130 were built around the country between 1907 and 1937, many near Oslo and most in beautifully situated farm properties in forests or at the shore.[61] Each part of the Labour movement had its own colony of holiday huts, indeed Breivik's

FIG 10.7 Utøya Labour Youth holiday camp, 1938.

target of Utøya was a holiday island owned by the AUF (Labour Youth Organisation) since 1933.

Councils were also active in organising holidays for children. In 1912, 1,414 children were given five-week holidays in 26 holiday *hytte* run by the *Kristiania Arbeidersamfung* (Oslo Workers Society) near Tønsberg.[62] When recession threatened to close the charitable holiday operation, the council took it over and bought extra land for more holiday homes.[63] In 1919 it also took over the *Feriekolonier* (Holiday Homes) movement and used 'social criteria' to decide which children would most benefit from 8–12 weeks in the country.[64] This might have acted as a template on Lindøya three years later, where families with the most children had priority in the allocation of hut sites.

In 1917, Oslo's first Labour council built modern public baths, seawater pools, parks, allotments and sports fields and spent 8.5 million kroner buying areas for recreation and new house building in working-class parts of Oslo.[65] It also rolled out a programme of *kolonihager* (allotments), creating a useful bit of civic competition with the less active Norwegian state.

Glasgow didn't have a Labour-controlled council until 1945, a quarter of a century after Oslo *kommune*.

The Norwegian working week was cut to 45 hours in 1959 and 42.5 in 1968 – and this, together with higher levels of pay and disposable income, produced a new wave of *hytte* construction. The number of cars increased 12-fold between 1949 and 1974.[66] And more 'milk roads' were built connecting villages to high pastures.[67]

The first tram in Oslo connected the city centre with the high moorland of the Marka, so workers could easily go skiing and walking. By contrast, the railway line connecting Glasgow to Milngavie (and the West Highland Way) operated with a Sunday ban for many years, apparently to deter city workers from disturbing folk in the leafy suburbs. So, in 1920s Norway, conditions were ripe for a massive increase in huts.

But these were not easy times.

There was dramatic conflict in the labour market, as food and fuel prices reached the highest levels ever seen in Norway.[68] Thousands of farmers lost their farms in forced sales, until neighbours took direct action to deter potential buyers, forcing banks to let the original owners return.[69] By 1918 food supplies were almost totally exhausted (at that time Norway produced only a third of the grain it consumed) and explorer turned diplomat, Fridtjof Nansen approached the American Food Administrator Herbert Hoover for supplies, which arrived later that same year, narrowly averting starvation.

In March 1921 a five-year period of compulsory arbitration expired. Employers and trade unions joined forces to oppose its renewal, setting the scene for a major strike. Within months Norwegian employers proposed a 33 per cent wage reduction and in May the Norwegian Seafarers Union called a strike, backed by most other transport unions. 120,000 workers joined Norway's first general strike which affected every sector bar rail, telegraph and hospital workers.[70] But the government quickly took control of unmanned ships and found workers to operate them under police protection. The strike soon foundered and in June 1921 the Federation of Labour agreed that all but seamen and transportation workers would return to work. Gradually those workers also returned to the workplace.[71]

Organised Norwegian labour lost the General Strike in 1921, just as Scottish workers had lost in 1919. But in Norway, the confrontation ushered in a period of cooperation and compromise which eventually brought major benefits to workers. Failure made the Labour Party leadership more cautious and in 1922 Labour MPs voted for compulsory arbitration legislation, in 1923, Labour quit Comintern and in 1927, the right of centre Social Democrats came back to the Labour fold. The reunited party won 59 of 150 seats in 1928 to form Labour's first government.

It lasted only two weeks, but when Labour returned to government in 1935 it stayed until 1965 (excluding exile during World War Two and one month in 1963). For most of the post-war decades, the party leader and Prime Minister was Einar Gerhardsen, often referred to as *Landsfaderen* (Father of the Nation) and generally considered to be the architect of Norway's successful post-war reconstruction.

Economically, the General Strike was a turning point too. In 1922, Norway's economy was judged 'one of the worst performers in the western world.'[72] But in 1935, two pivotal agreements enacted by the Labour government and supported by the Farmers' Party, helped turn that around. The Main Agreement set up rules for wage negotiations and collective agreements and gave workers the right to form unions and elect shop stewards – an accommodation between the forces of capital and labour.[73] The Crisis Settlement proposed large scale state investment in land clearance, industrial development, hydro-electric power stations, roads and railways – an accommodation between the forces of rural and urban, agricultural and industrial Norway. The agreements constituted a political and economic breakthrough and mirrored similar deals in neighbouring Sweden.

> The means of production would not be nationalised but the state would have greater power to regulate and control the economy.[74]

The pivotal agreements of 1935 built on subsidies for farming, fishing and public works initiated by previous non-socialist governments and the Concession Laws of 1906–9, which saw the newly independent Norwegian state effectively nationalise rivers bought up by foreign (often English) industrialists and investors.[75] The income from hydro dams thereafter flowed directly to county and municipal councils rather than private coffers or central government, thanks to the principle of local self government established 70 years earlier by those clever folk in the 'Peasant Parliament'. And when North Sea Oil was found in the '70s, its development in Norway followed the hydro template of public ownership:

> The natural resources on the Norwegian Continental Shelf should benefit the entire nation, its exploitation should be under national management and control [via] a state, not a private, oil company.[76]

As a result of this sequence of events, only made possible by independence, Norway's central and local government kept a controlling stake in land, hydro-electricity and oil, and used the proceeds to develop towns and local communities across the country. The scale of investment after 1935 was unprecedented and the social and political consequences of the agreements struck between labour and capital were far-reaching:

> First, they ended the era of deep-seated and destructive conflict in the labour market by establishing a robust framework for negotiations over wages and work conditions. Secondly, this framework spilled over to other areas of economic governance and contributed to the negotiated economy, which became a key aspect of the Scandinavian model. And it set the train running for the all-encompassing, universalist approach to social policy.[77]

Proposals to buy major oil fields in the British sector during the 1970s were apparently vetoed by Labour Prime Minister Harold Wilson – and the rest, as they say, is history.[78]

The first Labour government in Norway built upon an impressive framework of economic democracy established by its 'bourgeois' predecessors – a legacy of equity in the distribution of natural resources that has been entirely missing in Scotland. Sadly, but inevitably, Norway's 'negotiated economy' failed to emerge in Scotland, despite efforts by the Scottish Development Council and Scottish Economic Committee to produce industrial diversification and a uniquely Scottish approach. The thinking of British civil servants and planners during this period was overwhelmingly dominated by the belief that heavy industry had poor prospects and this 'discouraged investment and new ideas.'[79]

So, British industrial relations were (and still are) based on confrontation and exclusion, not compromise and agreement. And, as John Bryden points out, the consensus achieved by Norwegian Labour was not replicated on the centre-left of British politics, where working-class solidarity was weakened by religious conflict and the enduring urban-rural divide. Nor did the early promise of the co-operators (Scotland had half a million co-op members in 1916) translate into a political movement.[80]

This meant no window opened in Scotland during the interwar period for political and social change of the sort that appeared in Norway. Consequently, the two countries accelerated onto separate trajectories.[81]

After World War Two, Norway's economy bounced back to pre-war levels within two to three years, though regulation and rationing stayed in place. From the end of the war until the discovery of oil in the 1970s, Norwegian GNP rose annually by an average of five per cent and income was steadily equalised. The disposable income of a civil servant, for example, was 80 per cent higher than a worker in 1950 but only 60 per cent higher by 1975. Meanwhile, a married pensioner couple in 1960 had 30 per cent of an industrial worker's income, but 45 per cent by 1970.[82]

In Britain, Labour also swept to power after the war, winning 37 seats in Scotland and political dominance here for the next half century. Child allowances, state retirement pensions and unemployment benefit followed Labour's victory, with the crowning achievement of the NHS in 1948. But war activity masked the underlying weakness of Scotland's economy. Low wages, falling productivity because of under-investment by private owners and the confrontational nature of industrial relations left Scotland dependent on state intervention. By 1958, the Clyde shipyards launched only 4.5 per cent of world tonnage, compared with 18 per cent in 1947.[83] This left the whole apparently uncompetitive and strongly interconnected edifice of steel-making, shipbuilding and coal-mining ripe for abandonment, which duly happened under Margaret Thatcher's government in the 1980s.[84]

Scotland's workers' movement was as vigorous as the movement in Norway. Pretty much. It promoted the same wide range of cultural and sporting interests as the *arbeiderbevegelsen*, had the same emphasis on self-organisation, solidarity and education, the same formal, textual socialist underpinnings and a fairly unique infusion of moral and quasi-religious fervour. The workers' movement in Scotland also helped produce a Labour Party and a Labour Government. But British workers' organisations had to operate in a fundamentally different, more confrontational and less equitable democratic terrain. As the earliest hutters had already discovered.

CHAPTER ELEVEN

Plotlanders:
The hutting anarchists

ONE OF THE MOST influential developments for Scottish hutters in the 1920s was actually located in England. The 'plotlands' – a large area of tiny sub-divided sites with self-built huts – grew up over a 70-year period in the south of England, starting with the agricultural depression of the 1870s and spreading slowly to a peak of activity in the 1920s and '30s, before growth was brought to an abrupt halt by post-war planning regulation, enacted by a Labour Government.[1]

Yes, you read that right – a Labour Government.

The 1947 Town and Country Planning Act was the tin lid for the plucky plotlanders and many other 'makeshift' hutting communities. Was that an unfortunate by-product of well-inten-tioned planning legislation, or its primary purpose? It's hard to say. But land grabs by enterprising workers had seriously unnerved landowners in south-east England, whose narrow class back-ground contrasted starkly with the custodians of the Norwegian landscape – the *bønde*. Britain's first Labour Government was dealing with a landed elite more influential than anything expe-rienced in Norway. Perhaps that's why its post-war planning legislation and its clampdown on workers' modest, self-built holiday homes was so draconian, at a time when the Norwegian state was encouraging hut development on its own land.

Whatever the reason, this piece of the holiday homes jigsaw reveals the extent of opposition to hutting from every part of the political spectrum in Britain.

Lloyd George's redistributive budget of 1908, led to a quarter of land in England changing hands during the period 1918–22 with equally profound changes in Scotland.[2] A lot of marginal land was sold to speculators for development but areas like South Essex, with its heavy clay soil, Dungeness on the South coast with its saltmarsh, and the drained marshland of Canvey Island all came into the hands of land agents who subdivided them into rectangular plots for sale.[3]

At the same time, writers were highlighting the overcrowding and pollution in Britain's big cities. Richard Jefferies, author of the apocalyptic *After London*, saw the city as a deeply corrupting influence.[4] Jack London in *People of the Abyss*, painted a picture of the London working-class dropping like flies.[5] Parts of the workers' movement saw the resettlement of land as the only real alternative to poverty and regular unemployment.[6] A dire shortage of housing encouraged returning soldiers to take matters into their own hands and erect makeshift shanties on smallholdings created after the Addison Act of 1919. But for those who missed out, 'a little shack in the Essex plotlands might achieve... the mystical objective of acquiring a home of one's own.'[7]

The development of mass transport made the process easier. Steamers established the Thames estuary towns of Southend and Margate as venues for mass tourism and railways followed. This was the origin of the South Essex plotlands, with Laindon and Pitsea on the London to Southend line, and the stop at South Benfleet giving low tide access to Canvey Island.[8]

The absence of strict planning rules which attracted all sorts of entrepreneurial individuals. At Canvey Island, Frederick Hester built a tramway, with carriages marked 'Venice-on-Sea and Canvey', and a Wintergarten; 'an elegant glass structure, planted with choice fruit trees, flowering shrubs and climbers'.[9] Building did begin, but Hester was declared bankrupt in 1905, and the tramway and gardens dismantled.

Another entrepreneur was Leith born David Ogg, a marine engineer, who was apparently shipwrecked three times before settling in London to run a pub in the East End. He accepted plotland receipts to clear bad debts, and ended up owning several sites on Canvey Island, building his own grand hut complete with a railway carriage-supported balcony.[10]

The plotlands quickly developed an eccentric and individual character of their own. Some owners grew flowers and shrubs,

FIG 11.1 The Ogg's Lodge on Canvey Island.
Courtesy: canveyisland.org

others kept goats, geese, chickens and bees, or grew fruit and vegetables, enabling a number of inhabitants to be virtually self-sufficient during World War Two.

Early hutters in Scotland were well aware of these developments. The plotlanders activities earned praise in the *Dundee Courier* for letting the hard-pressed working classes avoid the commercialism of other holiday options:

> The lessee of a hut has no use for bathing machines, is a tepid supporter of the band… and contributes little to other forms of seaside brigandage. Loafing… is what all sensible doctors prescribe for a man who is taking a holiday from hard and sedentary work, and there is no better excuse than the possession of a hut.[11]

While plotlanders were deeply attached to their huts, other users of the countryside were horrified, particularly those with a proprietorial attitude to landscape like the National Trust, Council for the Preservation of Rural England, William Morris's Society for the Protection of Ancient Buildings and the Pure Rivers Society.[12] As French sociologist Pierre Bourdieu observed, such entitled groups always seem to have

> an obsessive fear of number, of undifferentiated hordes
> [who are] indifferent to difference and threaten to submerge
> the private spaces of bourgeois exclusiveness.[13]

In the late 1930s there was support for a 'Ministry of Amenities', with a watching brief over 'our visual background.' This prompted the Scott Report, whose wide brief was to review physical, social and economic development in the countryside.[14] Plotland landscapes were described as 'nameless messes... which have spoilt many a once-charming stretch of coastline' but not labelled a post-war priority. The report did however make farming the principal, protected pursuit of the countryside and restricted human development to the cities.

> It was strongly believed that urban development represented
> the major threat to the quality of a countryside whose char-
> acter depended on a prosperous agricultural sector... which
> was also seen as the only way to preserve the traditional
> appearance of the countryside.[15]

Happily, for the Norwegians, preserving the traditional appearance of their countryside meant keeping hydro dams and associated industries, keeping shipbuilding yards in every other remote fjord town, keeping sawmills and timber operations which used rivers for transport, keeping people on the land in small farms and building more bridges, ferries, tunnels and of course, *hytte*. Tradition is only a deeply conservative force in a deeply conservative country.

But another British government-commissioned wartime survey of the coastline was soon under way, conducted by the Cambridge geographer JA Steers who focused more closely on the plotlands. He described Canvey as

> an abomination... a town of shacks and rubbish... it caters
> for a particular class of people, and short of total destruc-
> tion and a new start, little if anything can be done.[16]

According to Hardy and Ward, genuine concern over the changing balance between public v private access to land did exist (as it did around the *hytte* islands of Oslo fjord), but class was the main driver of hostility towards the plotlanders.

> The Thames, with Eton, Windsor and Henley on its banks, must have seemed the undisputed sanctuary of a privileged caste. Suddenly, to find greengrocers from Acton and printers from Fulham making free with their 'squalid little huts', must have raised blood pressure to dangerous levels.[17]

The capacity for self-organisation exhibited by the hutters must have further heightened feelings of alarm. 'The organisation and fighting spirit of places such as Jaywick was almost legendary.'[18] There was hostility too from self-appointed arbiters of taste like naturalist and prolific author, Ronald Lockley:

> Nothing but a dictatorship will save the English coast in our time... when the millennium arrives, when battleships are turned into floating world-cruising universities, perhaps their guns, as a last act before being spiked, will be allowed to blow to dust the hideous, continuous and disfiguring chain of hotels, houses and huts which by then will have completely encircled these islands.[19]

But council leaders were listening and hobbling the viability of plotlands by withholding or delaying services and infrastructure. As a result, many were without water, drainage or gas for decades, even though (like Carbeth) hut owners paid rates. Roads and flood defences were only installed when plotlanders agreed to pay a significant portion of the costs.[20] But ironically this conflict with the authorities, and the absence of facilities served only to unite hutters:

> Community was built out of the shared hedonism of the summer holidays and a shared determination to overcome the brute necessities of the plotlands out of season, when coal trucks were unable to deliver in winter, or the only access to water was via a standpipe at the end of the road.[21]

With the aerial bombing of London in 1940, many East Enders moved permanently to their 'shanty' homes to escape danger and supplement rations with homegrown produce. But access to coastal plotlands like Jaywick Sands was quickly restricted, as a defence strategy against seaborne invasion. So during the war, some plotlands became ghost towns while others 'became virtually urban in their intensity of use'.[22]

Ironically though, it was the triumph of the Labour Party in the 1945 General Election that banged the first nail into the coffin of these makeshift workers' communities. After the war, abandoned army camps and vacant seaside properties were taken over by squatters during the 'Vigilante campaign', as committees of ex-servicemen installed homeless families and their furniture in unoccupied houses under cover of night.[23] Absentee property owners were slow to start legal proceedings and by 1946, government figures revealed that 1,038 recently-vacated military camps in England and Wales were occupied by 39,535 people organising their own communal services, along with 4,000 people squatting in camps in Scotland.[24] Minister of Health, Aneurin Bevan instructed councils to cut off supplies of gas and electricity to the camps, but even though local authorities were already directing desperate homeless families towards them. Described in the press as a 'communist stunt', the wave of squatting ended with injunctions, evictions and a few compromise solutions between authorities and settlers.[25]

The Scott and Steers reports denounced the plotlands as a form of rural blight, and Labour's new peacetime government, reflecting wartime tendencies towards centralisation and planning, was determined to act. A file ominously named *Removal of Shacks* mapped out ideas for dealing with the 'shacks and other sub-standard development', which were 'a national menace and a local disgrace'.[26] One civil servant drew attention to the wastefulness of 'shack blight' where the land could be used for much-needed food production. All of this, along with pressure for new public housing informed the 1947 Town and Country Planning Act.[27] Urban spread would henceforth be limited by rural Green Belts restricting development, and a wave of new town construction would take place beyond them. Local and central government were handed new tools to pursue their antipathy to the plotlands, blocking the creation of new sites and subjecting existing ones to removal, transformation or preservation – depending on the degree of official hostility.

The 1947 Act introduced compulsory purchase powers, which were used by councils in plotlands like Shoreham Beach to overcome 'untidy and unsightly' piecemeal development.[28] Although many county councils bitterly resisted New Town site designations imposed by central government, Essex County Council effectively killed two birds with one stone by locating Basildon New Town right on top of the plotlands at Pitsea and Laindon. Building began in 1952 after compulsory purchase orders were used to clear plotlanders off their sites.[29] Thus, within two decades the self-built plotland settlements were mostly cleared.[30]

Some plotlanders were able to upgrade their huts into permanent homes because they owned the land. But Ward observes that hutting settlements in Scotland lacked the security provided by land ownership or long leases and were easily 'extinguished' without a trace.[31] That process has never ended.

CHAPTER TWELVE

Barry Downs, Seton Sands: Evicted, gentrified and just hanging on.

SO, HERE WE ARE.

Given Britain's long history of elite control and Scotland's enduring tolerance of large sporting estates, it's no wonder this country has next to no huts. And no surprise that the authorities have largely stood back and watched while working-class families trying to maintain a link with nature have been harried, persecuted and broken.

I know that's emotive language. I think it's no exaggeration.

Pauline and James Rowling were unlikely land reform campaigners when I first met them in August 2012.

The 60-something couple lived together in a modest flat just off Glasgow's Maryhill Road, with a living room dominated by a second-hand photocopier. 'We sent that many letters to lawyers, MSPs – it was cheaper to buy a copier than go down the library.'

The couple had never visited Gigha, Eigg, Knoydart or any of the other famous community land buyouts. Yet their six-year struggle to occupy a modest hut on a scrappy field near Carnoustie gave the Scottish Parliament a second chance to protect the living working-class heritage of Scotland. MSPs didn't take it.

The valuation roll shows that some huts began on sites at The Downs, Barry, between Carnoustie and Monifieth on the Angus coast between 1937 and 1938.[1] Robert Sturrock was the first farmer to lease land for huts there. According to his daughter Doreen Paton, he was the only farmer locally to own his own land, instead of renting it from the Panmure Estate, which owned most land for ten miles around.[2] Sturrock had been in the Merchant Navy and sent savings home to his mother with the intention of buying land on his return. By 1935 he was able to buy the

350-acre Ravensby estate from the trustees of farmer Robert Colville Bowie.[3] Sturrock was described as a poultry farmer in the Sasine Register, prompted perhaps by a Department of Agriculture circular two years earlier that announced support for pig rearing, poultry farming and market gardening near the main centres of population in industrial Scotland.[4] The Land Settlement Act of 1934 confirmed this shift in policy, and provided funds for a thousand new holdings to be created near industrial centres.[5] It's not clear if Sturrock benefited directly, but it is clear that he ran Barry Downs as a commercial farm, not a base for rehabilitating wounded soldiers, despite repeated newspaper reports.[6] The significant thing about Robert Sturrock was that he could diversify into unconventional land uses because he owned the land and was his own master. But still, it was a regular camper, not Sturrock himself who had the idea of setting up huts.

Once again, I had a stroke of luck researching this story. Councils had no role in regulating interwar huts, so written records were generally in the archives of large landed estates. I did enquire about viewing material in the Dalhousie Estate Archive but was politely turned down. To be fair, the estate had not recently owned land at Barry Downs – probably the main reason huts blossomed. So, making friends at public libraries became my new strategy and I was lucky to encounter Joelle Gilbert at Monifieth Library who searched on my behalf. She came across a letter to *The Scotsman* from Doreen Paton, published two years earlier, which strongly objected to the idea Barry Downs was set up to help veterans returning from World War One. How did she know? The farmer, sadly deceased, had been her father.

It took me a couple of days to locate Doreen, who was a fount of information and helped me piece together this version of events.

A Dundee man, Andrew Jackson was the first to ask if he could put up a hut. Soon others came asking for plots and ground to the east was opened up.[7] The timing was significant. In 1937, there'd been a rent rebate for tenants of Dundee's new council flats, which included Andrew Jackson and the bulk of other

194   HUTS

hutters according to addresses on the valuation rolls.[8] So huts at
Barry Downs began a month after most hutters had one to two
pounds refunded to them by the council. It was also the year the
Holidays with Pay Act, recommended a week's annual paid
vacation for all full-time workers.[9]

The early days of Barry Downs, as recollected by Robert
Sturrock's daughter, Doreen Paton, contain striking similarities
to Carbeth. There was no hutting master plan, rather an ad-hoc
expansion of land and basic facilities as more hutters arrived.
Examination of the Valuation Rolls shows that huts were first
built by close neighbours of Andrew Jackson, in the Hilltown,
Dundee. Amongst the first 37 hutting families, many shared the
same home address and surname. Their occupations included
spinner, French polisher, brass moulder, fireman, millworker,
overseer, seaman, carter, labourer and mechanic. Like Carbeth
and Lindøya, skilled workers seemed to predominate and word
of mouth and family ties were important ways to find hut sites.
Like William Ferris at Carbeth, the original hutter at Barry Downs
also became caretaker for the whole camp:

> With expansion of the camp, Andrew Jackson had to relo-
> cate his original hut and agreed to keep an eye on things.[10]

And like Carbeth, the Downs expanded rapidly. There were 37
huts in 1937–8 and a similar number at a site closer to Dundee,
at Greenlawhill (described as Lucknow after 1961). This land
was also owned by an independent farmer rather than Dalhousie
Estate.[11] A local newspaper reported in 1938 that 200 people from
70 Dundee families were living in wooden huts set in rows to form
streets, unnoticed by the majority of passers-by since 'only the tops
were visible from the main road.'[12] Clearly, the need for hutting
discretion was as important in 1930s Angus as on Lindøya.

Numbers kept slowly rising until the early 1960s when there
were 159 huts across the two sites and a further 37 huts on the
coast at Buckiehillocks. These huts first appeared in 1949–50,
but by the summer of 1966 they had gone.[13] According to hutter
William Coupar:

The present tenant of the land is leaving and the ground will cease to be agricultural land. When this happens the railway authority is apparently under no obligation to maintain the level crossing, which is the only means of access to the site. There seems to have been a general build-up of opposition to us from all sides.[14]

This crestfallen hutter was right. After the passage of the 1947 Town and Country Planning Act, Angus County Council used its new planning powers to reject an application for more huts at Lucknow.[15] The Public Health Committee heard 'there did not seem to be any control whatsoever' amongst huts and shacks built on fields east and west of Carnoustie, 'and no steps were being taken to see that sanitary arrangements were right.'[16] Two years later, the Town and Country Planning Committee stopped work on huts without planning permission. In 1956 the Valuations and Ratings Scotland Act abolished owner's rates and levied them on occupiers instead. Doreen Paton recalls her father collected the rates and 'there was a lot of ill feeling.'[17] By 1978, Barry Downs had dropped to around 110 huts. But James and Pauline Rowling didn't enter the story till 1990, when numbers had been whittled down further to just 65 huts.

James Rowling was born in Springburn, one of a family of 13, and joined the army aged 19 after being threatened with an axe in the shop where he worked in Glasgow's Gallowgate: 'They wanted protection money and poured petrol over a shop further down the street. I decided to get out.'[18]

James left the army in 1976, got work in the haulage business and decided to spend a small payoff on a holiday for life, a caravan, which he towed up to Monifieth on the Angus coast: 'better weather than over here'.

The couple loved it even though there was restricted winter access. James would try to get an early finish on Friday delivery runs: 'I'd come home, have a shower and Pauline and 12-year-old grand-daughter April would load the car – then off we'd go. We were up in Monifieth almost every weekend and the whole of the Easter and summer holidays.'

FIG 12.1 James Rowling at Barry Downs huts.
Courtesy: Big Issue Scotland and Adam Forest

If James was on late shift the women took the Stagecoach bus to Dundee and then another bus to Carnoustie. It was a three-hour journey. But it was worth it. 'Every street corner on the Maryhill was a pub at that time. And for everyone else the pub was their only escape.'

But the Rowlings had something better. They had the wee caravan at Barry Downs. The couple didn't socialise much locally: 'We had good neighbours who understood we liked to get away and looked after the cat.'

Would they not rather have pitched the caravan away from everyone else, amidst some scenic splendour?

'No, we were far better off in the camp. We had friends. When the men went back to work on Sundays there was security for the women, cos we all knew one another, everyone helped to fix things and the kids all grew up together.'

It was the free, outdoor, cooperative, gregarious life they could not easily have found in Glasgow.

The Rowlings walked, flew kites on the beach, talked, saw dolphins at Broughty Ferry and took April to stables nearby. Pauline made friends with the hutters – after all she'd shared that long bus journey with them often enough.

So in 1990 the Rowlings decided to shift. By then Michael and Patricia Sharp owned the hutting site and James asked to buy a small hut near the access path, which had been accidentally burned by the last owner. The Rowlings bought it by paying off the £250 rent arrears of the previous owner and worked to fix it. 'We rebuilt it ourselves. Other hutters helped with wood, nails, know-how. We enjoyed making it. I did the sawing.'

That modest boast prompted a rare smile from Pauline.

Like the more famous Carbeth Hutters, the folk at Barry Downs quietly enjoyed their weekend escapes without much bother until a change of land ownership in 2005.

Just like Carbeth, there are several versions of what happened next.

Hugh Gentleman's report states that Barry Downs was gradually cleared by the new owners in 'a process of non-replacement, allied to a shift to partial use for caravans and caravan storage.'[19]

That's one way of putting it.

The new owner Andrew Young of Shoreline Management barred vehicle entrance to the site, cut off water supplies (which he later restored) and claimed the site breached health and safety rules. The hutters disputed this. He raised annual rents from £250 to £470 to upgrade the site. The hutters paid cheques which he returned, demanding they put concrete bases under the huts to make them more stable. The hutters pointed out the site is built on shifting sands (probably why it was surplus to requirements in the 1920s) and concrete bases would undermine not stabilise the huts. They were also advised concrete bases would require planning permission which they might not win. All the while James, Pauline and April were hardly able to use their hut.

In 2007, the hutters began a series of legal cases to prove they had tenancy rights. The expense was crippling for low-paid workers – and by September 2010 none had succeeded. Then, just like Carbeth ten years earlier, one by one the 45 remaining huts were mysteriously vandalised, with windows smashed during the week when the hutters were elsewhere. There were no witnesses and the police recorded no complaints. It was almost as if the huts had trashed themselves.

The hutters handed over around £44,000 to a law firm, despite that clear ruling from Professor Robert Rennie during the Carbeth dispute which said temporary tenants (like owners of huts, mobile homes and caravans) have almost no legal rights. James Rowling appealed to his local MSP, who decided the case didn't involve constituents and his MSP in Glasgow, who decided the case hadn't happened in his constituency. So James and the Barry Downs hutters fell neatly between two stools. And there was no helpful cavalry on the horizon. Angus Council did nothing.

James occupied the site until September 2011, though a decree awarded against him in his absence meant the landowner was legally empowered to 'eject' him. Eventually, Jim failed to appear for the final hearing because his own hut had been smashed up, he was reduced to representing himself and no other intact hut was left to try and occupy.

With nothing left to fight for, after years of pointless and expensive campaigning, James Rowling gave up.

Even so, all the hutters were issued with rates demands by Angus Council – though the Scottish Government's Small Business Bonus meant the amount charged was zero.

Over the next four years Jim begged councillors, MSPs and MPs for help – all to no avail. Despite the terrible state of the huts and uncertainty about who wrecked them, James was still keen to restart the community for a new generation of inner-city Scots.

Until he died suddenly in 2013. According to Pauline, heartbroken.

'A way of life was destroyed – there was a real community feel to the Barry huts which is a rare thing now. It was a cheap holiday for families living in the city, but it provided more than that and gave a lot of kids from urban areas the chance to experience a different life. That's all gone now.'[20]

Only the story of James Rowling's dogged fight for dignity lives on.

FIG 12.2 *Top*
Smashed hut at Barry
Downs.

FIG 12.3 *Above*
Panorama of Barry
Downs huts – all
vandalised.

FIG 12.4 *Right*
'Not abandoned' sign on
Barry Downs hut.

Seton Sands

The Seton Sands hut site on the Forth Estuary also started by accident and involved another unconventional landowner. In 1918 an Edinburgh academic, William Bruce bought most of the area around Seton Sands from the estate of Francis, Earl of Wemyss and March, for £10,000 – an interesting transaction. Bruce was a lecturer at the East of Scotland Agriculture College.[21] Francis Richard Charteris, tenth Earl of Wemyss (styled as Lord Elcho), was founder of the Liberty and Property Defence League,

> a thoroughly dogmatic pressure group for extreme laissez-faire, and a lobby group for industrialists and land-owners alarmed by Georgism [and its call for land taxes] trade unionism, socialism and elements in the Gladstone admin-istration.[22]

Fortunately, Lord Elcho was in no position to argue over what happened next. In 1921 some Boys' Brigade members had been camping nearby.[23] For most of the lads it was their first time away from the city's crowded tenements and the trip proved so successful they came back the following summer.[24] This time they were confronted by the local policeman who ordered them to move on. As they struck camp, the boys spotted a young farmer working in the neighbouring field and asked him to save their holiday by letting them camp. William Bruce Senior had recently acquired the land so that he could continue to farm while lectur-ing in the East of Scotland Agricultural College at Edinburgh University. He was used to students and enjoyed having young people around.[25] He also owned three farms near Blairgowrie (managed by one of his brothers). Indeed, Bruce managed to combine an enduring interest in farming with an ever-expanding portfolio of holiday huts, serving as National Farmers Union President in Scotland for 20 years.[26] Bruce was a liberal and an innovator and Lord Elcho would have hated him. In 1935 Bruce welcomed a government scheme for protection against unem-ployment amongst agricultural workers while other Lothian farmers were opposed. Around the same time he was elected to represent Scotland's sugar beet growers on the UK body and encouraged fellow producers to use processing facilities near Cupar or watch them be dismantled and moved to England.[27] Like William Ferris, he also sailed to Canada in 1932 – heading for Ottawa as NFU Scotland's representative at the Imperial Economic Conference. Perhaps a man with so many entrepreneurial and political interests (he stood unsuccessfully as a candidate in Caithness and Sutherland in the 1930s) could not be a very hands-on hutting manager, as complaints would later attest.[28]

Meanwhile, the Boys' Brigade members had returned home enthusing about the seaside delights of Seton Sands, so their parents decided to come as well in July 1923. Soon, 'The Sands' proved so popular that Bruce began to receive letters asking if he could provide more permanent accommodation (interestingly, the letter writers did not think to request land so they could build huts of their own).

In 1924 Bruce bought six old LNER passenger railway carriages and four old Edinburgh tram cars and made them available for rent at a few shillings per week or £3 a year. This part of his farm was sandy scrubland and no use for agriculture, so he cleared a

FIG 12.5 Huts at Seton Sands, 1930s.

further 52 acres and soon more tents, caravans, huts, converted bus bodies, tramcars and railway carriages were added. Bruce's son, William Junior, was put in charge of operations.[29] Very quickly, the camp became overcrowded with an average of 500 people per weekend by 1928 and 1,500 on Edinburgh and Glasgow Trades holiday weekends (around eight people per hut).[30] One of the site's big attractions was the comparative ease of access by public transport. Glaswegians travelled by train to Edinburgh Waverley and then by coastal tram to the end of the line at neighbouring Port Seton. From there they walked round the edge of the bay carrying belongings in suitcases and brown paper parcels with babies and toddlers in prams to reach the campsite. Some families banded together to hire a furniture van to transport them all the way there.[31] The number of campers grew rapidly from dozens to several thousand by the end of the 1920s with adverts in papers from the Borders to Dundee and beyond.

In 1927 William Bruce first explicitly mentioned huts as well as tents in the ads.

FIG 12.6 Ideal campsite advert, Seton Sands.
Courtesy: Falkirk Herald, *18 June 1927*

In 1933 holiday making at Seton Sands soared in popularity with the opening of a large, open-air, salt-water swimming pool nearby, on land bought by the council from the Earl of Wemyss. It was an Olympic standard length with changing cubicles at both ends, 1,500 spectator capacity on the other sides and a 33-foot diving stage – the highest in Scotland.[32] Pond Hall, built beside the pool, provided a council chambers, library, tearoom and function hall able to accommodate 800 people with a sprung ballroom floor, one of only three in Britain at the time.[33]

But wartime brought rationing, blackouts, concrete blocks

on the beach, and barriers at Seton Sands where travel permits had to be shown. Only ratepayers were allowed to stay in the huts, and only if their wives agreed to help on the land and children went to local schools.[34] As a result, camp occupancy levels dropped by 30 per cent.

After the war though, damaged huts were repaired and Seton Sands was soon back in business, attracting 3,500 holidaymakers during the Glasgow and Edinburgh Fair fortnights. In 1947 a joint stock limited company, Bruce's Camps Ltd was formed with over 600 chalets and caravans. Just like Lindøya, the camp which now covered 60 acres, was open from April until September. After 1954 it had running water.[35]

Seton Sands was so popular it was even possible to fly there using an air taxi service from Turnhouse (Edinburgh airport). SMT bi-planes landed on the sands at low tide and when demand for return flights was slack, enterprising pilots offered pleasure 'flips' round the bay for five shillings – half price for accompanied children.[36] William Bruce Junior (who became site manager after his father's death in 1951) often used the bi-planes to visit other family farms in Perthshire – timing the return journey to coincide with low tides. His daughter, Margaret Chapman, remembers an outgoing and (like all the other hutting landowners in Scotland) mildly eccentric man:

FIG 12.7 Huts at Seton Sands, 1950s.

Just as he enjoyed being a pioneer of air travel, my father always delighted in introducing modern attractions at the camp and we soon had an amusement marquee with early automatic slot machines, a fortune-telling machine and even a 'What the Butler Saw' peepshow which was considered very risqué at the time.[37]

But the camp was attracting negative comment. A 'local inhabitant' wrote to *The Scotsman* in 1949, complaining about 'troops of noisy hooligans wandering at will on the roads' – a view backed up by a resident of North Berwick who described:

A state of unparalleled squalor and dirt... at Bruce's Camp, which has a perennial border about five feet wide of dirty waste paper. Is one of the loveliest shores in the country to remain a plague spot? Are the summer lives of local inhabitants to be ruined without a hope of redress?[38]

The Head Planner between 1950 and 1975, Frank Tindall, had mixed feelings. At first his County Development Plan in 1950 sounded positive:

The camp at Port Seton fulfils a valuable regional need. Such huts are the poor man's equivalent of the weekend cottage, and are appearing around all big cities.[39]

Tindall even suggested the council should consider laying out new huts at the seaside near Aberlady and inland at Haddington, and if these were not enough, several small caravan sites and a large-scale holiday camp could also be built.[40] None of these ever materialised though, thanks to a lack of cooperation by landowners. In 1951, a survey showed that 129 of the 386 huts at Bruce's Camp were in poor or bad condition.[41] Tindall threatened parts of Seton Sands with closure, but changed his mind after giving a lift to a hutting family from Edinburgh:

Home was the fourth floor of a tenement block in Gorgie, and it made me appreciate the wonderful outlet that a weekend by bus to Seton camp provided for them and their children.[42]

In his biography, Tindall said this experience prompted him to protect and improve the camp. Doubtless, the support of this influential character was an important factor in the survival of Seton Sands. But hygiene concerns were growing. According to a grand-daughter of some original hutters:

> Compared with the latest caravans with their gas or electric central heating and ensuite facilities, our family's railway carriage was definitely primitive. We had to use the site's communal wash block and go outside to fetch all the water we needed from a standpipe in the grounds.[43]

It was the same old story that threatened Carbeth. The land-owner was unwilling to invest to meet new hygiene rules but the hutters were unable to make improvements themselves as tenants, and it was hard to lobby for improvements as a collection of individual hutters with individual leases and no joint, organising, Linøya-style Vel. By 1961, there were still 630 huts. That year, after many orders to improve conditions, Tindall offered a compromise that was also an ultimatum. The council would license Seton Sands, if the owners redeveloped the whole camp to eliminate sub-standard huts, install a water supply and sewerage to individual huts, improve roads, create firebreaks

FIG 12.8 Caravans replace huts at Seton Sands in the 1960s.

(after several devastating fires) and plant one tree beside each hut. Fifty sub-standard huts were demolished, and 72 large residential caravans were towed in to accommodate workers building the Cockenzie power station.[44] Clearly the future of the site now lay with caravans not huts:

> The general rise in living standards makes one consider whether something on the lines of a summer village should not be developed with proper little houses, each with water and electricity and sanitation laid on. The alternative is to convert large parts of the camp for caravans.[45]

And that's what happened.

William Bruce Junior died in 1957, and his children helped run the site as a caravan park until its sale to Bourne Leisure in 1973.[46] While many seaside resorts declined during the '60s, Seton Sands managed to buck that trend. But in the early '70s, with all-inclusive holidays on offer from Pontins and Butlins, the family decided to sell up.

The era of huts at Seton Sands was over.

Rascarrel

In 2007 at Rascarrel, in Kirkcudbrightshire, seven hutters dismantled or burned down their own huts, after a seven-fold rent increase.[47] They tried unsuccessfully to use the 1979 Land Regulation (Scotland) Act to prove tenancy rights, and like the Carbeth hutters, had also appealed unsuccessfully to the Scottish Parliament's Justice Committee.[48] Then, believing that restoring the land to a green-field site would at least stymy the landowner's plans for new luxury cottages by requiring a change of use, they destroyed their own huts. Planning permission for the new cottages was granted a year later, regardless. This dramatic act was the only way hutters could exercise any control over the land their families had occupied peacefully for a century. One of the hutters, Bill Allen, said his great-grandfather started the Rascarrel colony in 1936:

'He was a batman for an MP during World War One and was given permission to put an old roadman's wagon on the shore – whether it was a reward for services or what, I don't know.'[49]

The huts were in use until 2003 when the estate changed hands from Jim Hendry to his daughter and her husband. Thereafter, 'the relationship between the hutters and their landowner soured considerably.'[50] Sadly, that's the problem with hutting tenants on private land. So few outlive the landowner or farmer who first felt motivated to let hutters on their land.

Hopeman

Local historians suggest beach huts sprang up at Hopeman on the Moray coast during the 1800s and were 'initially for the gentry of Elgin to change their clothes and shelter should the weather deteriorate.'[51]

Thomas R Gordon-Duff of Drummuir owned the West Beach at Hopeman and huts were first recorded there in 1929.[52] The estate charged rents from 1931 but sold off much of its land in the 1950s. There were still 82 huts on the West Beach in 1978. But in 1984 a sharp decline followed the acquisition of hutting land by John and Margaret Geddes – only 23 huts remained in 1989.[53]

FIG 12.9 Hopeman West and East Beaches, 1980.

By contrast, the East (Braemou) Beach has been local authority owned since 1935 when Duffus and Drainie District Council became landowners.[54] Government reorganisation meant the huts were transferred to Moray Council who handed it over to Hopeman Community Council in 1981, which now administers 44 beach huts with a 10-year waiting list.[55] It's not clear why Duffus and Drainie District Council decided to buy the East Beach in 1930. But local government reform that year merged parishes to form larger, more powerful district councils, so a sense of civic duty may have prompted councillors to match the private huts already on offer on the West Beach.[56]

Lendalfoot

The hutting tradition at Lendalfoot in South Ayrshire started with the construction in 1929 of a stand-alone property known as 'the Hut'. It remains pretty much as built and is still owned by the same family, like most of the 26 neighbouring properties. The wooden huts are not confined to Carleton Crescent but extend south within Lendalfoot and to the Whilk Meadows and Games Loup. Nearby Carleton Fisheries, built in 1832, was let out to families for holidays in 1908. Some of the four cottages are now owned and occupied by the same families who first rented them. Around 1978, a new group of small wooden houses in the village of Lendalfoot was built, intended as a development of holiday properties but now a mix of holiday and permanent homes. In total there are around 53 wooden houses and 12 or more stone-built bothies/houses in the area. A number of properties are commercial holiday lets, but it tends to be the same families that come back year on year.

FIG 12.10 Lendalfoot – the original hut from 1929
and a bird's eye view of Carleton Crescent
Courtesy: Jimmy Stewart

Glendevon

Glendevon, in Perth and Kinross, had 15 huts in 1999, across five sites in a windswept glen, between Crook of Devon and Gleneagles. John Paterson, son of the farmer who first allowed huts after World War Two recalled:

> Families who built them were young couples with children, forced by the war-time housing shortage to live with in-laws. In 1958, the council caught up with the hutters and gave each hut a rateable value of £5. I had to pay their water charges.[57]

Many of the huts are still occupied.

Soonhope, Eddleston and Dunbar

The 47 huts at Soonhope were apparently built by miners from Rosewell, a mining village within cycling distance of the site behind the Peebles Hydro Hotel. Another group of huts near Eddleston north of Peebles also had a mining connection.[58] Twenty-four huts at Belhaven near Dunbar were built on a disused yard at Winterfield Mains farm after a golf course opened nearby in 1935 attracting tens of thousands of visitors.[59] It seems spare bits of land were opened up for camping and caravanning to relieve the pressure.

> On the plots there was a large degree of freedom and an eclectic mixture of old train carriages, roadmen's wagons, huts and tents.[60]

After 1947, numbers declined to 24 chalets. In the late 1990s the council did consider closing the site and incorporating the land into the golf course but finally decided not to. Perhaps the ghost of Frank Tindall lives on.

Carron Valley

Carron Valley, six miles west of Denny in Stirlingshire currently has 14 huts, built at the turn of the 20th century by miners from

Kilsyth and Kirkintilloch, both then 'dry' towns because of the danger of combining alcohol and machinery.[61] If anyone wanted a drink, they had to move outside that three-mile exclusion zone. The Carron Valley Hotel is three miles from Kilsyth at the top of the Tak-Me-Doon Road, so miners used to walk up and pitch tents. Some asked permission to build huts so they could spend the whole weekend on the moors. In 1990, the hutters were allowed to buy the land their huts stood on.

And that, along with a handful of stand-alone cabins and a few small clumps of huts, is the sum total of Scotland's hutting movement.

So many stories of hope and endeavour.

Yet so few huts.

CHAPTER THIRTEEN

Skaidi: Where rivers and snowmobiles meet

I NOW HAD CHAPTER and (largely unwritten) verse on how hutting was easy in Norway but virtually impossible in Scotland and the knowledge weighed heavily. More optimistic souls in the Thousand Huts campaign had been negotiating with Forestry Commission Scotland and after two years got the go-ahead to allocate 13 plots on a single site at Carnock Wood in Fife. I couldn't help calculating that it would take roughly 615 years and 100 days for Scotland to create a huts total of Norwegian proportions at such glacial rates of progress. And even though the patient Reforesting Scotland campaigners also got a change in legislation, so something called a hut can now get planning approval without meeting standards designed for a small house, some councils have still rejected every hut application. In any case, few folk can find the affordable bits of land needed to throw six and start the whole procedure. Today, ten years after the campaign was set up and despite a mammoth effort, there still aren't a Thousand Huts in Scotland. And though there are a few more beautiful, individually located and self-built cabins that do indeed steal your breath away, the huts total is probably smaller now than the 600 recorded in 2010, after evictions at Barry Downs and Rascarrel. Meanwhile, numbers in Norway have kept rising to just under half a million *hytte*.

All of which has left me wondering. Can Scots overcome the apparently insurmountable obstacles that stand between them and the ownership of wee weekend huts? And given the amount of disruption necessary to transform rural Scotland into a land of forests and huts, is it really worth the candle?

They say a little knowledge is a dangerous thing. So, it was no surprise that six years obsessing about huts had left me doubting everything. Maybe it's too late for Scotland to change?

Maybe time has moved on and what delighted folk in the 1920s doesn't engage their great-grand-children a century later? Or maybe it was time for another burst of snow, huts and optimism from Norway.

There was a standing invitation to go back to Hammerfest and chum Inger Lise and the Svendsen/Larsens to their *hytte* in Skaidi. Since frozen lochs and fjords and deep compacted snow actually make it easier to get around during the Arctic winter, it was a good time to go. Let's be honest. For uplifting companions, inspiring matter-of-fact hardiness and guaranteed minor daily dramas (try crossing an iced-over road with traffic driving past on the wrong side, in a whiteout), it's always a good time to head north. Inger Lise picked me up at the airport and chummed me to council offices, the local shipping depot, tourist office, fishing association hut and (the centre of all local knowledge and gossip) the hardware and fishing tackle shop.

More patient translation ensued and the local struggle for huts, 80 years ago, slowly unfolded.

Skaidi is a collection of around 800 huts which sit an hour's drive south-east of Hammerfest, on land *utparselllert* (divided up) by the Department of Agriculture, the same branch of the Norwegian State that owned Lindøya in 1922. Not one *hytte* at Skaidi dates from earlier than 1944 though, because that year retreating German forces burned every building in Finnmark to

FIG 13.1 Skaidi, Finnmark, 2010.

the ground, except for three churches. Modern-day Skaidi has no central organising *vel*, no restriction on year-round use and (given its Arctic latitude) no gardens. But like their counterparts on Lindøya, most Skaidi hutters are still content to rent land from the state. They've something else in common. Folk in Finnmark created their own hutting heaven by acting without permission – just like the *landliggerne* on Lindøya.

The *Vest-Finnmark jeger og fiskerforening* or VJFF (West Finnmark Hunting and Fishing Association) was founded in May 1924 to take over the management of the Repparfjordelva (Repparfjord river).

This excellent salmon river runs 70 kilometres from the Arctic plateau of Sennalandet to the sea near Kvalsund. In 1924 though, the river was badly run and fish stocks were perilously low. So, fishermen in Hammerfest applied to take over river management from Charles Robertson, the grandson of a Scot and the Norwegian government's Consul for Finnmark. The bid was rejected – the reasons given by the Fishing Commissioner were staggeringly offensive.

> As everyone knows the majority of the population of West Finnmark is comprised of Lapps and layabouts, a race that has little respect for Norwegian law and order, and the members of the Fishing Association in Hammerfest, are probably only as well behaved as the people just mentioned.[1]

The indigenous nomadic Sami people and their town-based descendants formed the majority of citizens in Finnmark, but until the early '90s were subject to persecution and 'Norwegianisation' by the authorities. After huge demonstrations opposing the creation of a hydro dam near Alta, attitudes in Oslo changed, and now the Sami (don't call them Lapps) are equal owners of land in Finnmark.

Back in the 1920s though, Robertson had become a member of the Government and while he was away in Oslo, VJFF members took matters into their own hands and restocked the river with salmon hatched in a private cellar in Hammerfest.[2] Nonetheless in 1931, the Agriculture Ministry again awarded the management contract to the largely absent Charles Robertson (the sort of bias towards the great and good that's still perfectly normal in Scotland.) But the *fylkesmann* (county governor) noticed the dramatic improvement in stocking levels on the Repparfjordelva and asked the VJFF to resubmit their application attaching a list of 93 union members who were all 'good citizens' with professional titles. This time the locals were successful. In 1938, even Charles Robertson paid tribute to the Association for transforming the river.[3]

But members had also transformed their own leisure lives. The men spent every spare moment on the Repparfjordelva and their tiny, seasonal fishing huts became so popular with family members that larger *hytte* were soon built further away from the river on state-owned land at Skaidi.[4] From 1938 a ferry ran from Hammerfest to Foldal, and hutters cycled, drove trucks, sledged and carried building material for the remaining ten (uphill) miles to Skaidi.[5]

Why Skaidi? Well even when the road south to Alta was built it was often blocked by snow and Skaidi was as far inland as Hammerfest folk could reach during the winter.[6] The glen between Skaidi and coastal Foldal has always been privately-owned by small farmers with summer grazing on the relatively fertile pastures.[7] But hilly, boggy, state-owned land at Skaidi was unused. It was also excellent for cloudberries (a national obsession).

Today the whole area contains about 1,200 *hytte* – more than the number of permanent residents in Kvalsund *kommune* (council) which gives Finnmark the highest rate of *hytte* ownership in Norway and thus probably the world, with roughly one *hytte* for every seven people.[8]

FIG 13.2 Pre- and post-WW2 versions of Myggheim *hytte*.
Courtesy: Hammerfest Museum

So, I was chuffed to join the Mathisen/Larsen/Svendsen clan (plus Inger Lise's dog Guffen), on their first trip of the winter out to Skaidi. We drove through the January night, spotting northern lights. (Christian indulgently stopped twice for me to try and get a photo. In vain.)

'We often stop as well. Especially when there are red or pink lights. That's unusual. Our grandparents used to say you could actually hear the lights when they started to fill the sky.'

Really? I could hardly get back in the car.

But we had a mission. The large four-by-four bumped along with four adults inside and a trailer on the back holding a huge empty water container and a snowmobile. Ola and Bjørg – Christian's grandparents – took their own car, with a similar trailer and contents. We reached Skaidi village – essentially just a few permanent homes, a hotel and a crossroads – and stopped at a huge petrol station to fill up on petrol and water. Low lights from hundreds of *hytte* winked through the low hedges that pass for forest in this Arctic tundra. Clearly, they accounted for the size of the garage and its year-round trade.

We reached the scrubby clearing that served for a Svendsen/Larsen car park about 8pm, though it had been pitch dark for four hours, so time seemed fairly irrelevant. Car doors were flung open and there was a flurry of head-torch activity. Even in the darkness this family moved like a well-oiled machine – they'd done the 'jump' to the *hytte* so many times before. The ski mobiles were filled with petrol, started up (the scary bit, since the whole weekend depended on them working) and trailers fastened to the back, loaded with water containers, food and other bulky items. Everyone pulled on their perfectly co-ordinated, black, padded, waterproof one-suits. Even in the dark I could sense that the labels matched the snowmobiles.

Nothing daunted, I pulled on my own new thermal kit, relieved that after my first trip to Hammerfest with the non-thermal boots and the boat trip round the *hytte* islands when my hands stopped working, I was finally, completely kitted out, even by Norwegian standards.

Wrong.

Christian looked carefully at my badly co-ordinated gear – the finest assortment Mountain Warehouse could provide. In the sale.

'Well, it'll have to do till we reach the hut but I have better gear you can use there. Put on this helmet.'

I felt slightly indignant. Minutes later though, I felt nothing at all. The snowmobile set off at a snail's pace (according to Christian) but even though relatively small amounts of the white stuff were being thrown about, and Arctic snow is incredibly dry, it doesn't stay that way on an exposed ankle, wrist and neck. So, I'd say my hands froze first, followed by my chin, feet and brain – fortunately though, in that order.

What then, you might wonder, is the attraction of using huts in the depths of winter? And actually, if huts are about 'getting away from it all', why do Hammerfesters have more pro rata than anywhere else in the world? They're already away from it all. They live in the world's northernmost town. How much more splendid isolation does anyone need?

That's why the Skaidi experience is so fascinating. It's a reminder, that for most Norwegians, the *hytte* isn't about splendid isolation at all. It's about real connection with family and friends, putting physical distance between time off and the world of work and getting completely immersed in the landscape and nature that sits on your hutting doorstep.

Despite the harsh climate, and maybe even because of it, Skaidi hutters are very aware of the passing seasons. Autumn/winter is for hunting, early Spring is for ice fishing, summer is for salmon fishing, walking (and swatting mosquitoes the size of small bats), autumn is for berry and moss picking and winter is for skiing and snow-mobiling. All this in a landscape that's frozen for three months of the year and permanently treeless.

But there are other reasons for Skaidi's existence.

Land has been available to locals at little or no cost for centuries. Finnmark 'county' has been owned by the State (just like Lindøya) since 1789 when the villages of Vardo and Hammerfest were given city status and the land between was taken over by the Norwegian government to stop annexation by incoming migrant Finns.[9] Many homeowners and farmers have since bought their land but even though most *hytte* owners still rent (with rolling contracts lasting 20 or even 100 years) they behave like owners when it comes to investment, expansion, improvement and sales decisions. Just like the inhabitants of Lindøya, Skaidi hutters view the state as such a fair and constant landlord, few have exercised the right to buy.

VJFF policy means fishing permits are cheap, with priority for locals (not wealthy incoming visitors or friends of the land-owner). On the other hand, boat-owning is less popular because of the extreme cold and danger of sailing on the open sea (which might explain the focus on land-based recreation in *hytte* instead).

When the first expansion of huts began after 1945, few other local opportunities existed for travel, holidays or entertainment. Even now Hammerfest is three hours flying from Oslo – Rome is closer to the Norwegian capital. So, huts offer affordable, reach-able holidays in one of the remotest parts of Western Europe.

The relatively dry climate means empty houses don't deterior-ate as they might in wet Bergen or wetter Scotland – so *hytte* can stay unused for months without going mouldy and damp (like poor old Drumnagarrow). Many people mentioned the change in climate at Skaidi (colder in winter, warmer in summer) as an attractive contrast and therefore another reason for going there.

FIG 13.3 A traditional Sami-style *gamme*.
Courtesy: Hammerfest Museum

Huts have also played a special role in the lives of Sami people and their descendants – *gamme* (turf huts) are sprinkled across Finnmark and act as temporary homes during reindeer herding.

When Bjørg's father Hagbart re-built Heimstad in 1947, he asked permission from the *Hulder* (people under the earth).[10] When he built the house and cattle shed (*fjøs*) he made a cross out of timber and asked aloud if he could build there. He looked the next morning to see if the cross had moved. If it had, he would have moved the building plans to a different place and asked again.

Since the Sami now have legal rights to herd reindeer on open land in Finnmark, they also indirectly helped Skaidi become a '*hytte* hotspot' since permission for 'stand-alone' huts in open country is now so hard to acquire.

The self-build tradition of building houses is also vital – teachers, fishermen, and all sorts of non-building professionals still expect to build large parts of their first homes and huts themselves. *Dugnad* (community labour) means help is supplied by friends, family and neighbours with only specialist work needed from paid professionals. In the post-war period when everything was being rebuilt in Finnmark, that self-build tradition was at its strongest.[11] Once people had 'self-built' whole family homes, rebuilding their *hytte* must have been a doddle. The long Arctic winters offered time to plan, and a sense of social, personal and even moral purpose surrounded the rebuilding of those burned out huts.

Wood was often 'recycled' from the temporary barracks used to house returning citizens after the Nazi occupation and one local man explained how his father had bought half a barracks for the equivalent of £5, sawed it into sections and rowed across a freezing fjord, with the sections perched precariously on his tiny rowing boat, before reassembling them as a new *hytte* on the other side.[12]

Since then, snowmobiles have revolutionised the way Skaidi *hytte* are used, making it easier to move about in winter than summer, when the frozen ground thaws to become incredibly boggy. Give any of the blokes an opportunity and they will reel off prices, towing capacity and horse power of each machine. But since it's impossible to walk in deep snow and hard for beginners to cross-country ski beyond compacted trails, you can easily forgive the techie chat. The snowmobile is a lot more than a gadget. It's like a horse in the days before cars – or a second turbo-charged pair of webbed feet.

And though it's tempting to go crazy and zoom around like something out of a Bond movie, hutters don't generally do that. Rules were introduced in 1978 forcing snowmobile users to stick to officially marked trails, and folk mostly do.[13]

Anyway, we reached Bjørg's *hytte* and after unpacking, Christian and Ola drove their ski mobiles into the wooden shed beside the *hytte*. It took a few minutes to appreciate the skill behind the simple design. Bjørg's *hytte* is built on stilts, partly to improve ventilation and partly to let folk drive snowmobiles straight into the adjoining shed when there's a metre of packed snow outside.

'How do you know how high to build the front door?'

'Well the snow is really quite predictable. We just followed our neighbours and I guess their parents also learned the hard way.'

Christian suggests a sweepstake on how long it'll take after

FIG 13.4 Wooden barracks in Hammerfest, 1945.
Courtesy: Hammerfest Museum

lighting the wood-burning stove before the thermometer soars from minus 18 to 0.

An astonishing five minutes later (with no-one foolish enough to bet against the *hytte*-heating champion) the house was fairly toasty, my inadequate outdoor wear had been consigned to a black bin bag, and I was fully kitted up in Christian's 'old' outfit.

I was shown the procedure for using the outside earth toilet. The family ritual is to leave the door open so everyone knows someone is there. Actually, it's surprisingly warm – Bjørg's loo seat is made of foam plastic which is warm to the touch. But you wouldn't exactly sit there reading a book.

Back inside the *hytte*, the central wood-burning stove was roaring away and we talked for hours about dogs, snowmobiles, forests, Liverpool FC and what Scots did with their spare time instead of going to huts. It reminded me so strongly of that easy, free-flowing conversation between total strangers 25 years earlier, when I'd accidentally first-footed Alan Campbell in Drumnagarrow, amidst the winter snows of Glenbuchat.

I promised to send pictures.

'We love those funny houses in Scotland with a fireplace in the wall that faces the wind. Why do you build houses so that all the heat escapes? Is it some kind of offering to Loki?'

Much laughter.

'I'm sorry. It must seem like we are all picking on you.'

It kinda did.

'But why do Scottish people build in stone not wood when you have such a wet climate?'

I don't know. I don't know why any of the self-defeating things that have become 'tradition' managed to slip through our door.

Talking of which, I was slightly dreading the moment I would have to leave the igloo atmosphere to join my black binbag in one of the tiny bedrooms radiating like a cartwheel around the wood-burning stove.

'Will it warm up fairly fast in the bedrooms?'

They laughed and looked at each other.

'You have no idea. You'll have to kick the sleeping bag open, it'll be so hot'

Christian got up and opened all the doors to the five bedrooms. Minutes later we were all stacked inside our separate rooms... sweltering.

The next morning after breakfast (coffee and smoked salmon), Inger Lise was determined to get me out and visiting on the back of her snowmobile. After a few near misses with the small trees I'd airily dismissed as bushes, I learned to shift my weight to counter balance Inger Lise and the contours of the hill.

We arrived with a swoosh outside the *hytte* of Ken Andre Olsen, a 40-something welding and metalwork teacher and his wife Marianne, a primary school teacher.

'Are they expecting us?'

'No, but it's fine.'

The couple made coffee (would I ever sleep again) and cuddled up on a sofa with six-year-old daughter Sophie, gamely tolerating this adult intrusion.

How did you get this *hytte*?

Ken: We bought and then 'extended it' to 150sqm over two years. Really, I bought it for my parents (then in their late 70s) who had a *hytte* on Seiland. Dad had two heart attacks and

FIG 13.5 Inger Lise Mathisen and myself go visiting.
Courtesy: Christian Svendsen

there's no mobile phone signal on the island so I was always worried when he didn't answer. The journey by boat took one and a half hours whereas this *hytte* is close to the road. I thought it would be ideal. But my dad is an old seaman and when he saw it, he said, 'Where can I put my boat?' and never used it. You've got to love dads.

So, what are the differences between home and *hytte*?

Marianne: We clean in the cabin because we want to – we clean at home because we must. At the cabin we just visit other people, like you've visited us now. At home we always call first.

Ken: Non-*hytte* people stay in town and go to clubs. It's very boring. They see the same things all the time. The height of someone's weekend is to go and have coffee onboard the *Hurtigruten* (coastal steamers that ply endlessly up and down the Norwegian coast). Young boys become *rånere* (boy racers) who drive slowly round town. Then they come to the *hytte* and become boy racers on snowmobiles. That's better.

Any mod cons?

Ken: I've got the earliest type of snowmobile from the 1980s – it carries a home-made device which makes trails so Sophie can go cross-country skiing safely. I've got two other snowmobiles, a wagon, a sleigh and a mosquito killing machine (which answers the question about summer conditions).

So, is this really a *hytte*?

Ken: There's no washing machine and no dishwasher. But the wooden floor cost more than the one at home and we have a new flat screen TV. We do have a Cinderella (an indoor toilet which operates by incinerating the (ahem)… material, and was in truth the main reason we'd come around), but the men still use the outdoor toilet.

Naturally.

Next stop was Vidar Antonsen, a former mechanic.

Have you always had a *hytte*?

Vidar: I started going to the cabin my dad built south of Skaidi in the '60s. I loved it but stopped going from 18 to 24, like a lot of young men.

What happened then?

FIG 13.6 Ken, Marianne and Sophie Andre Olsen's *hytte*.

I grew up. When I came to build my own *hytte* I wanted to be in Skaidi. I'm a social man. I like going around, having coffee – and all my friends are here.

(Indeed, there is an issue of critical mass. If 50 per cent of the Hammerfest population moves to Skaidi each weekend there's very little point staying in town. Even funerals are held midweek to ensure a turnout.)

So, what's different about the *hytte*?

Vidar: The difference for me isn't the inside, its what's outside. I fish for salmon in the summer and hunt for grouse and hare from September till March (though no-one shoots in the very dark days). It's forbidden to use the snowmobile to go hunting to conserve numbers and for safety. So, hunting has to be on foot or skis. I'm about to go on a trip of 11 kms with 15 other guys into the *fjell* (mountainous interior). This is quality time. We'll put a small oven on the sledge. Then when we arrive, we'll clear a hole in the snow, put in birch branches, then put in reindeer skins – this is the Sami way – then put a tent on top and pack snow around it for insulation. Then we spend the weekend ice fishing. It's great companionship.

Do people think you're mad?

Vidar: No, a lot of other people would like to come too.

Have you heard of Ray Mears?

Vidar winces. Lars Monsen is better (and Norwegian). He crossed Canada with a dog and gun, coast to coast. He camped for a year.

Point taken. So that's why you come to the *hytte* – for adventure.

Vidar: No, I need a place to chill out. If I was at home at weekends, I'd be restless. Feeling I should be doing something but without anything to do. Town doesn't allow all the activities we have here and town is connected with 'paid work' in my mind.

I have a dream to go fishing in Scotland. I'm not sure why – but I know it's very expensive.

The allure and disappointing reality of Scotland summed up in one neat sentence.

Anyway, back on the snowmobile and the next stop is young Linn Tørseth Nilsen, and her girlfriend Fay. Linn, a member of the Næss clan, uses the house but it belongs to her stepfather Torstein. A framed photo shows the first cabin, built by Torstein's aunt Dagmar Naess and Harald Hofseth before it was burned down in 1944. Later it was given to Torstein who built a cabin, but demolished it in 2001 and rebuilt with a larger house – the mother ship around which both families have assembled their own satellite communities.

The Naess/Hofseth clans get together for Easter and weddings with around 60 people present – and there's a Naess Games every summer for up to 100 family members and a quiz night where they all text in from individual cabins. Linn and Fay say they stick to skiing and picking berries (but not mushrooms).

I wondered aloud when the pre-war photo of the first cabin had been taken and Fay promptly strapped on skis, donned a thermal jacket and set off for the neighbouring *hytte* to get an answer from the nearest Naess.

Meanwhile, Inger Lise and I were invited to rest up on the deerskin-covered bench outside, amidst the snow, coorying mugs of steaming hot chocolate.

FIG 13.7 Hot chocolate at
the Naess *hytte*, Skaidi.
Courtesy: Linn Naess

FIG 13.8 Ove Høddo's old *hytte*.

FIG 13.9 One man, his *hytte*
and his dog.

I could have fallen asleep there, but we had one more visit. Ove Hoddø's family have a glazier's business and it's his trade too. When we arrived, he was in the middle of building a new and fairly lavish *hytte*, beside an older cabin built from packing cases and spare wood by his

FIG 13.10 Ove Høddo's new *hytte* being self-built.

god-mother Astrid Reinholdsen and her parents. Astrid is in her late '70s now, has no car and can't manage regular visits, but she and a friend do come every summer to collect cloud-berries (no-one lets on the location of their best berry sites). Ove has always come to clear snow from the roof and ten years ago Astrid said he could inherit the house and the land.

So Ove is using her old house as a base to build a new *hytte* and says he might turn hers into a snowmobile shed when he's finished (all present are horrified at this), because the new *hytte* must be an extension of the old one not to break the rules. Ove insists his new house is not as big as it could have been (and according to Inger Lise, that means it's still a *hytte* because he's shown some restraint) though it does have fabulous floor to ceiling windows.

We come back home, peel off the thermal layers, set the fire, have baked salmon for tea (and breakfast and lunch but having lived off one giant lump of mature cheddar many weekends at Drumnagarrow, I wasn't complaining).

The trip had done what I hoped it would do – confirmed that in our northern climes, Bjørg, Ola, Mariann, Christian and Inger Lise are not so unusual.

We are.

All over Scandinavia, families (complete with bidie-ins, step-children, their friends and passing strangers) have permanent homes in nature, places where non-work identities dominate – self-built, hutting safe havens.

FIG 13.11 Mariann and Aurora (Inger Lise and Christian's daughter)
at Skaidi.
Courtesy: Christian Svendsen

Leaving this little oasis of contentment in Skaidi, I was reminded
of the ever-smiling Tutta and Ola Normann on Lindøya.

I'd always wondered why they didn't resent being forced to
end island summers, by law, every October.

'Ah, but we've had enough by then. It's fine to leave. After
three months on Lindøya, we're completely satisfied.'

That simple sentence had stopped me in my tracks.

And now, hearing its echo in Skaidi, I finally understood the
great attraction of securely-owned huts everywhere. Weekend after
weekend, year after year, generation after generation, they produce
deeply satisfied people.

People filled up by nature, conviviality, friendship and family
japes. People sated with time away from the daily grind that
without booking, saving, planning, paying through the nose or
imposed conditions.

People whose experience of satisfaction is not drug, booze
or food-based, expensive or transient.

What's that like?

What's it like to have holidays that don't short-change, package, commodify or disappoint? What's it like to have vast reserves of affordable, genuine satisfaction on tap every summer and every weekend?

What's it like to walk away from paradise with a smile, knowing you can soon return because it belongs to you and your family. And their families to come. Amidst tens of thousands of other families, just like yours. Not as a perk of wealth or social connection but as the shared birth-right of citizens. What's it like to have this emotional outlet in perpetuity? What's it like – to have enough?

These are not questions Scots generally ask.

Our leisure lives don't deliver deep satisfaction, but we make do. What else is there?

Some of us grab short, expensive or borrowed vacations. Others grab fleeting days here and long weekends there. Some grab disposable tents, twelve packs and ghetto blasters for a few nights of two-fingers-to-the-world dirty camping. Without a share of Scotland's natural bounty, we grab whatever's within reach. But without feeling entitled to time and space, whenever we need it, right here in our own country, we are rarely satisfied.[14]

This is the secret of Lindøya, Skaidi and Carbeth.

In daring to shape their leisure lives, without advice or instruction, and against all odds, the bold hutters of the interwar years gave their children, grand-children and great-grandchildren the ultimate legacy – time and space that's not subject to any direct control by outsiders.

It's something we all need.

CHAPTER FOURTEEN

The Cloch

HOME AGAIN. Buoyed up and borne down by seeing so clearly what Scots are missing. Scotland and Norway may be North Sea cousins, but in social terms we are oceans apart. Very different patterns of land ownership have created very different patterns of employment and population. Small farms in Norway tend to be owned, giving Norwegian farmers freedom to diversify, whilst Scottish farms are still generally tenanted and constrained. The location of wealth and power, has long been distributed across Norway, but politically and economically concentrated in Scotland. Natural resources were nationalised in Norway, but privatised in Scotland. Norway had one of Europe's broadest franchises in the nineteenth century – Scotland one of the narrowest. The Norwegian Parliament made the state responsible for providing 8 hours of rest, relaxation and sleep when it imposed limits on the working day in 1919 – such a comprehensive package of workers' leisure rights has never been enacted by any British parliament.

Essentially, Scotland and Norway have become mirror images of one another – and though Scotland has valiantly resisted, the British state has embedded society within the market while Norway has embedded the market within society, to the enduring benefit of its people.

With such powerful institutional, economic and political barriers, it's astonishing Scots created any hutting communities at all. But they did because of determined individuals like William Ferris, a few, relatively open-minded, small-scale landowners and a unique historical situation. In the 1920s, men and women returned from war expecting to find a 'land fit for heroes'. Land prices had crashed and the government was encouraging market gardening, smallholdings and other forms of rural diversification. Meanwhile a plethora of radical movements was encouraging working class Scots to challenge the combined might of the landed and professional classes and reach into countryside locations hitherto regarded as physically and culturally off limits. Indeed, growth in hutting on both sides of the North Sea maps the years of Labour's primacy in each country with the creation of the welfare state, intervention to alleviate land shortages and the advent of universal suffrage. But progress faltered in Britain and structural inequality combined with underinvestment to cause post-war economic decline. Crucially, Scotland's hutters remained precarious tenants of the land, not secure tenants or outright owners like almost every hytte owner in Norway after WW2. Today, 82 per cent of hutters in Scotland are tenants – 80 per cent of hutters in Norway are owners. This dramatic difference has dampened down hutting demand in Scotland. Insecure, rented and badly maintained sites don't attract the influential and decision-making middle classes. So professionals tend to view huts as valueless and unsightly and that just makes the situation of hutters worse. It's a vicious circle.

Essentially, for a short period between the 1920s and 1950s, rural Scotland was not considered to be the sole preserve of the landed classes. But once Britain's post-war dalliance with social- ism, home rule and land reform were over, it was back to busi- ness as usual.

This is the crux of the difference. In the 1920s, the Norwe- gian Government was indeed engaged in a 'social experiment'. It was an experiment called genuine, full-throated, empowered and locally rooted democracy.

But that didn't happen here and almost every aspect of Scottish life is the poorer, including those canaries down the coalmine – our tiny cohort of wee wooden huts.

Over ten years I'd been to see most of the sites listed by Hugh Gentleman in his massively useful research. Yet an acci- dental visit as I was driving from Gourock to Ardrossan was perhaps the most heart-wrenching.

And that's surprising, because no-one could call the Cloch huts beautiful.

These shacks lie four miles west of Gourock Ferry terminal – lash-ups of corrugated iron and recycled bits of old tanks, constructed to withstand weather, vandalism and the ocean's highest tides. Seven huts, perched defiantly between the A770 and the Irish Sea, in that customary position sought by skint Scots trying to relax in their own country – the edge. Meanwhile, across the road, wooded acres stretched up to the inevitable, invisible Big Hoose.

Wood was neatly chopped up beside one hut, faded plastic chairs were stacked by another and – beyond a chasm created by the winter's torrential rain – there was a self-built pier of railway sleepers inching into the tide. A poor man's jetty with small boats padlocked beyond. These possessions were meagre but precious. The Cloch hut owners had obviously fought hard to inhabit this precarious fragment of land. I was about to leave when a wee car drew up and Archie got out. He caught me standing with a clipboard, flipping through Cal Mac booking papers to find my check-in time for the Arran ferry. Archie stared at the clipboard, looked at me and instinctively backed away.

'I'm not here from the council or anything. Sorry about the clipboard – it's just got my ferry tickets on it. I'm doing research about huts in Scotland and saw these in the passing. When were they built?'

Archie visibly relaxed, introduced himself and told his story.

Seven friends jointly pay £200 per annum to the Laird to rent the foreshore upon which these wee huts sit. They began life as tents further down the coast until a small factory was built on the site after the war and campers were 'offered the chance' to erect sheds on this tiny crumbling fringe of coastline instead.

'Why do you think the huts were moved here?'

'Because it's a suntrap, I imagine – the best place on the coast. We're able to stay because we keep the site so tidy.'

Clearly, we inhabit different worlds. To me this looks like unusable land cynically offloaded so the better site could be developed commercially and the hutters along with their ramshackle constructions hidden from view in this sunken corner of coastline.

'This bit here,' Archie continued, 'this is work Junior has done all on his own. Junior's had 13 hip operations – he's on the sick now. But he built this flood defence himself.'

FIG 14.1 Cloch huts.

I followed Archie's gaze to a mound of stones which looked set to be washed away in the next high tide.

'Come back at the weekend. You can see how we've kitted out the huts inside.'

Above Archie's proud possession a Saltire fluttered in the breeze.

It was heart-breaking and impressively defiant at the same time.

Such a tiny bit of unwanted, marginal, borrowed ground is all a retired working man like Archie can ever hope to have in massive, empty, modern Scotland – two precious yards squeezed between the exhaust fumes of cars on a busy coast road and the cold Irish Sea. A couple of miles further south sits Inverkip Marina – an upmarket haven where second homes sell for a quarter of a million pounds apiece. It seems the fabulous landscapes of Scotland are still available only to the very affluent or the very hardy – and not many in between.

Anywhere else, certainly in all the Nordic nations, this scene would be very different. No-one's weekend hut would be crammed into a tiny, eroding space by a frisky sea, no-one would have their hut reinforced with ugly bolts against the likelihood of vandalism, few folk would own over-sized, pseudo-suburban homes for a weekend getaway and any forested hill by the sea within an hour's travel of Glasgow would be discreetly covered with hundreds of wooden huts, hidden in mature forests.

Standing by those weather-beaten shacks I could have wept over the sheer enduring injustice of it all. But instead I visualised a different Scotland.

I imagined that Archie could have more. More security, more space, more like-minded folk around him, more of a right to be there, more beauty. I could imagine the hillside covered with wooden huts, crafted and built by Archie and Junior's children and neighbours in the forgotten housing estates of Greenock. The two pioneers themselves would doubtless insist on retaining their ringside seats at the very edge of the ocean. But I could see their grand-children playing in the woods and later down by the sea, swimming and squealing with the cold, gathering sticks for an evening stony beach barbecue and rehearsing a few songs since the old ceilidh tradition was popular once again. I could see Scots relaxing, stretching out in space and not getting 'oot their brains' – Scots acting, at last, as if they actually own the place.

I could imagine the difference in confidence and behaviour as Archie's descendants finally dare to expect their interests will come first, not last after protected species, landowners, sheep, deer, wind turbines, conserved landscapes, national parks and famous monuments.

And not just here at the Cloch. I could visualise this easy connection with land all over Scotland. I could imagine the moment herded Scots stop arguing amongst themselves in the squeezed margins of Scotland and walk forward into the empty country-side around them. Not in anger but by right. By right of legisla-tion passed by the Scottish Parliament.

This won't happen tomorrow. We are still too fearful of intervening in the sacred market, too uncertain that our current distance from nature and chronic land scarcity really matter. But they really do.

Attachment to people is regarded as a human right. Without a caring, nurturing, constant human presence, babies falter, fail to feed and may even die.

Attachment to nature is seen rather differently. In Scotland it's become an optional extra. Nature is an alien place full of mud, wellingtons and scowling farmers driving tractors at ten mph. Nature occurs on land – something which was once important, way back when. Now, a Google generation tells itself, we are post-place. Stuff matters. And stuff can be consumed anywhere.

I notice this doesn't make anyone very happy. I notice that Scots are the only northern nation without a hut or cabin culture. I wonder if we know what we are missing.

Without land-anchors, our experience of nature is often synthetic, controlled, random and slightly inauthentic. A day trip here with the kids whining 'are we there yet'. A weekend there, to consume listable, collectable worldly pleasures. We drive lightly and aimlessly over land we hardly know, 'dearly held' by people we never meet and place names we no longer understand.

We experience no subtle change in weather, wind direction or outlook. We do not reach a place beyond the daily grind – we do not find our makeshift selves. Because that takes time and trust.

Like any good love affair, it takes a series of small adventures to forge a meaningful bond between person and place.

Each choice, each decision, each flash of anxiety, each sigh of relief, each logistical problem overcome, each shared delight forms part of a weave. Binding us tighter, faster and closer to that place and no other – tighter with each passing year.

That strong connection, that recurring immersion in another particular place, that regular return to low-impact living, that relaxed reconnection with all the important people in our lives – that can all happen despite the obstacles cast up by Scotland's history.

But first, we have to want it.

POSTSCRIPT

Huts to relish

WHAT COULD THE future look like?

Some enterprising folk have managed to find small plots of land and built some fabulous huts. This could easily be reproduced – but woodlands currently offer exemption from death duties, so it's very hard for ordinary Scots to outbid investors. But receptive landowners and farmers exist now as they did in the 1920s and '30s when Carbeth, Seton Sands and Barry Downs were started. The trick is to find them and win them over.

The Thousand Huts campaign has been helping would-be hutters do that since it was set up in 2011 by the charity Reforesting Scotland, which works towards a future of sustainable communities in a well-forested land. Campaigners believe that hut life brings people closer to nature, cultivates practical skills in low carbon living, helps foster a spirit of community and co-operation and brings physical and mental health benefits – particularly important given high levels of obesity and anxiety in children and teenagers. Crucially, Reforesting Scotland believes that hut life helps grow a sense of empowerment and dignity through the creation and enjoyment of simple, low-impact building and living.

The Thousand Huts folk campaigned successfully for a new planning policy that supports low impact huts for recreational use with lighter-touch building regulations. So now folk who can find the land can hope to get planning permission to build a safe, sustainable and affordable hut.

The campaign has produced publications to support prospective hutters and hut site developers, including a 40-page guide to huts and planning permission, a 70-page technical guide to good practice in hut construction, and a Voluntary Code of Good Conduct between hutters and landowners to help create fair leases and formal agreements that protect the rights of both parties. All are available to download at www.thousandhuts.org.

The campaign's also obtained planning permission for a

Pilot Hut Site of 12 huts on public forest land, and has helped create a new Carnock Hutters Group to take the site forward. All their sites are taken though – sorry.

New huts are starting to pop up all over Scotland though, with more in the pipeline once planning permission is achieved. The pilot study site near Saline is still in development with many valuable lessons being learned along the way. Hopes are high that dozens of government-owned sites will get the go-ahead for hutting, once this pilot site has been successfully completed.

More info, advice, events and contact info via: www.thousandhuts.org.

Finally, have a look at some of the huts the Thousand Huts campaign has helped folk build.

Alan Reeder – His forester's hut in the West Highlands was designed by Cormac Seekings and constructed on site by Cormac and friends using local wood over a seven-year period. It was built (mostly without power tools) from timber felled on site – except for the windows (recycled) and the roof shingles (left over from another project). There's still no electricity today and running water comes fresh from the burn.

Jack Hughes and Lucinda Eccles designed this hut for a client in
Fife. It was built by a group of friends and fellow architects from
Glasgow School of Art.

Elaine Robinson's hut in Newcastleton built in 2017 by Peter Caunt of Quercus Design. This was the first hut built under the new 'hut-friendly' planning policy.

This hut in Fife shared by four Edinburgh couples with young children, was built in the second half of 2019.

The hut at Plot 19 Cash Wood, Fife.

The pilot hut on Falkland Estate, Fife, designed by architect Alastair Baird and built in 2018 using all estate Larch timber. It became a demonstration hut for folk wanting to build 'Baird' huts in nearby Cash Wood.

Woodsman's hut near Nethy Bridge.

Thousand Huts website homepage.

Endnotes

Introduction

1   Robbins, J, *Ecopsychology: How Immersion in Nature Benefits Your Health*, Yale School of Forestry & Environmental Studies, 2020; also www.learn.eartheasy.com/articles/how-to-take-a-forest-bath/

2   Fridjhof Nansen, inaugural address as Rector of the University of St Andrews, 1926.

Chapter One

1   Buchan, D and Moreira, J (eds), *The Glenbuchat Ballads*, Mississippi: University Press of Mississippi, 2011

Chapter Three

1   *Dagens Næringsliv*, 27 January 2003

2   Statistics Norway, www.ssb.no/en/natur-og-miljo/statistikker/fritidsbyggomr/aar

3   Buchan, D and Moreira, J (eds), *The Glenbuchat Ballads*, Mississppi: University Press of Mississippi, 2011

4   www.nrscotland.gov.uk/files/statistics/household-estimates/2017/house-est-17-publication.pdf accessed June 2015

5   Statistics Norway, 2018 (The most recent time huts were properly counted in Scotland was 1999.)

6   UK Census, 2011 (A planned question on second homes in the census was dropped, but figures showed a decrease in Scotland's second home total to 25,700 in 2017, after councils were able to raise the level of council tax payable on second homes. The 2017 survey contained no mention of huts.)

7   Ibid.

8   Vagner, J, Müller, DK and Fialova, D, 'Second home tourism in light of the historical-political and socio-geographical development of Czechia and Sweden', *Geografie*, 116: 2, 2011, pp.191–210 & Hall, CM and Müller, DK, 'Introduction: Second Homes, Curse or Blessing? Revisited', in Hall, CM and Müller, DK (eds), *Tourism, Mobility and Second Homes: Between Elite Landscape and Common Ground*, Toronto: Channel View, 2004, p.10

9   Aanesland, N and Holm, O, *Boplikt: Drøm og Virkelighet* (Residence Requirements: Dream and Reality), Oslo: Universitetsforlaget, 2002, p.108

10   www.newsinenglish.no/2019/12/31/hytte-dream-stirs-climate-nightmare/ accessed 31 December 2019

11   www.ssb.no/en/natur-og-miljo/statistikker/fritidsbyggomr/aar accessed April 2020

12   Gentleman H, *Huts and Hutters in Scotland*, released by Research Consultancy Services via Scottish Government, Edinburgh, 1999, p.19

13   Statistics Norway, 2013 (Eight per cent of those in the lowest income quintile were *hytte*-owning households in 2009 while 36 per cent in the highest earning quintile owned a *hytte* (or several). Top earners were also twice as likely to own a *hytte* as those on an 'average' income.)

14   *Fritidshus* (Holiday Houses) report 1970, www.ssb.no/a/histstat/sagml/sagml_20.pdf accessed April 2016

15   Gentleman, *Huts and Hutters*, p.113

16   Ibid., p.82

17   Statistics Norway, 2017

18   Robert Rennie in email response, 4 November 2011

19   www.theguardian.com/uk/scotland-blog/2013/mar/20/scotland-carbeth-hutters-
     buyout accessed March 2014

20   Kaltenborn, BP, 'The Alternate Home: Motives of Recreation Home Use', *Norsk
     Geografisk Tidskrift*, 52:3, 1998, p.52

21   Wolfe, RI, 'Summer Cottages in Ontario' in Coppock, JT (ed.), *Second Homes
     Curse or Blessing*, Oxford: Pergamon Press, 1976, pp.19–28

22   Nordin, U, 'Second Homes' in Aldskogius, H (ed.), *National Atlas of Sweden:
     Cultural Life, Recreation and Tourism*, Stockholm: Almquist & Wiksell, 1993,
     pp.72–79

23   Bjerve, BJ, *Planning in Norway 1947–56*, Amsterdam: North Holland, 1959,
     pp.47–59 ('A resolution adopted by the *Storting* [the Norwegian parliament] on 5
     April 1949 prohibited the construction of cabins and summer homes. Furthermore,
     a temporary supplement to the tax laws in 1950 (not abolished until 1954) made
     repairs and maintenance expenses non-deductible for income tax.')

24   Statistics Norway, 2010 ('In 1970 there were 190,000 holiday cottages in Norway,
     1 for every 7 houses. Almost 75 per cent were built after 1945 – often by the owner
     in his newly acquired holiday time.')

25   www.visitnorway.com/uk/media-press/ideas-and-features/hiking-in-norway

26   www.mountainbothies.org.uk/mba-history.asp

27   www.visitnorway.com/things-to-do/great-outdoors/fishing/freshwater

28   www2.gov.scot/Topics/Justice/law/17975/Abolition accessed June 2015

29   General Registers of Scotland, www.gro-scotland.gov.uk/press/2014/scots-pop-
     highest-ever.html accessed January 2015

30   Wightman, A, *Forest Ownership in Scotland: A Scoping Study*, Edinburgh: Forest
     Policy Group, 2012, p.2

31   Ibid., p.13 ('59.6 per cent of European forest holdings are less than 1ha in extent
     (Scotland = 6.3 per cent). Over 93 per cent of privately-owned forestry in Scotland
     is held in holdings of over 100ha.')

32   British Waterways, www.northsearegion.eu/files/repository/20141203134901_Bran
     ding&Crosspromotionbetweenpartners-Waterways_for_Growth_-_March_
     workshop_per cent2803_versionper cent29.pdf accessed July 2017

33   DeSilvey, CO., *'When Plotters Meet': Edinburgh's Allotment Movement 1921–
     2001*, Masters dissertation, Edinburgh: University of Edinburgh, 2001, p.vi

34   Ibid., p.1

35   Ibid., p.2

36   Geddes, on the outskirts of Edinburgh his 'Vacant Lands Cultivation Scheme',
     found a further 450 unused acres

37   McDaid, H and Reid, L, *Portobello East Junction Allotments*, self-published
     booklet, 2000

38   ECA, File 144/1 DRT 14 (Public Parks Committee), 12 June 1919

39   ECA, File J20/8, report by the Town Clerk in regard to 'Statutory Provisions
     Relating to Garden Allotments', February 1920

40   De La Rue, B, et al., 'Finding Scotland's Allotments', 2007, pp.3–4, www.sags.org.
     uk/docs/ReportsPresentations/AuditReport07.pdf

41   NAS, AF 43/352, minutes of proceedings for Agricultural Land (Utilisation) Bill
     1930, Allotments Conference, 22 November 1930

42   NAS, AF 66/100, draft official letter from the Office of Works, Westminster to the
     Under-secretary for Scotland, March 1932

43 ECA, File 144/1 DRT 14 (Public Parks Committee), letter to the Edinburgh Town Clerk from the Edinburgh and Leith Federation of Garden Allotment Associations, 12 April 1929

44 DeSilvey, 'When Plotters Meet', p.23

45 ECA, File 186 DRT 14 (Public Parks Committee), minutes of the Garden Allotments Committee, 18 April 1929

46 NAS, AF 66/96, letter to the Editor, The Scotsman, from JG Roberts, Secretary, Barrhead Allotments Association, 26 November 1931

47 The Scotsman, 27 April 1932

48 NAS, AF 66/96, Correspondence between Department of Agriculture for Scotland and the Scottish Office

49 NAS, AF 66/96, letter from Archibald Fischer to Secretary of State for Scotland, 8 July 1932

50 Thorpe, H, Departmental Committee of Inquiry into Allotments. Cmnd., 4166, Parliamentary Papers, London, 1969

51 ECA, File CA/30/1 DRT 14 (Civic Amenities Committee), 'Review of Garden Allotments to be included in the Quinquennial Review of the Development Plan', drafted 1963 (The review notes 1,508 Corporation plots, 1,150 in permanent, and 358 in temporary, areas.)

52 VWA, SAGS Conference Report, 1965

53 ECA, File CA/30/1 DRT 14 (Civic Amenities Committee), letter to the Town Clerk from the Federation of Edinburgh and District Allotments and Gardens Associations, 29 November 1964

54 ECA, File CA/30/1 DRT 14 (Civic Amenities Committee), memo from the Superintendent of Parks to the Town Clerk, 29 December 1964

55 ECA, File CA/30/1 DRT 14 (Civic Amenities Committee), memo to the Edinburgh Town Clerk from the Director of Parks and Recreation, 15 December 1965

56 ECA, File CA/30/1 DRT 14 (Civic Amenities Committee), memo from the City Chamberlain to the Town Clerk, 3 June 1968

57 Statistics Norway, 2010

58 The Economic Impact of the Holiday Park Sector in Scotland, report for the Scottish Caravan and Camping Forum, 2014 (Scottish statistics are harder to access than Norwegian figures and not directly comparable. Non-SCCF caravan sites exist, but the Scottish total also includes chalets, lodges, wigwams, yurts and pods.)

59 Bevan, M, Mobile Homes in Scotland, Edinburgh: Scottish Government, 2007, pp.1–2

60 Rodnick, D, Norwegians: A Study in National Culture, Washington: Public Affairs, 1955, p.39

61 Ferguson, T, Scottish Social Welfare 1864–1914, Edinburgh: Harcourt Brace, 1958, p.246

62 Jordan, TE, The Degeneracy Crisis and Victorian Youth, New York: Suny, 1993, p.42

63 In the public and private sectors combined.

64 Rodger, R, Scottish Housing in the 20th Century, Leicester: Bloomsbury, 1988

65 According to the 2001 Spanish Census more than 82 per cent of households were homeowners, the greater part being outright owners. Tenants accounted for just over 11 per cent.

66 86.1 per cent in 2008, according to Trading Economics, www.tradingeconomics.com/norway/home-ownership-rate accessed May 2015

Chapter Four

1 Lyngø, IJ and Grimstad, I, 'Sommerliv på Lindøya 1850–1922', Byminner, 2, 1992

2   Grönvold, A, *Norske Musikere*, Oslo: Aschehoug, 1st edition, 1883, p.94 ('It
     boasted just one tiny room, and was poised on the edge of the fjord, in the midst of
     the exquisite beauty of Ullensvang, with the dark, deep fjord below, and the
     glittering ridge of the Folgefonna glacier on the other side of the water. Grieg
     returned there every summer, and sometimes in the winter too, for the peace and
     tranquillity he needed for his work.')
3   Klepp, *En Stat i solen*, pp.76–77
4   Interview with Anne Marie 'Tutta' Normann, 2011
5   Leonard Normann – Ola's grandfather – was a typographer at a newspaper and an
     active union man. He used the *kolonihager* to grow vegetables, apples and pears
     and bought a tiny kiosk so the family could live there over the summer. Ola's father
     Trygve and mother Edith finally built a *hytte* on the old kiosk site in 1969.

Chapter Five

1   'We are lucky the government owns the islands. I trust the government – I don't
     trust the *kommune* the same way. When they need more money, they sell
     something.' Anne Marie 'Tutta' Normann, Chair Lindøya Vel 1989–2010, 2011
2   Lyngø, IJ, *Hyttelivets*, p.44 (From 1849 the Association for Shooting
     (Skarpsskytten) and the Oslo Hunting Club (Christiania Jægerklubs) used Lindøya
     – both were private men's clubs.)
3   *Lindøya Vel*, 75th anniversary publication, p.21
4   Lyngø, *Fritid er sosial sak*
5   Lyngø, *Hyttelivets*, p.46
6   Borgen, *St Hallvard*, pp.10–19
7   Blom, H, *Indre Oslofjord – i gamle og nye bilder*, Oslo: Norlis, 2005, p.48
8   Borgen, *St Hallvard*; The island was so subtly undulating that it gave space for 13
     houses and no one could see one from the other, sometimes we'd glimpse a roof
     with a spire.
9   Blom, *Indre Oslofjord*, p.49
10   Gjerland, L, *Oslos øyrike før og noe*, Oslo: Dreyers Forlag, 2006, p.85
11   Ibid., pp.84–85
12   *Byminner*, 2, 1992
13   Stensby, P, 'Hvor skal utstillingen ligge?', Oslo: *St Hallvard*, 2, 1989, pp.32–39
14   *Aftenposten*, 21 May 2009
15   Mathisen, B, *Nakholmen Vel 1923–1998*, Oslo, 1998, pp.9–15
16   Ibid., p22 and footnote 220
17   Lyngø, *Fritid er sosial sak*, p.116
18   Tvedt, *Oslo Byleksikon*, p.186
19   Klepp, IG, 'Søndre Skaerholmen – det tapte paradis', in *Badeliv* (*Byminner*, 2),
     Oslo, 1997, p.28
20   Gjerland, *Oslos øyrike*, Oslo, 2006, pp.65–67 (He notes the masts used to stick out
     at low tide and were blown up when the outdoor swimming pool was constructed
     lest it reminded swimmers of the site's former life.)
21   Ibid., pp.65–68
22   www.lokalhistoriewiki.no/wiki/Langøyene (Oslofjorden) accessed June 2011
23   Gjerland, *Oslos øyrike*, pp.65–67
24   Johansen, T, Elvrum, F and Larsen, O, *Nakholmen Vel 25th Jubileum*, Oslo, 1948,
     p.49 ('Simple people have long used the islands as a residence during the holidays on
     average two to four days a week. It is important for us to look forward to having our
     Sunday trips to the islands. Everywhere else in the fjord the right to land is forbidden.')

25 Ibid. ('My stepfather had a tent (on Rambergøya) and was living in it (during the summer). He had a motorboat in Akerselva and ten kids and my stepmother. But when he went out to Rambergøya in 1920, he was not allowed to be there. So, they moved the tent and the kids and boat all together, and came to Lindøya.')

26 Lyngø, IJ, Hyttelivets, p.49

27 SBED 569 in Lyngø, IJ, Hyttelivets, p.54

28 SBED 568 from State Forests Direktoratet Sakspakke pp.565–85 (Statens øyer i Oslofjorden)

29 Lindøya Vel, p.14

30 Direktor Sørhus interviewed in the island joint newspaper Øy og vi (The island and us), 1931, p.30 ('The first year I was in the forest office, we got complaints every Monday morning in the warm summer [about] what had been going on on Lindøya and how impossible it was for the guard to keep the island in order, prevent trees being destroyed, and meet minimum standards with regard to order and sanitary considerations.')

31 Stagg, East Norway, p.56

32 Libaek and Stenersen, A History of Norway, p.103

33 www.lindoya.org/historie/hytteutviklingen accessed October 2011

34 Lyngø, IJ, Hyttelivets, pp.52–55

35 Ibid., pp.55–56

36 Ibid., p.55

37 Lindøya Vel, p.21

38 Alsvik, B, Friluftslivet i Indre Oslofjord, Tobias, 2, Oslo Byarkivet, 1999

39 Lindøya Vel, p.17

40 Huts could be no more than 25 square metres for a two-storey house and 35 metres square for a single storey house. The height to the roof ridge was to be 4.8 metres and 3.6 metres respectively – bigger than the hut sites on Lindøya.

41 Warnings were posted all over the island declaring, 'if this regulation is not observed, you will forfeit your application to live on Lindøya.' Ironically given the commune's actions at Langøyene, one poster warned of punishment for anyone putting rubbish into the sea, citing 1894 public health regulations. Lindøya Vel

42 Mathisen, B, Nakholmen Vel, 1923–98, p.22

43 Ibid., p.45

44 Semi structured interview with Oddmund Ostebø, June 2013

45 Mathisen, Nakholmen Vel, p.112

46 Ibid.

47 Lyngø, IJ, Hyttelivets, p.44

48 Tidens Tegn, 1922 ('Instead of meeting with beautiful un-spoilt nature, now people on the steamer float into our once proud fjord surrounded by huts painted in a rainbow of terrible colours.')

49 Witoszek, N, The Origins of the 'Regime of Goodness', Oslo: Universitetsforlaget, 2011, pp.78–80

50 Kjeldstadli, Den delte byen, p.431

51 Social Demokraten, 31 July 1922

52 Lyngø, Hyttelivets, p.60

53 Rolland, CS, Langåra – et sommerparadis i Oslofjorden, Oslo: Oslo University, 2006

54 Tvedt, Oslo Byleksikon, p.106

55 Lyngø, Hyttelivets, pp.59–60

56 Ibid., p.61

57 Klepp, IG, *En Stat i solen*, PhD dissertation, Oslo, 1990, pp.105–06

58 Sub committees in 1973 included; 1. Price Committee – audit of the shops' pricing.
    2. Building Committee – control of repairs. 3. Working Committee – maintenance
    work imposed by the Vel Board. 4. Light Committee – measuring power
    consumption per cabin and total consumption. 5. Water Committee — opening and
    closing water supplies in the spring and fall, and maintaining pipelines and public
    toilets. 6. Supervisory Committee — overseeing hedge height and width, and
    ensuring trees that might be a danger to the mains are notified to the nearest
    rodemester to ensure removal. 7. Electricity Committee – troubleshooting at the
    island substation. 8. Traffic Committee – liaison between the ferry company and
    islanders. 9. Tractor Committee – maintenance and use. 10. Colour Committee –
    ensuring cabins are painted according to the agreed colour plan, www.lindoya.org/
    historie/øyas-administrasjon/ accessed November 2013

59 Borgen, *St Hallvard*, p.13 ('Here there was no speculation with property. Sales were
    straightforward though very few came on the market [and] the spectre of
    unemployment forced [some] to divorce from their *hytte*.')

60 Klepp, IG, 'Hytta som leilighetens mannlige anneks' in Klepp, A and Thorsen, LE
    (eds.), *Den mangfoldige fritiden*, Oslo, 1993, p.94

61 Ibid. ('Technology is so impressive we think it master and we servants. But on the
    islands, we reconnect with humanity, even if there is always the threat of an
    architect springing out from town with concrete-filled plans which could knock
    human life out of existence here.')

62 The biggest association is currently the mini-golf club. The bridge club has been
    started and closed twice. It opened in 1947, closed in 1960, was revived in 1972
    and closed in 1995. www.lindoya.org/historie/hytteutviklingen/ accessed November
    2013

63 Kjeldstadli, *Den delte byen*, pp.430–31

64 www.lindoya.org/historie/hytteutviklingen/ accessed November 2013

65 Aftenposten, 15 November 1960

66 Klepp, *En Stat i solen*, pp.36–50 (The original rent of ten kroner per cabin was
    raised to 50 kroner in 1957, 100 kroner in 1971 and 1,000 kroner in 1981.)

67 www.aftenposten.no/norge/i/Vbqn4/Oslos-dyreste-hytter-har-utedo accessed June 2017

68 www.statsbygg.no/Nytt-fra-Statsbygg/Nyheter/2012/13-tomter-i-Oslofjorden-solgt/
    accessed June 2016

Chapter Six

1   Aase, A, 'In Search of Norwegian Values', in Maagero, E and Simonsen, B,
    Norway: *Society and Culture*, Oslo, 1998, p.14

2   Also found in the Orkney and Shetland Islands of Scotland, which were
    dependencies of the Norwegian Crown until the 15th century. Udal tenure
    comprised a set of inheritance rules assuring the hereditary right of descendants.

3   Only 3 per cent of Norwegian land is cultivated.

4   Derry, TK, *A History of Scandinavia*, London: Allen & Unwin, 1979, p.142

5   Lunden, K, 'Recession and New Expansion 1350–1814', in Almås, R, *Norwegian
    Agricultural History*, Trondheim: Tapir, 2004, pp.144–232

6   Larsen, K, *History of Norway*, New York: Princeton, 1948, p.310

7   Lunden, K. 'Recession and New Expansion 1350–1814', pp.144–232

8   NOS, Utvandringsstatistikk NOS VII 25, Oslo, 1921

9   Helvig, M and Johannessen, V, *Norway: Land, People, Industries*, Oslo: Tanum,
    1970, p.47

10 Ibid.
11 Witoszek, N, *The Origins of the 'Regime of Goodness'*, Oslo: Universitetsforlaget, 2011, p.56 (Allodial ownership is real property (land, buildings, and fixtures) owned independently of any superior landlord.)
12 Johnston, T, *The History of the Working Classes in Scotland*, Glasgow: Forward, 1920, pp.186–87
13 Return of Owners of Lands and Heritages Scotland 1872–3, Comptroller-General of the Inland Revenue
14 Dickinson, WC, *Scotland from the Earliest Times to 1603*, Scotland: Nelson, 1961, p.21
15 Ibid.
16 Kidd, C, *Subverting Scotland's Past: Scottish Whig Historians and the Creation of an Anglo-British Identity, 1689–1830*, Cambridge: Cambridge University Press, 2003, p.35
17 Kidd, *Subverting Scotland's Past*, p.40
18 Chambers, R, *A Biographical Dictionary of Eminent Scotsmen*, Glasgow, Vol 2, Part 2, Glasgow: Blackie & Sons, 1855, p.355
19 Hunter, J, *The Making of the Scottish Crofting Community*, Edinburgh: Birlinn, 1976, pp.61–62
20 Ibid., pp.96–97
21 Ibid., pp 96–97
22 Ibid., p.47
23 Bryden, J, et al, *Northern Neighbours*. p 11
24 Riddoch, L, *Riddoch on the Outer Hebrides*, Edinburgh: Luath Press, 2007, p.23
25 Mather, AS, *State-aided Land Settlement in Scotland*, Aberdeen: Aberdeen University Press, 1978, p.10
26 Leneman, L, 'A Land Fit for Heroes', *The Scottish Historical Review*, 67:184, Part 2, 1988, pp.156–71
27 McIntosh Gray, A and Moffat, W, *A History of Scotland: Modern Times*, Oxford: Oxford University Press, 1999, p.28
28 Devine, TM, *The Scottish Nation*, London: Penguin, 1999, p.453
29 Ibid.
30 Gray, M, *The Fishing Industries of Scotland, 1790–1914: A Study in Regional Adaptation*, Oxford: Oxford University Press, 1978, pp.7–9
31 Mahoney, E, *The Guardian*, 19 September 2001
32 Devine, *Farm Servants*, p.20
33 Devine, *The Scottish Nation*, p.454
34 Ibid., p.455
35 Ibid., p.455
36 Johnston, T, *Our Scots Noble Families*, Scotland: Argyll Publishing, 1999
37 Devine, *The Scottish Nation*, pp.455–56
38 Ibid., p.458
39 Statistics Norway, NOS Census of Agriculture and Forestry, 1989
40 Land Reform Review Group Final Report, May 2014, pp.159–60, www.gov.scot/publications/land-reform-review-group-final-report-land-scotland-common-good/pages/61/
41 Ibid., p.29
42 Ibid., p.159
43 Wightman, 2013

Chapter Seven

1   Bryden, J, et al, *Northern Neighbours*, p.37
2   Lunden, 'Recession and New Expansion', pp.144–232
3   Skirbekk, G, *Multiple Modernities*, pp.84–86, www.gunnarskirbekk.no/bøker/ Multiple%20Modernities% 20book.pdf accessed July 2019
4   Fougstad, CA, *The Norwegian Storting*, 1834 ('there is no place on Earth where the common man has gained a comparable freedom. This phenomenon has awakened much attention. Some have called it the true development of freedom and the bringing to life of the constitution in common minds. Others have called it the triumph of ignorance and the forerunner of barbarism.')
5   Østerud, *Agrarian Structure*, p.129 (Tenants outnumbered freeholders by three to one in 1660 while in 1750 freeholders were twice as numerous as tenants. By 1890 scarcely one out of ten of the total registered rent comprised large estates.)
6   Bryden, J, et al, *Northern Neighbours*, pp.10–11
7   Most of the articles in the *Eidsvold* constitution remain unaltered, some have been revised and the *Grundlov* (fundamental law of the Norwegian state) continues in operation today.
8   Og, FA, *The Governments of Europe*, Oslo: Gutenberg Press, 1913
9   Political parties did not exist until 1884 when first *Venstre* (Liberal Party) and then *Høyre* (Conservative Party) were established.
10 Lunden, 'Recession and New Expansion', pp.142–232
11 Heidar, K, *Norway: Elites on Trial*, Boulder: Westview, 2001, pp.18–19
12 Brox, O, *The Political Economy of Rural Development: Modernisation Without Centralisation?*, Utrecht: Eburon Academic Publishers, 2006, pp.12–13
13 Women were excluded, but their independence petition collected almost 250,000 signatures.
14 Danielsen, et al, *From the Vikings to Our Own Times*, p.335
15 Kirby, DG, 'Revolutionary Ferment in Finland' in *Scandinavian Economic History Review*, 26:1, 1978, pp.15–35 (This view was also shared by non-socialist parties in inter-war Norway).
16 The Moscow-based communist organisation calling for armed uprising by the working classes.
17 Heidar, *Elites on Trial*, pp.20–21
18 Bryden, J, et al, *Northern Neighbours*, p.29
19 Goksøyr, M, 'Phases and Functions of Nationalism: Norway's Utilization of International Sport in the Late Nineteenth and Early Twentieth Centuries' in *The International Journal of the History of Sport*, 12:2, 1995, pp.125–146
20 Ibid.
21 Bryden, J, et al, *Northern Neighbours*, p.44
22 Lewis, WA, 'Economic Development with Unlimited Supplies of Labour', *The Manchester School*, 22:2, 1954, pp.139–91

Chapter Eight

1   Goksøyr, M, 'Norway's Utilisation of International Sport' in Mangan, JA (ed.), *Tribal Identities*, London: Routledge, 1996
2   Ibid.
3   Ibid., p.142 ('Constitution Day brought sport and nationalism together. Sport was used as a deliberate means to extend the popularity of celebrations.')
4   Ibid., p.143
5   Rouse, P, 'Sport on a Partitioned Island: 1920 to the New Millennium' in

Sport and Ireland: A History, Oxford: Oxford University Press, 2015, pp.243–328

6   Nansen, F, *Adventure & Other Papers*, California: Books for Libraries Press, 1967, p.38

7   Nansen, F, *The First Crossing of Greenland*, USA: Interlink, reprint 2003, p.83

8   Faarlund, N, 'Friluftsliv – a tradition alive in Scandinavia' in Liedtke, G and Lagerstroem, D (eds), *Friluftsliv*, Aachen: Meyer and Meyer, 2007

9   *Norsk Skyttertidene* 5/1903

10 Reynolds, EE, *Nansen*, Harmondsworth: Penguin, 1949, pp.272–74

11 Vittersoe, G, 'Norwegian Cabin Life in Transition' in *Scandinavian Journal of Hospitality and Tourism*, 7:3, 2007, pp.266–80

12 Bent, M, *Coastal Express: The Ferry to the Top of the World*, Virginia: Conway Maritime Press, 1987, p.12

13 Rokkan, S and Urwin, RW, 'The Politics of Territorial Identity: Studies in European Regionalism' in *Urban Studies*, 26:3, Jun 1989, pp.340–55

14 Hroch, M, 'From National Movement to the Fully Formed Nation' in *New Left Review*, 1:198, 1993

15 Gjerdåker, B, 'Continuity and Modernity' in Almås, R, *Norwegian Agricultural History*, Trondheim, Tapir, 2004, pp.234–93

16 Rees, E, 'Det egentlige Norge – hytte I norsk litteratur 1814–2005' in Jorgensen, FA, Gansmo, HJ and Berker, T, *Norske hytte i endring*, Trondheim: Tapir, 2011, p.23

17 Witoszek, N, 'Nature, Knowledge and Identity', in Teich, M, Porter, R and Gustafsson, B, *Norway in Nature and Society in Historical Context*, Cambridge: Cambridge University Press, 1997, pp.214–15

18 Ibid, p.214

19 Ibid, p.214

20 https://norwegianacademy.com/nynorsk-or-bokmal/ accessed March 2016

21 Westergaard, JH, 'Scandinavian Urbanism: A Survey of Trends and Themes in Urban Social Research in Sweden, Norway and Denmark' in *Acta Sociologica*, 8:4, 1965, pp.304–23

22 MacLellan and Smith, *Tourism in Scotland*, passim

23 Boswell, J, *Tour to the Hebrides*, Amazon Media, p.2

24 Seaton, *History of Tourism*, p.1

25 McCrone, D, *Understanding Scotland: The Sociology of a Nation*, Oxford: Routledge, 2002, p.133 (The Act of Proscription 1747 says: 'No man or boy, within that part of Great Briton called Scotland, other than shall be employed as officers and soldiers in his Majesty's forces, shall on any pretence whatsoever, wear or put on the clothes commonly called Highland Clothes (that is to say) the plaid, philibeg, or little kilt, trowse, shoulder belts, or any part whatsoever of what peculiarly belongs to the highland garb; and that no tartan.' Carrying weapons had already been banned in the Disarming Act of 1716.)

26 Gibson, JG, *Traditional Gaelic Bagpiping 1745–1845*, Montreal: 1998, p.127

27 MacLean, CI, *The Highlands*, London: Batsford, 2006, p.63

28 Riddoch, L *Blossom*, Edinburgh, Luath Press, 2013, p.295

29 McCrone, *Understanding Scotland*, pp.129–30

30 Simpson, E, *Going on Holiday*, Edinburgh: National Museums of Scotland, 1998, p.24

31 Seaton, AV, 'History of Tourism in Scotland' in MacLellan, R and Smith, R (eds), *Tourism in Scotland*, London: International Thomson, 1998, p.8

32 Seaton, *History of Tourism*, p.32

33 Slee, B, 'Tourism and rural development in Scotland' in MacLellan and Smith, *Tourism in Scotland*, pp.93–112

34 Simpson, *Going on Holiday*, p.26

35 Wolfe, *Second Homes: Curse or Blessing*, p.4

36 Gunn, N, *Highland River*, Edinburgh: Canongate, 1997

37 McGrath, J, *The Cheviot, the Stag and the Black Black Oil*, first performed in Aberdeen, 1973

38 Simpson, *Going on Holiday*, p.30

39 Devine, *The Scottish Nation*, p.459

40 Ibid., p.30

41 Ibid., pp.9–10

42 Marshall, D, 'The Problem of the Picturesque' in *Eighteenth-Century Studies*, 35:3, 2002, pp.413–37

43 Green, D (ed.), *Cobbett's Tour in Scotland*, Aberdeen: Aberdeen University Press, 1984

44 Fraser Darling, F and Morton Boyd, J, *The Highlands and Islands*, (London: Collins, 1977), p.23

45 Slee, 'Tourism and rural development', p.94

46 Smout, TC, *Scotland Since Prehistory: Natural Change and Human Impact*, Aberdeen: Scottish Cultural Press, 1993, p.116

47 Simpson, *Going on Holiday*, p.27

48 Ibid., p.43

49 Brown, CG, 'Popular Culture and the Continuing Struggle for Rational Recreation' in Devine and Finlay, *Scotland in the 20th Century*, p.226

50 Hall, CM, Müller, DK and Saarinen, J, *Nordic Tourism: Issues and Cases*, Channel View; 2008, p.175 ('In Sweden the cabin-movement (Sportstugerörelsen) caused the construction of many simple cabins on the outskirts of rapidly growing urban areas. Hence, during the 1960s, 1970s and the early 1980s second home construction boomed and added cottages to locations on the urban outskirts and amenity-rich areas all over the Nordic countries.')

51 McFarlan, DM, *First for Boys: The Story of the Boys Brigade 1883–1983*, Glasgow: Collins, 1982

52 Eager, W McG, *Making Men: The History of Boys Clubs and related movements in Great Britain*, London: University of London, 1953

53 Dedman, M, 'Baden-Powell, Militarism, and the Invisible Contributors' to the Boy Scout Scheme, 1904–1920' in *Twentieth Century British History*, 4:3, Oxford: Oxford University Press, 1993, pp.201–23

54 McDevitt, PF, *May the Best Man Win*, New York: Palgrave, 2004

55 *A Military System of Gymnastic Exercises for the Use of Instructors*, 1862; *Training in Theory and Practice*, 1866; *A System of Physical Education Theoretical and Practical*, 1869

56 Ibid.

57 *Dundee Courier*, 22 August 1918

58 Ibid.

59 *Hawick News and Border Chronicle*, 15 November 1918

60 *Dundee Courier*, 7 February 1921

61 *Dundee Courier*, March 1920

62 Pimlott, JAR, *The Englishman's Holiday: A Social History*, Michigan: Harvester Press, 1976, p.214

63 Libaek and Stenersen, *A History of Norway*, p.100

ENDNOTES

64 *Daily Express*, 13 April 1938
65 Report of the Committee on Holidays with Pay, Part V, 96, April 1938
66 'Low Rating of Holiday Camps', *The Caterer and Hotel Keeper*, 7 July 1939
67 Dawson, S, 'Working-Class Consumers and the Campaign for Holidays with Pay' in *Twentieth Century British History*, 18:3, 2007, pp.277–305
68 Matless, D, *Landscape and Englishness*, London, Reaktion, 1998
69 Beaven, B, *Leisure, Citizenship & Working-Class Men in Britain, 1850–1945*, Manchester: Manchester University, 2005, pp.59–60
70 Dawson, 'Working-Class Consumers', p.283
71 Thane, P, *Divided Kingdom: A History of Britain, 1900 to the Present*, Cambridge: Cambridge University Press, 2018
72 Ward and Hardy, *Goodnight Campers*, p.57
73 Dawson, *Working-Class Consumers*, p.283
74 SRO ED14/460 Education Scotland Bill
75 *Ministry of Education, Community Centres*, 1944, 16, pp.3–4
76 Simpson, E, *The Cairngorm Mountaineering Club*, National Museums of Scotland; Edinburgh, 1997
77 Maclean, I, 'Mountain Men: The Discovery of the Hills by Glasgow Workers During the Depression' in B Kay (ed.), Odyssey, Edinburgh: Polygon, 1996, pp.79–87
78 Thomson, IDS, *May the Fire Always Be Lit: A Biography of Jock Nimlin*, UK: Ernest Press, 1995, pp.24–26
79 Haldane Grenier, K, *Tourism and Identity in Scotland 1770–1914*, Oxford: Routledge, 2005, p.110
80 Harrison, D and Sharpley, R, *Mass Tourism in a Small World*, Wallingford: CAB International, 2017, p.97
81 Ibid.
82 Simpson, *Going on Holiday*, p.53

Chapter Nine
1 Ballance, C, *The Fire that Never Went Out*, self-published booklet, 2000, p.7
2 Jamieson, F, *Carbeth Character Appraisal, final draft report*, Stirling: Stirling Council, 2000, p.4
3 Tribute to William Ferris by Dr TJ Honeyman at his funeral, 28 September 1963
4 Ibid.
5 *Kirkintilloch Herald*, 27 April 1927 (Barns-Graham wrote a letter urging 'all Conservatives, Liberals, and Socialists... to unite in demanding that Scotland shall, at an early date, be allowed to manage her own affairs). & *Motherwell Times*, 16 May 1947 (Ferris writes supporting the creation of the Scottish Tourist Board because 'as far as the London administration is concerned, Scotland is not on the map.')
6 Semi-structured interview with Allan Barns-Graham (Junior), 2015
7 Obituary of Mr Allan Barns-Graham of Limekilns, *Glasgow Herald*, 27 June 1957
8 Dryden, A, *Strathblane 1870–1970: A Century of Change*, Strathblane: Strathblane Library, 2012, p.6
9 Ibid., p.24
10 Dryden, *Strathblane*, p.25
11 Ibid., p.26
12 Ironically, having finally unlocked the key to William Ferris's life, I found that copies of his letters were also in a hitherto undiscovered part of the Carbeth Archive.
13 Semi-structured interview with Murray Ferris, February 2015
14 Letter dated 13 December 1918, C Company, Ballinrobe, Co. Mayo, Ireland,

Carbeth Archive
15 Ibid.
16 Semi-structured interview with Allan Barns-Graham (Junior), 2015
17 Letter dated 14 July 1919 from 26 Glebe St, Glasgow, Carbeth Archive
18 Dryden, *Strathblane*, p.158
19 Scottish Parliament, Justice and Home Affairs Committee, Column 24, 26 October
   1999, www.archive.parliament.scot/business/committees/historic/x-justice/or-99/
   ju99-0702.htm
20 Jamieson, *Carbeth Character Appraisal*, p.43 (The author, recommending the
   award of conservation status by Stirling Council, comments: 'the socialist and
   philanthropic principles of Allan Barns-Graham may be in danger of being diluted,
   leading to gentrification.')
21 Interview with ABG Junior, 2012
22 Carbeth Hill Camp, Rules & Conditions issued by William Ferris, Secretary for
   Allan Barns-Graham, 1923
23 Carbeth archive
24 Email from former Green MSP and Carbeth hutter Chris Ballance, June 2013
25 Ballance email, June 2013
26 *Dundee Evening Telegraph*, 19 September 1935 (Ferris represented 150 hutters in
   court and won them the right to vote in forthcoming general and local government
   elections. The objector was West Stirlingshire Unionist Association, which later got
   the decision reversed on appeal.)
27 *Milngavie and Bearsden Herald*, 27 August 1920
28 *Milngavie and Bearsden Herald*, 11 July 1930
29 *Dundee Evening Telegraph*, 5 July 1948
30 Moir, DG, 'Scottish Youth Hostels', in *Cairngorm Club Journal*, 1933
31 Jamieson, *Carbeth Character Appraisal*, p.8
32 *Stirling Observer*, 18 September 1941
33 Ibid.
34 *Falkirk Herald*, 1 November 1941
35 Undated letter by May MacGregor, 1980s, Carbeth Archive
36 Ibid.
37 The Mitchell Library, Carbeth Guthrie archives box TD 1075 Box 12 3/3
38 Undated letter by May MacGregor, 1980s, Carbeth Archive
39 Undated letter by Netta Wallace, Carbeth Archive
40 Undated letter by Robert Maxwell Beveridge, Scarborough, Ontario, Canada,
   Carbeth Archive
41 Ibid.
42 Simpson, JW, Auditor, Kilmarnock, 31 March 1935, Carbeth Archive
43 Carbeth Swimming Pool Balance Sheet (The number of adult members falls from
   164 to 31 when the prices double from 2/6 to 5s in 1936.)
44 Jamieson, *Carbeth Estate Area Character Appraisal*, p.14
45 Tribute to William Ferris by Dr TJ Honeyman at his funeral, 28 September 1963
   (Interestingly, in every other account of the Scottish Tourist Board's formation,
   Ferris's name is omitted.)
46 Dryden, *Strathblane*, p.158
47 Jamieson, *Carbeth Character Appraisal*, p.12
48 Dryden, A, *Strathblane 1870–1970: A Century of Change*, Strathblane: Strahblane
   Library, 2012
49 Ibid., pp.12–13

50 Mitchell, IR, *Walking Through Scotland's History*, Edinburgh: National Museum of Scotland Publishing, 2007, p.133

51 *The Herald*, 7 June 2011

52 Mitchell, *Walking Through Scotland's History*, p.133

53 Ibid., p.13

54 Ibid., p.14

55 Scottish Parliament, Justice and Home Affairs Committee, Column 235, 26 October 1999, www.archive.parliament.scot/business/committees/historic/x-justice/or-99/ju99-0702.htm accessed January 2012

56 Patrick's *Herald* obituary recorded that he'd been Honorary President of the Possilpark Festival and held Mission Services 'for many years for a number of his tenants.' But just like the obituary of his father ABG Senior 30 years earlier, it omitted any reference to the unique hutting community on his land.

57 Ibid., p.14 (Allan Barns-Graham inherited the estate in 1987.)

58 Scottish Parliament, Justice and Home Affairs Committee, Column 244, 26 Oct 1999, www.archive.parliament.scot/business/committees/historic/x-justice/or-99/ju99-0702.htm accessed January 2012

59 *The Herald*, 7 June 2011

60 Ibid.

61 Gentleman, *Huts and Hutters*, www.chrissmithonline.co.uk/files/huts-and-hutters-in-scotland-1999-draft-research-materials.pdf accessed February 2012

62 Scottish Parliament, Justice and Home Affairs Committee, Column 241, 26 October 1999, www.archive.parliament.scot/business/committees/historic/x-justice/or-99/ju99-0702.htm accessed February 2012

63 Ibid., Column 244 (Ballance observes that he applied to sell his hut and the estate said a transfer charge of £1,500 or £1,750 would be applied because it was in a particularly nice spot.)

64 Letter by Deputy Justice Minister Hugh Henry to Pauline McNeill MSP, 3 February 2004

65 Ibid.

66 Ibid.

67 Letter by Hugh Henry, 3 February 2004

68 William McQueen, VC Carbeth Hutters Association, letter to members of the Scottish Parliament, 23 February 2004

69 Jamieson, *Carbeth Character Appraisal*, Stirling Council, 2000, p.39

70 Ibid., p.39

71 According to the *Cambridge Dictionary*, 'arcadia' describes 'a mountainous region of ancient Greece', and 'a real or imaginary place offering peace and simplicity.'

72 Environmental Quality Committee, Stirling Council, Minutes, 8 February 2001

73 Jamieson, *Carbeth Character Appraisal*, p.10

74 *The Herald*, 7 June 2011

75 A loan from Triodos bank eventually made the buy-out possible after years of fundraising, www.theguardian.com/uk/scotland-blog/2013/mar/20/scotland-carbeth-hutters-buyout accessed May 2015

Chapter Ten

1 *Labour Leader*, April 1895

2 Glasier, L, *Young Socialist*, January 1906

3 Reid, F, 'Socialist Sunday Schools in Britain, 1892–1939', in *International Review of Social History*, 11:1, 1966 (In 1892, a Social Democratic Federation (SDF) member opened the first British SSS amidst the Battersea dock strikes. But it didn't

trigger the wave of school openings that followed the Glasgow launch.)

4   Gerrard, J, *Radical Childhoods: Schooling and the Struggle for Social Change*,
    Manchester: Manchester University Press, 2014, p.47

5   *Socialist Sunday Schools: Aims, Objects and Organisations*, National Council of
    British Socialist Sunday Schools (henceforth NCBSSS) (undated), William Gallacher
    Memorial Library/Democratic Left Archive (WGML, Glasgow), p.6

6   Interview with Rose Kerrigan in Rafeek, NC, *Communist Women in Scotland: Red
    Clydeside from the Russian Revolution to the End of the Soviet Union*, London:
    Tauris Academic Books 2008, pp.26–35

7   Reid, 'Socialist Sunday Schools', p.32

8   Gerrard, *Radical Childhoods*, p.106

9   Semi-structured interview with Murray Ferris, February 2015

10 Reid, 'Socialist Sunday Schools', pp.18–46

11 *The Glasgow Herald*, 2 May 1960

12 Rafeek, *Communist Women*, p.63

13 Socialist Sunday School Collection, www.archiveshub.jisc.ac.uk/search/
    archives/0550d3b8-9a35-3b4c-918c-060891673dob accessed April 2019

14 Glasier, L, *Socialist Sunday Schools: A Reply to the Sabbath School Teachers'
    Magazine*, Glasgow: Glasgow and District Socialist Sunday School Union, 1907,
    pp.19–20

15 Gerrard, *Radical Childhoods*, p.23

16 Interview with Marion Henery in Rafeek, *Communist Women*, p.98

17 Jones, SG, 'Sport, Politics and the Working Class', Manchester: Manchester
    University Press, 2008

18 *Daily Record*, 2 February 1939

19 *Sunday Post*, 7 August 1938

20 Pye, D, *Fellowship is Life: Story of National Clarion Cycling Club*, London:
    Clarion Publishing, 1995, p.63

21 *Dundee Evening Telegraph*, 20 August 1901

22 Gawsfor, *Daily Record*, 2 February 1939

23 Pye, *Fellowship is Life*, p.65

24 Ibid.

25 Ibid.

26 *Falkirk Herald*, 17 July 1909

27 *Scottish Referee*, 8 July 1910

28 Pye, *Fellowship is Life* (Wartime circulation plummeted from 60,000 to 10,000.)

29 Ibid.

30 McGurn, J, *On Your Bicycle: The Illustrated Story of Cycling*, York: Murray, 1999,
    p.7

31 Ibid.

32 Price, R, *Labour in British Society*, New York: Croom Helm, 1986, p.73

33 Savage, M, 'Urban Politics and the Rise of the Labour Party, 1919–39' in Jamieson,
    L and Corr, H (eds), *State, Private Life and Political Change*, London: Palgrave
    Macmillan, 1990

34 Rafeek, *Communist Women*, p.19

35 www.libcom.org/history/articles/40-hours-strike-1919 accessed May 2014

36 Finlay, R, *Modern Scotland 1914 to 2000*, London: Profile, 2004, p.51

37 Gallacher, W, *Revolt on the Clyde*, Glasgow: Lawrence & Wishart, 1978

38 Macaskill, K, *Glasgow 1919: The Rise of Red Clydeside*, Glasgow: Biteback, 2019

39 *Motherwell Times*, 18 February 1921

40 www.hansard.parliament.uk/commons/1923-03-27/debates/30c41388-7883-49f1-a3ba-ed116296dfc8/NoticesOfMotion accessed March 2018

41 Reid, 'Socialist Sunday Schools', p.29

42 *The Young Socialist*, Winter, 1964 (The SSS movement began earlier and endured longer in the West of Scotland than elsewhere in Britain despite helping to produce generations of Scottish activists, councilors and MPs. There's no dedicated archive in Scotland to showcase the scale and impact of civic socialist organisations, apart from Glasgow University's William Gallacher Memorial Archive.)

43 Libaek and Stenersen, *A History of Norway*, p.82 (So was 10 per cent of the total industrial workforce.)

44 Kjeldstadli, *Åtte timer arbeid*, pp.76–77

45 Ibid.

46 Ibid.

47 Ibid., p.79 (Max Vogel of the Norwegian Foundry Company in 1914 said 'regular holidays are the cheapest and most rational way to keep workers wholesome, capable of work, fresh and exuberant.')

48 Libaek and Stenersen, *A History of Norway*, p.100

49 Kjeldstadli, *Åtte timer arbeid*, p.78

50 Lyngø, *Fritid er sosial sak*, p.22

51 Kjeldstadli, *Åtte timer arbeid*, pp.79–80

52 Thingsrud, L, 'Arbeideridrett i kamptid. Et tilbakeblikk på AIF i Akershus' in *Akershus' Årbok*, Haermuseet 1989

53 Riordan, J, 'The Workers' Olympics' in Tomlinson, A and Whannel, G, *Five Ring Circus: Money, Power and Politics at the Olympic Games*, London: Pluto Press, 1989, pp.98–112

54 Kjeldstadli, *Åtte timer arbeid*, p.80

55 Ibid., p.80

56 Labour Youth magazine, *Arbeider Ungdommen*, 1929

57 Kjeldstadli, *Åtte timer arbeid*, pp.71–93

58 Ibid., pp.81–82 ('Norwegian workers did not support military but moral rearmament.')

59 Bjørgum, J, *Store Norske Leksikon*, 2011, www.snl.no/Martin_Tranmæl accessed May 2017

60 Kjeldstadli, *Åtte timer arbeid*, p.79

61 Ibid. (The Tailors Union bought a farm on Nesodden in 1920, the Oslo Waiters Association bought Upper Bleker Asker in 1927 and the electrical fitters built a holiday home in 1929 on Bjork Island in Langen, Enebakk.)

62 Somdal-Åmodt, T, *På vei til sommer'ns feriekoloni, Tobias* 2, 1999, pp.16–18

63 Hodne, O, *Folk og Fritid*, Oslo: Novus, 1994, pp.18–19

64 Ibid., pp.20–21

65 Ibid., p.18

66 Ibid.

67 Gjerdåker in Almås, *Norwegian Agricultural History*, pp.234–93

68 Libaek and Stenersen, *A History of Norway*, pp.103–05

69 Ibid., p.102

70 Danielsen, *From the Vikings to Our Own Times*, p.362

71 Bunker, J, *A History of the SIU*, Seafarers International Union, 1983

72 Grytten, *Economic Policy*, pp.3–7 (Total unemployment rose from one per cent in 1919 to eight per cent in 1926. In manufacturing it reached more than 18 per cent the same year.)

73 Libaek and Stenersen, *A History of Norway*, p.113

74 Ibid., p.113
75 Bryden, J, et al, *Northern Neighbours*, p.107
76 Ibid., p.100
77 Brandal, N, Bratberg, O and Thorsen, DE, *The Nordic Model of Social Democracy*, Basingstoke: Palgrave Macmillan, 2013, pp.109–14
78 www.bbc.co.uk/news/uk-scotland-north-east-orkney-shetland-14895693 accessed January 2019
79 Bryden, J, 'Scottish Agriculture 1950–1980' in Saville, R, *The Economic Development of Modern Scotland 1950–1980*, Edinburgh; John Donald, 1985, p.15–17
80 MacDonald, CMM, 'A Different Commonwealth: The Cooperative Movement in Scotland' in Mulhern, MA, Beech, J and Thompson, E (eds), *The Working Life of Scots*, series: Scottish Life and Society (7), Edinburgh, 2008, pp.161–78
81 Bryden, J, et al, *Northern Neighbours*, p.48
82 Kjeldstadli, K, 'Åtte timer arbeid' in Klepp, IG and Svarverud, R (eds), *Idrett og fritid*, Oslo: Univeristy of Oslo, 1993, p.78
83 Devine, *The Scottish Nation*, p.571
84 This is a necessarily brief summary of complex processes in each country. Far more detailed descriptions are available in *Northern Neighbours* (Edinburgh: Edinburgh University Press, 2014), the book I co-edited with Professors John Bryden and Ottar Brox – particularly the chapters written by John himself, extracts from which are printed here and the whole of which has hugely influenced my own outlook on Scotland's restricted development.

Chapter Eleven
1   Hardy and Ward, *Arcadia for All*, pp.18–25
2   Szczelkun, *The Conspiracy of Good Taste*, p.46
3   Ibid., p.46
4   Jefferies, R, *After London*, first published 1885, Book Jungle, 4 July 2008, passim
5   London, J, *People of the Abyss*, originally published 1903, Echo Library, 1 January 2007, passim
6   Belchem, J, *Popular Radicalism in Nineteenth-Century Britain*, New York: Palgrave, 1996
7   Hardy and Ward, *Arcadia for All*, pp.16–18
8   *The Plotlands Experience: Self-Build Settlements of Southeast England*, 2003, OASE 59
9   Daly, A, *The History of Canvey Island*, 1903, quoted in Hardy and Ward, *Arcadia for All*, pp.120–22
10 Hallmann, RA, A *Dynasty of Oggs*, www.canveyisland.org accessed November 2016
11 *Dundee Courier*, 27 August 1913
12 Szczelkun, *The Conspiracy of Good Taste*, p.47
13 Bourdieu, P, *Distinction: A Social Critique of the Judgement of Taste*, Paris, 1979, p.469
14 Hardy and Ward, *Arcadia for All*, pp.49–50
15 Hodge, I, 'Countryside Planning' in Cullingworth, JB, *British Planning: 50 Years of Urban and Regional Policy*, London: Routledge, 1999, p.91
16 Steers, JA, 'Report on the East Anglian Coast: Hunstanton to East Tilbury', Public Record Office, 1943 in Hardy and Ward, *Arcadia for All*, 1984, p.120
17 Hardy and Ward, *Arcadia for All*, p.185

259

18 Szczelkun, *Conspiracy of Good Taste*, p48
19 Lockley, RM, in Szczelkun, *Conspiracy of Good Taste*, p.48
20 Hardy and Ward, *Arcadia for All*, p.281
21 Ibid., p.51
22 Hardy and Ward, *Arcadia for All*, p.152
23 Lund, B, *Housing Politics in the United Kingdom: Power, Planning and Protest*, Bristol: Policy Press, 2016, p.1
24 Ward, C, *Cotters and Squatters: The Hidden History of Housing*, Nottingham, Five Leaves Publications, 2002, p.159
25 Ibid., p.160
26 Ministry file *Removal of Shacks* etc Public Record File HLG/92/81 (ref 91647/15/2), April 1946
27 Hall, P and Ward, C, *Sociable Cities: The Legacy of Ebeneezer Howard*, London: Wiley, 1999, pp.50–55
28 Hardy and Ward, *Arcadia for All*, p.97
29 Ibid., pp.203–09
30 Hall and Ward, *Sociable Cities*, p.197
31 McNab, I, www. hutters.uk/2014/08/18/arcadia-for-all-by-dennis-hardy-and-colin-ward/ accessed September 2020

Chapter Twelve

1 Valuation Roll, County of Angus 1937–8, entry 142, p.100 (Gross annual value of 36 huts is £42 5s. Gross annual value of Sturrock's own farm land is less – £32 6s 4d.)
2 Semi-structured interview with Doreen Paton, 2012
3 Sasine Register, 1935, National Register Office, Edinburgh
4 Hansard HC, vol 303 cc 1456–7, 28 June 1935, www.api.parliament.uk/historic-hansard/commons/1935/jun/28/department-of-agriculture-scotland accessed June 2018
5 Mather, AS, 'The Rise and Fall of Government-assisted Land Settlement in Scotland' in *Land Use Policy*, 1985, p.220
6 'Barry huts not for war veterans', letter by Doreen Paton in *The Scotsman*, 2 May 2010 ('May I repeat that the huts at the Downs, Barry, were never in any way connected to war veterans returning home.')
7 Interview with Doreen Paton, 2012
8 Valuation rolls show Andrew Jackson lived at 10 St Salvador Street with the code DCC which 'usually means council housing' according to Iain Flett, Dundee City Archivist, 2010.
9 County of Angus proceedings 1937–8, principal minutes
10 Interview with Doreen Paton, 2012 ('We never had any trouble with vandalism as in those days nearly everybody came from Dundee and were known to each other.')
11 This might be due to the impact of death duties but no evidence was found in archive search.
12 *People's Journal*, 23 July 1938, front page
13 Valuation Roll Country of Angus, 1949–50, lists huts 139–169, p.138
14 'The Battle of Buckie is Over', *People's Journal*, 17 April 1965
15 County of Angus Proceedings, 4 January 1950
16 *Arbroath Herald and Advertiser* for the Montrose Burghs, 24 January 1947
17 'Barry Huts Not for War Veterans', letter by Doreen Paton in *The Scotsman*, 2 May 2010
18 Gentleman, *Huts and Hutters*, p.33
19 Interview with James and Pauline Rowling, 2013

20 Baker, S, *Fourth Statistical Account of East Lothian*, 2000, www.el4.org.uk/parish/
    cockenzie-port-seton/economy/ accessed December 2016

21 Bristow, E, 'The Liberty and Property Defence League and Individualism' in
    Historical Journal 18:4, December 1975, pp.761–89

22 Baker, S, *Fourth Statistical Account of East Lothian*, 2000

23 Hendrie, WF, *Discovering the Firth of Forth*, Edinburgh: John Donald, 1998

24 *The Scotsman*, 21 July 1920, p.6

25 *Dundee Courier*, December 1951

26 *The Scotsman*, 25 January 1935

27 *Falkirk Herald*, 24 February 1940

28 Baker, *Fourth Statistical Account of East Lothian*, 2000

29 *The Scotsman*, 27 November 1928, p.11

30 Hendrie, WF, 'Sands of Time' in *Scots Magazine*, New Series 153:2, August 2000,
    pp.168–172

31 Marshall, J, *Holidays in East Lothian with Focus on Seton Sands*, dissertation,
    Stirling: Stirling University, 2012, p.26

32 Baker, *The Fourth Statistical Account of East Lothian*, 2000

33 Baker, *The Fourth Statistical Account of East Lothian*, Volume 5, 2000 p.163

34 Marshall, J, *Holidays in East Lothian with Focus on Seton Sands*, dissertation
    Stirling: Stirling University, 2012, p.32

35 Hendrie, 'Sands of Time', pp.168–172

36 Ibid., p.169

37 *The Scotsman*, 4 August 1949

38 ELCC, Development Plan, 11 December 1950, p.8, paragraph 40

39 Ibid.

40 Marshall, J, *Holidays in East Lothian with Focus on Seton Sands*, dissertation,
    Stirling: Stirling University, 2012, p.32

41 Tindall, F, *Memoirs and Confessions of a County Planning Officer*, Midlothian,
    1998, p.37

42 Hendrie, WF, 'Sands of Time' in *Scots Magazine*, New Series 153:2, August 2000,
    pp.168–72

43 Baker, *The Fourth Statistical Account of East Lothian*

44 ELCC, Planning department coastal survey, Box A16, 1961, p.21

45 Hendrie, WF, *Discovering the Firth of Forth*, Haddington, John Donald, 2002,
    pp.181–202

46 *Galloway News*, 10 July 2008, p.1

47 Correspondence from Christine and Norman Milligan, J1/S2/04/13/11 Annex E,
    2 February 2004

48 Lloyd, M, *Inside Housing*, 4 March 2005

49 *The Herald*, 23 December 2004

50 McPherson, J, *Hopeman 1805–2005*, Hopeman: Hopeman Community
    Association, 2008) pp.23–24

51 *Northern Scot*, 20 July 1929

52 VR125/1/14, 1979, pp.49–55 – Estate bought by J. Dean Anderson per Wink &
    Mackenzie, Elgin

53 *Northern Scot*, 4 July 1931, p.8

54 *The Scotsman*, 3 May 2013, www.scotsman.com/news/odd/the-scots-beach-huts-
    with-a-10-year-waiting-list-1-2919219 accessed April 2017

55 Lockhart, DG, 'Hopeman, Moray: Houses, Harbours and Holidays' in *Scottish
    Local History* 89, Autumn 2014, p.36

56 Gentleman, *Huts and Hutters,* p.20 and p.40
57 *Reforesting Scotland Magazine,* Issue 43, 2011, p.15
58 Information sheet by David Anderson, librarian East Lothian Council, March 2014
59 Ibid.
60 Gentleman, *Huts and Hutters*, p.40
61 Interview Sheila Laidlaw, Craigannet Farm, June 2014

Chapter Thirteen

1   Nielsen, R, *Der laksen biter,* Hammerfest, 1999, p.16 (Freshwater Fisheries
    Commissioner Landmark explained why VIFF failed to win the river management
    contract.)
2   Ibid., pp.16–18
3   Ibid., p.20 ('It is my impression that salmon populations increased sharply after the
    association took over.')
4   Ibid., p.21
5   Friberg, L, *De grae skipene,* Hammerfest, 1991, p.56
6   Ibid., p.59
7   Interview with VJFF official, Jan Hartvigsen, 2011
8   www.ssb.no/a/histstat/nos/nos_b867.pdf accessed November 2016
9   www.idunn.no/heimen/2017/01/finnmarkshandelen_i_en_brytningstid_17891811_
    hva_kan_toll accessed October 2015
10 The *hulder* could originate from a Christian story about a woman who hid some of
    her children when God came to visit because she hadn't washed them. God decreed
    they would be hidden from humanity – they became the *hulder.* Or they may be
    descendants of Lilith, the mythical and rebellious first wife of Adam.
11 Interview with Bjørg and Ola Larsen, Hammerfest, 2010
12 Semi-structured interview with Snorre Sundquist, Regional Director, Husbanken,
    The Norwegian State Housing Bank, 2010
13 www.lovdata.no/dokument/NL/lov/1977-06-10-82 accessed November 2015
14 www.scotsman.com/news/opinion/columnists/rise-dirty-camping-scotland-
    concernlesley-riddoch-1409397

List of Figures

List of Tables

Timeline

1397	Norway enters the Kalmar Union with Denmark and Sweden.
1523	Sweden leaves Kalmar Union with Denmark and Sweden and Norway becomes part of Danish state.
1707	**Treaty of Union – England and Scotland become a single state.**
1814	Danes lose control of Norway in Treaty of Kiel after backing Napoleon.
	Norway declares independence, publishes a constitution and enfranchises all male landowners.
	Norway is forced into a personal union of crowns under the King of Sweden but keeps its own constitution and parliament.
1821	Nobility is formally abolished by Norwegian Parliament.
1833	Peasant farmers form a majority of MPs in Norwegian Peasant Parliament.
1835	70 per cent of Norwegian land is owned by individual farming families.
1848	Den Norske Turistforening or DNT (Norwegian Trekking Association) founded.
1854	**Balmoral completed for Queen Victoria – fashion for Highland hunting lodges begins.**
1883	**Boys' Brigade founded in Glasgow by Sir William Alexander Smith – world's first voluntary uniformed organisation for boys.**
1887	**Allotments Act.**
1889	**Scottish Mountaineering Club formed.**
1896	**Glasgow Socialist Sunday School launched – first in Britain.**

1896	Camping Section of the Clarion Field Club starts activity on Arran.
1905	Union with Sweden is dissolved – Norway becomes independent country.
	Campers start rowing over from Oslo's East End to the island of Lindøya.
1906–9	Concession Laws effectively renationalise Norway's rivers.
1908	**Ladies Scottish Climbing Club founded.**
1917	Bolshevik Revolution in Russia.
1917	First socialist controlled Oslo Council builds swimming baths, seawater pools, parks, allotments and sports fields.
1918	**William Ferris writes to the owner of Carbeth asking permission to build a hut.**
1919	**William Ferris and others start camping at Carbeth.**
1919	Norwegian Labour becomes a revolutionary party and joins Comintern.
1922	**Allan Barns Graham permits huts at Carbeth.**
	Huts start at Seton Sands, East Lothian.
1929	**Carbeth Swimming Pool or Lido opens. (closed 1972)**
1937	**Huts start at Barry Downs, Carnoustie.**
1938	Holidays with Pay Act – week's annual paid leave, but not compulsory.
	Billy Butlin opens his first 'luxury' holiday camp at Clacton-on-Sea.
1947	**Town and Country Planning Act.**
1957	**Allan Barns Graham, Carbeth owner dies.**
1965	**Mountain Bothies Association (MBA) formed.**
1963	**William Ferris dies.**
1975	**40-hour week with 20 days' annual paid holiday (still not compulsory).**

1997   Allan Barns Graham's grandson takes over Carbeth and decade-long rent strike begins.

2000   Hugh Gentleman's Scottish Executive-commissioned research on hutting is published, showing around 600 huts in Scotland. (Around half a million in Norway).

2000   Scottish Parliament rejects Carbeth hutters' petition for help.

2001   Stirling Council awards Carbeth huts conservation area status.

2007   Hutters at Rascarrel, Kirkcudbrightshire burn down huts, after massive rent increase.

2009   28 days of paid annual holiday (thanks to European Working Time Directive).

2011   One Thousand Huts campaign established.

2012   Evictions end hutting at Barry Downs.

2013   Ten-year rent strike at Carbeth ends with £1.75m purchase of land.

Index

Norwegian terms and people are in italics.

Some other books published by **LUATH** PRESS

Blossom: What Scotland Needs to Flourish

Lesley Riddoch

3rd edition · 978-1912147-52-6

Paperback · £11.99

Dispensing with the tired, yo-yoing jousts over fiscal commissions, Devo Something and EU in-or-out, *Blossom* pinpoints both the buds of growth and the blight that's holding Scotland back. Drawing from its people and history as well as the experience of the Nordic countries, and the author's own passionate and outspoken perspective, this is a plain-speaking but incisive call to restore equality and control to local communities and let Scotland flourish.

Blossom *is an account of Scotland at the grassroots through the stories of people I've had the good fortune to know – the most stubborn, talented and resilient people on the planet. They've had to be. Some have transformed their parts of Scotland. Some have tried and failed. But all have something in common – they know what it takes for Scotland to blossom. We should too...*

McSmörgåsbord: What Post-Brexit Scotland Can Learn from the Nordics

Lesley Riddoch

978-1-912147-00-7 Paperback £7.99

The Nordic countries have a veritable smörgåsbord of relationships with the European Union, from in to out to somewhere in between.

So, what does that mean for Scotland?

Would an independent Scotland need the support and shelter of another union – or could the nation stand alone like the tiny Faroes or Iceland?

The tough questions have already been faced and resolved by five Nordic nations and their autonomous territories within the last 40 years. Perhaps there's something for Scotland to learn?

Riddoch on the Outer Hebrides

Lesley Riddoch

978-1-906307-86-8 Paperback £12.99

Riddoch on the Outer Hebrides is a thought-provoking commentary based on broadcaster Lesley Riddoch's cycle journey through a beautiful island chain facing seismic cultural and economic change. Her experience is described in a typically affectionate but hard-hitting style; with humour, anecdote and a growing sympathy for islanders tired of living at the margins but fearful of closer contact with mainland Scotland.

Luath Press Limited

committed to publishing well written books worth reading

LUATH PRESS takes its name from Robert Burns, whose little collie Luath (*Gael.*, swift or nimble) tripped up Jean Armour at a wedding and gave him the chance to speak to the woman who was to be his wife and the abiding love of his life. Burns called one of 'The Twa Dogs' Luath after Cuchullin's hunting dog in Ossian's *Fingal*. Luath Press was established in 1981 in the heart of Burns country, and now resides a few steps up the road from Burns' first lodgings on Edinburgh's Royal Mile. Luath offers you distinctive writing with a hint of unexpected pleasures.

Most bookshops in the UK, the US, Canada, Australia, New Zealand and parts of Europe either carry our books in stock or can order them for you. To order direct from us, please send a £sterling cheque, postal order, international money order or your credit card details (number, address of cardholder and expiry date) to us at the address below. Please add post and packing as follows: UK – £1.00 per delivery address; overseas surface mail – £2.50 per delivery address; overseas airmail – £3.50 for the first book to each delivery address, plus £1.00 for each additional book by airmail to the same address. If your order is a gift, we will happily enclose your card or message at no extra charge.

Luath Press Limited
543/2 Castlehill
The Royal Mile
Edinburgh EH1 2ND
Scotland

Telephone: 0131 225 4326 (24 hours)
email: sales@luath.co.uk
Website: www.luath.co.uk